# The Trinity and Creation
# in
# Karl Barth

Gordon Watson

# The Trinity and Creation

# in

# Karl Barth

Gordon Watson

Adelaide

Cover design by Astrid Sengkey with photo of Karl Barth supplied by Victor Pfitzner

ATF Press

An imprint of the Australasian Theological Forum Ltd
P O Box 504
Hindmarsh
SA 5007
ABN 90 116 359 963
www.atfpress.com

# Contents

# Foreword

One of the most striking and, indeed, defining features of recent theology has been the renaissance in explicitly trinitarian thought. It is now commonplace for theologians to present the doctrine of the Trinity as the *sine qua non* of a cogent exposition of Christian thought. Analyses of the doctrine's essential significance for theological epistemology and method, for interpreting salvation, worship, theological anthropology, society, the arts and, indeed, ontology more generally can be found in the writings of a diverse group of theologians. A list of those who have written explicitly on the doctrine would include the following: Karl Rahner, Hans Urs von Balthasar, Eberhard Jüngel, Jürgen Moltmann, Robert Jenson, the Torrance brothers, John Zizoulas, Colin Gunton, Cornelius Plantinga, Catherine Mowry LaCugna, Miroslav Volf, Paul Molnar, Bruce Marshall, Jeremy Begbie and David Bentley Hart

*The Trinity and Creation in Karl Barth* is a profoundly significant contribution to this major debate for a host of reasons. I shall highlight just a few. First, it is an analysis of the thought of the theologian who was the key intellectual impetus behind this revival of trinitarian theology—one, indeed, who is now universally recognised as the theological giant of the modern era. Second, Watson explores the relation of the doctrine of the Trinity to the doctrine of creation and thus to the whole structure and character of God's engagement with the contingent order. Watson's research, in this regard, was ahead of its time given that he was writing on this topic and expounding its importance long before others began popularising this theme! Third, it explores—and brings into sharp focus—the integrity of the biblical and traditional interpretations out of which the dogma of the Trinity developed. Finally, it offers an insightful and deep-thinking critical assessment of whether Barth went far enough in his trinitarian vision of the theological task. Barth's study of St Anselm had led him to find, in the trinitarian dogma, the means of integrating the method and the material content of theology. Watson raises the question, in dialogue with the Greek Fathers, as to whether Barth's adoption of the principle *fides quaerens intellectum* did not lack a further essential element, namely, a *fides quaerens adorationem*. The questions this raises clearly have important consequences not only for the structure of Barth's thought but also for the viability of his understanding of the Trinity within an ecumenical context.

This volume began its life as a doctoral thesis written under the guidance of the late Professors TF and JB Torrance. An earlier edition, was one of the eight books that TF Torrance recommended for reading on Karl Barth's theology. This new revised edition shows the mature reflection over an academic career of a leading contemporary theologian and Barth scholar on the ramifications and implications of what is doubtless the most significant theological development since the Reformation.

Professor Alan J Torrance
Chair of Systematic Theology
St Mary's College
University of St Andrews
Scotland
Easter 2009

# Acknowledgments

Every attempt has been made to credit the sources of copyrighted material used in this book. If any such acknowledgement has been inadvertently omitted or miscredited, receipt of such information would be appreciated.

The author gratefully acknowledges the help given in the preparation of the second edition of this book by the ATF Press in particular Mr Hilary Regan and the editor, Revd Dr Victor Pfitzner, without whose perspicacity and wisdom the work would be much the poorer.

The author also thanks the editors and publishers of *The Scottish Journal of Theology* for permission to use material from his following articles:

1. 'Karl Barth and St Anselm's Theological Programme', *SJT* 30/1 (1977): 31–46.
2. 'The Filioque—Opportunity for Debate?' *SJT* 41/3 (1988): 313–330.
3. 'A Study in St Anselm's Soteriology and Karl Barth's Theological Method', *SJT* 42/4 (1989): 493–512.

I am indebted to the late Rev Professor TF Torrance, the co-editor of the English translation of Karl Barth's *magnum opus*, the great *Church Dogmatics*, and a man recognised in the English speaking world as the pre-eminent authority on Barth's theology. He kindly recommended this book for reading as one of only a few in the plethora of published works on Barth.

This study was originally publsihed in 1995 under the title *God and the Creature: The Trinity and Creation in Karl Barth*. In its revised form, it contains corrections and additional material, in particular, three Appendixes. Some more recent studies have been noted and added to the Bibliography.

# Introduction
## Second Edition

That theology has a method must be assumed since theologians believe that what they present coheres in some way with the received deposit of Christian teaching. While it may be true that some theologians develop a non-theological method,[1] for Karl Barth there must be a direct connection between the material content of theology and its method.[2] Thus for him the dogma of the Trinity does not derive its importance from its recognition as a central Christian dogma, but from the fact that it articulates the reality which makes all Christian theology possible: namely, God reveals God's self as Lord.

Whatever one may say about the shortcomings of Karl Barth's theological method, this should not detract from the fact that Barth's *Church Dogmatics* established the dogma of the Trinity as central to the church's theological agenda in the twentieth century. Pope Pius XII described Barth as the greatest theologian since St Thomas Aquinas![3]

The problems raised by the relationship between God and creation focus on the relevance of the Augustinian western tradition of trinitarian thought. Barth's grounding of the dogma of the Trinity in the doctrine of revelation concentrates on the relationship of God's own being who God is as God with God's relationship with the creature. The pervasive inclusivity of this relationship, in which God's being is, prototypically, the basis of the creature's being and life, can call into question the importance of its created purpose for its integrity as a creature. The creature's contingency and created purposiveness is essential to its being who it is. If this is called into question then the relationship between God and the creature can appear to be meaningless.

In what follows, it is proposed that the Trinity needs to be appreciated in the context in which it is located by the church: the church's liturgical and doxological experience. In this particular context, the relationship between God and the creature can take account both of God's sovereign approach to the creature and of the creature's created integrity in its response. It is to the Eastern

---

1.  See Francois Wendel, *Calvin: the Origins and Development of his Thought* (London: Collins, 1963), 357ff.
2.  Barth, *Church Dogmatics* 1/2, 863 ff.
3.  See the biographical note inside the front cover of K Barth, *Fragments Grave and Gay* (London: Collins, 1971).

church's trinitarian vision that reference is made with a view to clarifying and resolving some of the inadequacies of Karl Barth's presentation.

The intention of this work is both ecumenical and historical: to allow a conversation between the Augustinian Western tradition of Christianity, both Catholic and Reformed, and the Eastern tradition of the one church. It is also an attempt to elucidate the relevance of the dogma of the Trinity for the issues which impinge on the church's understanding of creation's purpose in social and cultural contexts, which in many ways deny it.

W Gordon Watson
Port Macquarie, New South Wales
Pentecost 2008

# Chapter One

# The Place of the Trinity in Barth's Developing Theology

Barth understood the Trinity to be of foundational significance for the theological road he was beginning to tread, as the claims of his first academic appointment made its demands upon him. His first series of lectures make this plain, as do his letters to his friend Eduard Thurneysen.[1]

> In regard to the incarnation it is best at any rate to proceed cautiously that one may not run his head into the exclusive 'Jesus Christ'–pit of the Lutherans. Everything depends on this denominator, but the denominator 'somehow' under everything. A Trinity of being, not just an economic Trinity! At all costs the doctrine of the Trinity! If I could get the right key in my hand here, then everything would come out right; but one is always coming to premature conclusions which then take their revenge somewhere.[2]

The significance of the Trinity for Barth, at this stage of his theological journey, was that it provided the means of understanding how, by God's own action, the mystery of the *Deus dixit* of revelation might be understood. By means of a Trinity in which there is an identification of the 'economic' Trinity with the Trinity of 'being', he attempts to show that God's revelation is not quantifiable by means of such distinctions as between revealed and natural theology, and between revelation and reason. Such distinctions were, for Barth, characteristic of neo-Protestant and Roman Catholic theology.

---

1. K Barth, *The Göttingen Dogmatics* (Grand Rapids: Eerdmans, 1990), 89–91, 96–97. These lectures were given in 1924 and 1925. When Barth moved to Münster, he gave a second series of lectures in 1926 and 1927. These latter were published in 1927 under the title *Die christliche Dogmatik in Entwurf, 1. Die Lehre vom Worte Gottes, Prolegomena zur christlichen Dogmatik* (München: Kaiser, 1927).
2. K Barth and E Thurneysen, *Revolutionary Theology in the Making: Correspondence 1914–1925* (London: Epworth, 1964), 176.

> Either God speaks, or he does not. But he does not speak more or less, or partially, or in pieces, here a bit and there a bit. This is a contradiction in terms, an anthropomorphism, a basic naturalizing of revelation which fits Schleiermacher very well . . . And even in Thomas Aquinas the insights one can gain into God's nature apart from revelation have the significance only of a possible and necessary ancillary construction that pays secondary honor to the truth of revelation.[3]

Barth opposes to this the view that 'if God *speaks*, then *God* speaks and we have to do with the one Logos that the prophets and apostles received'.[4] Therefore, he understands the Trinity, in this context, as bringing to understanding the action of God in revelation as an action in which God remains the sole subject of the event.

> If we say that the content of revelation is identical with God alone, wholly God, God himself, the word 'God' can only denote what was called God in the doctrine of . . . the Trinity . . . It is *this* God who in his inexhaustible vitality, that is, in his indestructible subjectivity, makes superfluous and meaningless the question whether there is some special content of revelation alongside the fact that it is *his* revelation.[5]

A merely 'economic' Trinity would therefore suggest to Barth the possibility of a quantification of revelation, either by pious self-consciousness or by reason. Barth was familiar with both of these alternative views of revelation in neo-Protestantism and Roman Catholicism. It is precisely this that he sets out to oppose with a revitalised exposition of the nature of the *Deus dixit* of revelation in the dogma of the Trinity. It would take Barth another six years before he felt he had 'the right key in his hand', that is, a 'Trinity of being, not just an economic Trinity' as the foundation of his monumental theological construct, *Die Kirchliche Dogmatik.*[6]

---

3.    Barth, *Göttingen Dogmatics*, 92.
4.    *Ibid.*
5.    Barth, *Göttingen Dogmatics*, 95–96.
6.    K Barth, *Die kirchliche Dogmatik*, Volumes 1–4, 1932ff. The authorised English translation, *Church Dogmatics*, edited by TF Torrance and G Bromiley, 1936ff. will be

With the publication of his book on St Anselm in 1931, we reach a turning point in Barth's understanding of his theological method, one that will have decisive implications for his understanding of the nature and place of the Trinity in the structure of his theological work.[7] The evidence presented in Barth's own writing of this period supports the view that, whatever change took place at this time, it was in great measure related to his attempt to relativise theological problems associated with understanding God's relationship with the world by means of a deeper understanding of the dogma of the Trinity.

## *Die christliche Dogmatik*

As Barth proceeded with his work as a theological teacher in Münster, he looked back on this second attempt at writing a Christian dogmatics and concluded that it was

> a readoption of the line Schleiermacher—Ritschl—Herrmann, and because in any thinkable continuation of this line I can only see the plain destruction of Protestant theology . . . I can therefore only say No here.[8]

The method Barth adopted in this work, in order to counter the systematising of theology by anthropological presuppositions, was a radical dialectical method. This method was developed by Barth himself. For example, if a comparison is made between the second edition of *The Epistle to the Romans* and *Die christliche Dogmatik*, one can see that the later work presents the incarnation as having a certain historical reality. It is not simply a mathematical point in time, simply the place where non-historical eternity intersects but does not extend into time

---

followed unless otherwise indicated (henceforth referred to as *CD*).

7.　　K Barth, *Anselm: fides quaerens intellectum; Anselm's Proof of the Existence of God in the Context of his Theological Scheme* (London: SCM, 1960). Some commentators draw a distinction between different phases of Barth's development at this stage. See for example, TF Torrance, *Karl Barth: An Introduction to his Early Theology 1910–1931* (London: SCM, 1962), 48ff, 133ff. Cf H Urs von Balthasar, *Karl Barth: Darstellung und Deutung seiner Theologie* (Köln: Hegner, 1951), 71ff, 93ff. However, others maintain a more fluid relationship between Barth's earlier and later development. See JD Smart, *The Divided Mind of Modern Theology* (Philadelphia: Westminster, 1967), 224.

8.　　Barth, *CD* 1/1, x.

and history, making the empty tomb a matter of indifference in terms of its significance for the Christian faith.[9]

At the urging of his friend Eduard Thurneysen and to fulfil his need to develop a program of lectures at the University of Münster, Barth set about rewriting his previous efforts.[10] His point of departure is, as in his previous lectures, the necessity and possibility of Christian speech about God. Barth states the issue in the form of a dilemma. Of necessity, the church must speak about God to be the church, yet because the church brings to its task its own human language it cannot speak about God. The resolution of the dilemma is to be found in the action of God. It is found in the freedom of God to speak the truth concerning himself. Theology begins at the point of the church's most acute embarrassment, its attempted speech about God. Consequently, as opposed to all forms of direct communication, Christian speech about God can only be described as a venture.[11] Barth opposes a theological simplicity that believes and ventures to meet the contemporary church's desire to speak directly and to arrive at self-certainty.[12] Thus, if the Word of God 'happens' through the human words of the preacher, it is as the commission of God, pressing upon the church to proclaim the Word of God, coincides with God's permission. This is God's personal presence as *actus purus*.[13]

In terms of the other side of the equation—the human recipient or hearer of the Word of God—this cannot be understood within the framework of a neutral anthropology. This side of the relationship, too, is constituted by the action of the Word of God. Anthropology must be defined by the structure of the relationship presupposed by the presence of the Word of God; it is only in God's presence that persons come to self-understanding.[14] The Word of God is both the question to and the answer of human existence; from the human side of knowledge of this event, the given answer poses the question of meaning for human existence. Who are human beings in terms of the answer, the address, of the Word of God to the human situation? This is the methodological starting

---

9.   Barth, *The Epistle to the Romans*, second edition (Oxford: Oxford University Press, 1950), 29ff, 40ff, 91, 92, 204. Cf also Barth, *The Word of God and the Word of Man* (London: Hodder & Stoughton, 1928), 196,197, 285, 286; also Barth, *The Resurrection from the Dead* (London: Hodder & Stoughton, 1933), 142–146.
10.  Barth, *Göttingen Dogmatics*, XVI.
11.  Barth, *Die christliche Dogmatik*, 55.
12.  *Ibid*, 56.
13.  *Ibid*, 63, 64.
14.  *Ibid*, 66, 67, 70, 71, 75.

point for a Christian anthropology. It entails understanding human existence not as a static ideal but as an event. Thus, knowledge of it is a gift.[15]

Barth finds support for his analysis of the situation of the church before God and the place of theological reflection in St Anselm's understanding of the certainty of knowledge of God only in God.[16] Anselm did not grasp this concept out of the air. It follows necessarily from an analysis of the situation of the preacher and the hearer.[17]

It is for these reasons that Barth insists that dogma cannot be understood either as a reflection of the self-consciousness of the individual Christian or of the church. Likewise, it cannot be considered as objective verbal statements. Dogma can only be conceived as eschatological reality for which the church must hope and pray.[18] The event structure of the Word of God entails this. It also involves a particular way of understanding the doctrine of the Trinity.

If the 'root' or the foundation of the Trinity is found in the event nature of the Word of God in the situation of the preacher and the hearer, this fact will decisively shape its configuration.[19] The event structure of the Word of God precludes an admixture in human knowledge of God of revealed and natural knowledge, as though God's being can be quantified by the creatures' knowledge of the creation. Likewise, there can be no hidden metaphysical hinterland apart from the act in which God is known. God is wholly present in revelation or God is not present at all.[20] Here we find the same concern as that which Barth had voiced to his friend Thurneysen, a concern for a Trinity of 'being', not just an 'economic' Trinity. An 'economic' Trinity would presuppose a distinction between the being of God as revealed and the being of God who is apart from revelation.[21] The event structure of revelation, which configures Barth's understanding of the knowledge of the Word of God, precludes consideration of any such distinction that is not presupposed by the event of revelation itself.

Understood in terms of the event of revelation, the Trinity provides Barth with the basis for understanding within a circle of knowledge which follows

---

15. *Ibid*, 96.
16. *Ibid*, 98.
17. *Ibid*, 102, 108
18. *Ibid*, 123–125.
19. *Ibid*, 131, 132.
20. *Ibid*, 135.
21. Cf C Welch, *The Trinity in Contemporary Theology* (London: SCM, 1953), 239.

the contours of God's own being. God is both the object and the subject of the statement 'God speaks'. There is, then, a qualitative difference between human reason or religious self-consciousness on the one hand, and revelation and faith on the other.[22]

Barth's rejection of a distinction between an economic Trinity and a Trinity of 'being', on the basis of a definition of revelation in terms of 'event' or 'act', entails that Barth develops a particular view of the relationship between revelation and its historical content. Any direct relationship with the fact of revelation by means of the historical content of revelation apart from faith, which presupposes the freedom of God in the act of revelation, is excluded. Such a relationship would presuppose a freedom of the creature for God not included in the event of revelation itself. Therefore, we must make a distinction between *Übergeschichte* and *Urgeschichte* to understand the historical nature of God's revelation.[23] The former refers to 'that eternal event between God the Father, Son and Holy Spirit'.[24] This distinguishes it from the event in which God gives himself to be known in the form of the creature. This revelation of God, while it consists of all that involves the event of the divine *Übergeschichte*, since it is the personal presence of God as *actus purus*, is nevertheless not itself *Übergeschichte*. Revelation is something 'more' than the 'history' that is God's eternity.[25] The Word of God assumes this 'more than eternity' and, in so far as this happens, revelation is historical. Because God's free action presupposes revelation, the statement that revelation is historical cannot be reversed. No examination of history can lead to the revealed God.[26] History as God's revelation must be understood as a special history; it is in fact *Urgeschichte*.

Barth's formulates his view of history here in terms of dogmatics, not a theory of history in general. Revelation considered from the point of view of a theory of history remains ambiguous, even mythological.[27] Put positively, world history from the point of view of revelation can be said to reflect or echo the *urgeschichtliche* event. In this sense, revelation can be said to be the *Urbild* of all history, general history is the periphery of this middle point.[28] In like manner,

22.   Barth. *Die christliche Dogmatik,* 139, 206, 207.
23.   *Ibid,* 231, 232.
24.   *Ibid*; author's translation.
25.   *Ibid,* 232.
26.   *Ibid,* 233.
27.   *Ibid,* 236, 237.
28.   *Ibid,* 237, 238.

the church in its distinction from the world, as the sphere in which the Word of God is actualised, reflects the greater distinction between *Urgeschichte* and history.

Of particular intersect in this context, as shedding light on Barth's view of history and historical relationships, is his understanding of the relationship between Jesus and the apostolic band. They become who they are as witnesses not through the relationship which they form with Jesus, considered as an historical figure. Their authority derives from direct meeting with the *urgeschichtliche* event without historical co-ordinates. The difference between the apostles and the patriarchs of the Old Covenant does not lie in the apostles' relationship to the events of AD 1–30, but in their relationship to the *urgeschichtliche* content of that time, and thus not to Jesus character as a historical figure, but to his character as a witness.[29]

Barth thus achieves in this account of the event structure of revelation, associated with his view of the doctrine of the Trinity, an understanding of the relationships between the reality of God's presence in history on the one hand, and history and human language and relationships on the other. Barth has given an account of the revelation of God, which, while safeguarding the freedom and non-objectivity of God in terms of the structure of worldly reality, is yet able to see a relationship between God and the creature as the object of this activity.

It may indeed be true that Barth leaves many questions unanswered, and that the influence of Kant through Barth's teacher W Herrmann of Marburg is obvious at many points in his exposition. He is not unaware of these questions.[30] But, in his own way, Barth has succeeded in confronting what he saw as the danger of the dominant neo-Protestant theology of his day, the co-positing of God and the creature with God in terms of an ontology which denied God's freedom and therefore God's grace. It is true that with the severe dialectic inherent in Barth's method of understanding the event nature of revelation, God's being in becoming the God of the creature, that 'an existentialism of some kind was bound to arise if only to anchor the event (of revelation) down to earth or to clothe it with flesh'.[31] But Barth has begun to move in directions which were to become formative for his later dogmatic thought. He grounds the event structure of the Word of God in the being of the Trinity so that knowledge of the

---

29.   *Ibid*, 245–249.

30.   Barth, *CD* 1/1, 14ff, 159.

31.   TF Torrance, *Karl Barth: an* Introduction, 144ff.

creature and the creatures' world presupposes a relationship with God that is founded in his self-election to be the God of the creature.[32]

### Barth and Schleiermacher: the question of neo-Protestantism

We have already spoken of neo-Protestantism's co-positing of God with the creature in a neutral concept of being as forming the object of Barth's polemical posture. To appreciate the meaning of Barth's stance we must understand something of the thought of that theologian, which epitomised for him this neo-Protestant co-positing. This person whom Barth highly respected as a theologian is F Schleiermacher.[33]

Barth spent some time towards the end of 1923 studying Schleiermacher.[34] From this study emerged two rather lengthy essays.[35] He saw Schleiermacher as a theologian concerned with the nature of the inexpressibility of the divine reality.[36] All expressions of this reality in words are at the same time a profanation of that reality. All dogma must therefore be considered as descriptions of human self-consciousness and is not to be considered as descriptions of something particular in the nature of God.[37] Theology is thus directed by Schleiermacher towards an 'X' that combines an equilibrium of opposing forces. The divine reality is the absolute subject/object, the highest knowledge in its identity with the highest being. It stands over against our existence in the duality of reason and nature. It is never identical with but is related to our knowing and being.[38] The divine reality is reached by no finite knowing. However, there is a correlate to the absolute given foundation to finite knowing and being. It is the unity of feeling beyond the psychological realms of thinking and willing. This

32.  Barth, *Die christliche Domatik*, 137,138,150,152–155,178,191–194,197–198.
33.  Barth, 'Liberal Theology: Some Alternatives', in *Hibbert Journal* 59 (1960–1961): 216, 217: 'There is no doubt that Schleiermacher, whether we look backwards or forwards in the history of theology, was the prince of all anthropocentric, and so all liberal, theologians.' see also158–160. Also Barth, *From Rousseau to Ritschl*, 308: 'Anyone who has not loved here, and is not in a position to love again may not hate either.'
34.  K Barth and E Thurneysen, *Revolutionary Theology in the Making: Correspondence 1914–1925* (London: Epworth, 1964), 158–160. Cf JD Smart, *The Divided Mind of Modern Theology*, 145.
35.  Barth, *Theology and Church* (London: SCM, 1962), 136ff, 159ff.
36.  *Ibid*, 161.
37.  *Ibid*, 163, 164.
38.  *Ibid*, 168.

phenomenon of feeling is related to thinking and willing as the ground of their certainty. In this function of feeling Schleiermacher finds the original foundation established even in us.[39] However, as soon as this original foundation enters the sphere of discursive thought there remains only a refracted image of the original foundation.[40]

While Barth is conscious of the strong tendency in Schleiermacher towards an undifferentiated unity, a 'placid silence', he realises that the actuality of the individual held a place of significance in his scheme of thought. Against Schelling, Schleiermacher speaks of 'the lofty arbitrariness of Christianity'.[41] This seemingly inimical characteristic in Schleiermacher's thought is explained in terms of the fact that the original ground of being does not teach but acts. 'What makes Revelation is not that it is true, but that it is effective.'[42] Effectiveness here means the modification of the individual religious self-consciousness. God is to be understood as the non-objective cause whose effects are objective in terms of feeling, as opposed to being simply cognisable.

The historical figure of Jesus is understood by Schleiermacher in terms of his power to impart to others the strength of his God consciousness in the form of absolute dependence upon the ground of being.[43] As it is through Jesus that one comes to an experience of absolute dependence, it must be concluded that his God consciousness is not only prototypal but archetypal. For if humanity itself had the power to produce this archetypal God consciousness, its actual condition of sin, the incomplete feeling of dependence, would be inexplicable. The possession of such an archetypal God consciousness in Jesus can only be explained in terms of a divine creative act. Jesus Christ does not help people because he is a Redeemer; he is the Redeemer because he helps them.[44]

Barth's criticism of such a Christology is that communion between God and the creature is established by a concept of human nature which serves as the higher order in which a move is made from the sensuous to the spiritual. Its logic can be summarised thus; we

---

39. Barth, *Theology and Church*, 170.
40. *Ibid*, 174, 178.
41. *Ibid*, 178.
42. *Ibid*, 179; see also 181, 189, 196, 197.
43. *Ibid*, 187.
44. Cf R Bultmann, *Essays Theological and Philosophical* (London: SCM, 1955), 280, 281.

substantiate an existent divine life, conclude from this divine an activity witnessing to it, and from this activity deduce a correspondingly endowed active being.[45]

Barth sees nothing but a contradiction between Schleiermacher's concern for the individual and a Christology which derives its significance from a 'higher order of human nature'.[46] Schleiermacher allowed himself to be pushed into a mystico-naturalistic corner where the historical element in Christianity could play only a questionable role. This conclusion is a tentative one and is open to revision in the light of a continuing debate with Schleiermacher.[47]

Barth's conclusion, though tentative, is concerned to defend the unity of theological knowledge as grounded in God's being and act in the event of revelation. This unity cannot be considered as existing within the relative differences of intra-mundane relationships, such as the relationships in which individuals may stand with one another.

It is a paradoxical fact that Barth's criticism of Schleiermacher is exactly what Schleiermacher strove so energetically to avoid: the identification of God with a state of being in contingent existence.[48] The possibility of the reduction of Schleiermacher's theology to anthropology is grounded in his emphasis that God is exempted from any direct relationship to the sphere in which we have only relative knowledge. By exempting God as the Absolute from such a relationship, Schleiermacher is forced to make God wholly other. God is One with whom there must be strictly non-cognitive relation.[49]

It should be observed in passing—since there will be occasion to return to this point—that Barth is not free from the same difficulties he sees in Schleiermacher. In the alternative he proposes, it has already been noted that the sharpness of

---

45.  Barth, *Theology and Church*, 190.
46.  *Ibid*, 189.
47.  *Ibid*, 199. Cf Barth, *From Rousseau to* Ritschl, 307.
48.  Cf F Schleiermacher, *The Christian Faith* (Edinburgh: T&T Clark, 1928), Section 4, 17–18. We agree with the judgment that 'there can be no doubt on the one hand his [Schleiermacher's] critical idealism was the obverse side of a very serious realism, for his doctrine of dependence was intended to be a decisive expression of the ultimate objectivity of God which must not be confounded with our own objectivity'; TF Torrance, 'Hermeneutics according to FDE Schleiermacher', in *Scottish Journal of Theology* 22 (1968): 264.
49.  JB Torrance, 'Interpretation and Understanding in Schleiermacher's Theology: Some Critical Questions', in *Scottish Journal of Theology* 22 (1968): 279ff.

the dialectic involved in Barth's understanding of the event nature of revelation leads to some form of existentialism in order to ground revelation in history.[50] It will be of continuing interest to examine how successful Barth is in addressing this important issue. For the moment, we note how Barth dealt with this question in *Die christliche Dogmatik*.

## Schleiermacher and Barth in *Die christliche Dogmatik*

It is with reference to the dogma of the Trinity that Barth formulates his criticism of Schleiermacher. For Barth, the Trinity is to be understood in relation to the question as to the possibility of human speech about, and hearing of, God's Word. In this point of departure, he emphasises two fundamental characteristics of God's activity, which Schleiermacher found difficult to express. These are the objectivity of the self-revealing God as the subject of revelation, and the relationship of this presence of God to human speech about God.[51]

Barth again emphasises that Schleiermacher's theological method can only lead to a situation in the church where the phenomenon of religious self-consciousness and the possibility of revelation are one and the same thing.[52] This implies that an essential and general element in human nature is one with the divine.[53] Consequently, the creature does not need God in order to be with God. There can then be no question of the existence of an irreparable guilt of the creature before God, but only of a blank, direct and quantitatively differentiated relationship between creatures and God. It is inevitable in this context that such a God will be objectless, since the relationship in which this God stands with the creature is one of an unending circle of natural life, of One in all and through all. Whether this One is called personal, depends on personal inclination and imagination. Schleiermacher never concealed the fact that his preference did not run in this direction. Ultimately, the idea of God is not necessary at all.[54] God is understood in terms of the relationship presupposed by the feeling of

---

50.  See above, 5. Cf also H Urs von Balthasar, *Karl Barth: Darstellung und Deutung seiner Theologie*, 213.
51.  See *Die christliche Dogmatik*, appendix 1.
52.  *Die christliche Dogmatik*, 306. Cf *From Rousseau to Ritschl*, 355.
53.  *Ibid*, 307.
54.  *Ibid*, 309: Eine Religion ohne Gott kann besser sein als eine andere mit Gott', since, 'Gott ist nicht alles in der Religion, sondern Eines, und das Universum ist mehr'.

absolute dependence; God is the whence of the feeling of absolute dependence. It is only meant as symbolic if this whence is conveyed as an object.[55]

Against such an interpretation of God in relationship to the creature Barth emphasises the sheer actuality of God's personal presence in the act of revelation. Only thus, from the point of view of the preacher and the hearer, can it be made clear that faith in God is a hazardous venture. The relationship between God and the creature must be understood as a drama, a struggle, the continuity of which must be sought and found in God alone.[56]

Schleiermacher maintains, however, that

> it would be part of the perfect truth that God would make himself known as He is in himself [his essence]; but such a [revelation] could neither emerge externally out of some given fact, and even if it were to reach a human soul in such an incomprehensible way, it could not be comprehended or held in thought by it and, if in no way perceived or held, could not be effective.[57]

The contrary is the case, according to Barth. This is precisely what has to happen and does happen in the existential struggle of faith in relationship with God's Holy Spirit. In this either/or struggle created by the actuality of the personal presence of God with the creature there stands the subjective possibility of revelation, and nowhere else.[58]

The strategic placement of the Trinity in Barth's presentation may be said to derive from his concern to oppose Schleiermacher's 'objectless' theology with its anthropological presuppositions. Barth understands the 'root' of the doctrine of the Trinity to consist in 'God's self-grounded speech'.[59] In all forms of revelation, even the ungrounded event of the person of Jesus Christ, it is God alone who speaks. The secondary forms of revelation, the humanity of Jesus, the Scriptures considered as human documents, and the preacher's word, must be understood as relative to the revelation of God's own personal speech. In this, God 'does not yield his honour to any other. Never and nowhere does this

---

55. *Ibid*, 310.
56. *Ibid*, 313.
57. *Ibid*, 314, 315; author's translation.
58. *Ibid*, 315.
59. Barth, *Die christliche Dogmatik*, 131; author's translation.

form become the subject of revelation.'[60] So God is either wholly revealed in revelation or not at all. There can be no quantifying of God's personal presence in revelation. Natural theology is excluded precisely for this reason. It attempts to divide the knowledge of God between natural and revealed knowledge. This is shown to be an impossible enterprise by the manner and fact of God's *self*-revelation. The hiddenness of God in the event of God's self-revelation is not co-determinate with the limits of the structures of human cognition. The hiddenness of God, God's incomprehensibility, is rooted in the freedom of God to speak, to be present in revelation. 'He who recognises the revealed God, he and only he also recognises the hidden God.'[61]

Barth expounds this fundamental feature of revelation within the context of developing an understanding of the Trinity. The subject and the object of the statement, 'God speaks', is God. To impugn this conclusion is to question the reality of God's Lordship in the event of revelation. If God is revealed to the creature then God is the One who speaks, the word who is spoken and the hearer in the event of revelation.[62] The creature who receives revelation cannot be understood as presupposing any continuity with or in this event. If there were a continuity, this would have to be understood as an efflux or continuation of the person of God in history, which would be a contradiction in terms. Against any such suggestion, it must be rigidly affirmed that God is both subject and object in the act of revelation.[63] Barth may have thought that his exposition of the doctrine of the Trinity within the framework of this very tight dialectic, based on an analysis of God's Lordship, was the '*Nagel*', (nail) which co-ordinated his argument against the neo-Protestant co-positing of the creature with God. However, the very structure of his presentation prevented the Trinity from having the strategic importance he intended for it. This basic weakness became evident when Barth read the reviews of *Die christliche Dogmatik*.[64]

On the one hand, Barth was criticised for not developing a consistent anthropology that would correspond to his doctrine of God and serve as the basis for his exposition. On the other hand, he was criticised for attempting an existentialist proof of the doctrine of the Trinity because of the structural relationship between the dogma of the Trinity and the situation of the preacher

---

60. *Ibid*, 134; author's translation.
61. *Ibid*, 137; author's translation.
62. *Ibid*, 139.
63. *Ibid*.
64. See Barth, *CD* 1/1,141ff, 153, 159, 194ff.

and hearer. In these critiques, he was faced with a contradiction. He realised that his critics from both sides could find a basis in his writing for their point of view.

Barth's intention, in developing the doctrine of the Trinity in terms of the situation of the preacher and the hearer of the Word of God, was clearly to understand how the creature participated in the actuality of God's self-revelation. However, when God's revelation is expounded in terms of the actuality of God's presence without consideration of a corresponding continuity of the historical existence of the creature, the question of the meaning of revelation is bound to arise. Again, in attempting to counter Schleiermacher's wordless revelation by emphasising the locus of revelation in the situation of the preacher and hearer and thus the possibility of its verbal form in history, Barth gave credence to the suggestion that he was attempting to prove the existence of God by finding a congruence between the nature of the Word of God and human existence.

> The Word of God is not only speech but address. Here we can neither hurry here not there, neither to heaven or the abyss in order to hear it. Rather, because it has come to us, 'it is in your mouth and in your heart'. That means that listening man is included in the concept of the word of God, just as much as the speaking God. He is 'posited with it', as Schleiermacher's God is posited with the feeling of absolute dependence. One does not speak of God's word unless thereby one speaks of its being heard by man . . . That is precisely why the word of God is a concept accessible only to existentialist thinking.[65]

It was patently obvious to Barth that he had to solve the question of a genuine relationship between God and the creature on the basis of God's act of revelation, whilst at the same time avoiding the pit of an independent anthropology. If this was to be accomplished, while remaining true to the direction of his developing thought, a more diligent search had to be made into the reality of the *being*

---

65.   Barth, *Die christliche Dogmatik*,111; author's translation. The final form of the material presented in *Die christliche Dogmatik* does not deviate significantly from the programmatic sketch given to the project in 1924. See Barth and Thurneysen, *Revolutionary Theology in the Making*, 182, 183. See also Barth's comment, 'Das Korrelat der Wahrheit der Offenbarung, des Wortes Gottes, ist der Mensch.' More precisely, it is the 'Einzelnen! Er is das Korrelat der Wahrheit.' *Ibid*, 139.

of God in the *act* of self-revelation. This would entail a re-examination of the relationship between theology and philosophy and the place of the doctrine of God in the dogmatic enterprise.

Barth's thoughts about the former question may be seen in the series of lectures he gave at Dortmund in 1929.[66] The latter question would be dealt with by Barth in his critical study of St Anselm's *Proslogion* in the following year.[67]

## The relation between theology and philosophy: *Schicksal und Idee in der Theologie*

In these lectures, Barth attempts to clarify the relationship between the two poles of human thought that emerged as the basis for the critical appraisal of the *Die christliche Dogmatik*. On the one hand, there were those who criticised him for attempting to justify the doctrine of the Trinity in terms of the structure of human existence, through his analysis of the situation of the preacher and the hearer as the *Sitz im Leben* of the dogma. Did this method tie the existence of God to human existence as a kind of fate (*Schicksal*)? On the other hand, there were those who criticised Barth's effort as projecting a timeless ideology, unrelated to the historicity of human existence, an *Idee*.

Barth saw that these twin problems were not a peculiarity of theological thought. Philosophy had perennially concerned itself with this question, which entailed the issue of how the knowing subject is related to the object of knowledge. The presupposition of the question in the theological context should be how theology can become 'an objectively ordered exploration of the truth in relation to God as the Object of the church's proclamation.'[68] Theological knowledge is thus tied to its Object in terms of its structure and truth. Theology is not concerned with 'the truth of God as such'; it is concerned with the truth of God 'in the special sphere of the church.'[69] Meant is not the church in general,

---

66. Barth, *Schicksal und Idee in der Theologie*. Gesammelte Vorträge, Band 3 (Zürich: Ev Verlag Zollikon, 1957), 54–92.
67. K Barth, *Fides Quaerens Intellectum: Anselm's Proof of the Existence of God*. See in this connection G Watson, 'Karl Barth and St Anselm's Theological Programme', in *Scottish Journal of Theology* 30/1 (1977): 31–45 and G Watson, 'A Study in St Anselm's Soteriology and Karl Barth's Theological Method', in *Scottish Journal of Theology* 42/4 (1989): 493–512.
68. Barth, *Schicksal und Idee in der Theologie*, 55; author's translation. Cf Barth, *Dogmatik im Grundriss*, 12.
69. *Schicksal und Idee*, 55; author's translation.

an empty sphere above the church and its confessions. This is so since the God who is confessed by the evangelical churches is the God who has 'given Himself to be found by us'.[70] Since God's gracious approach to the creature defines both the sphere of knowledge and the objectivity of God, the objectivity of God is not at the disposal of humankind. Theology 'therefore has God as an object, but as an object only in so far as it has him as subject'.[71] This is of decisive importance when it is recalled that theology as a human activity is not carried out in heaven but on earth, amidst the other human disciplines which attempt to understand the reality of the world as it is experienced by specific cultures. If theology has a place within the spectrum of human intellectual endeavours, then we must understand that this is not because it is dependent upon the characteristics of human knowledge as such. Theology as a human undertaking is dependent upon the 'miracle' of God's gracious condescension to be known by the creature.[72] Thus, those characteristics which shape the structure of human thought in other areas of knowledge must, in theology, play a different role.

This may be seen in the history of theology. There are those theologies that emphasise that aspect of human thought which, in understanding 'reality', draws attention to the fact that things objective to the knower as well as the knowing subject 'are'. Such theologies may be characterised as 'realist'. It is assumed that, since God and creatures exist and 'are', a link exists between God and the creature simply in terms of this fact. God then becomes the creatures 'fate'. A state of mutual reciprocity is posited by the fact of the existence of God and the creature. This theological realism found classic expression in Thomas Aquinas and the doctrine of the *analogia entis*. Barth understood this to mean that

> all being as such has a part in God, in utmost dissimilarity as a mere creature, yet most similar to the Creator in that it, too, has being: *analogia entis*.[73]

---

70.  *Ibid*, 56; author's translation.

71.  *Ibid*.

72.  *Ibid*, 58.

73.  *Ibid*, 62; author's translation. It may well be true that Barth has basically misunderstood Thomas at this point. On this question see Barth, *CD* 1/1, x, and 2/1, 82. Cf B Mondin, *The Principle of Analogy in Protestant and Catholic Thought* (The Hague: Nijhoff, 1963); EL Mascall, *Existence and Analogy* (London: Longmans, Green, 1949); TF Torrance, *Theology in Reconstruction* (London: SCM, 1965) and *Theological Science* (Oxford: Oxford University Press, 1969).

Christian theology takes the legitimate concerns of realism into account, that is, the assertion that the God of the Christian tradition not only exists, but also exists within the mode of being which characterises nature and history in general. Christian theology must also add certain definite qualifications to the understanding of this givenness of God's existence. These qualifications are based on the fact that the subjective and objective givenness of being, which is presupposed by realist theologies, needs to be understood in terms of the subjective and objective realities included in the event of revelation itself, not as an independent or so called 'neutral' ontology. Although *similitudo Dei* may be experienced in the natural world—such as in the I-Thou relationship—its truth, however, is to be understood as grounded in the reality and actuality of God's gracious approach to the creature. It is this condescension that makes possible the conceiving of God existing as subjectively and objectively present to the creature. Thus, theology does not ask if it is to speak realistically of God, but 'in what way it may speak realistically'.[74] Theology will speak of God's revelation and God's objectivity as 'revelation and not a state of being revealed'.[75]

Here Barth is progressing toward a view of revelation, which has a Christological content that enables him to relate the creatures experience of earthly reality to the divine disclosure. However, at the same time he safeguards the distinction between God and the given actuality of the creature on the basis of God's freedom in the act of God's self-giving. This overcomes some of the obvious difficulties associated with Barth's use of existentialist categories in *Die christliche Dogmatik*. There, Barth postulated a correlation between God's act of revelation and human existence, considered from the point of view of the preacher and the hearer. This correlation was only prevented from developing into a full-blown ontology by a sharp dialectic reinforcing a doctrine of forensic justification.

However, Barth still faced significant problems. If the focus of God's triune life is the basis for describing the relationship between God and the creature—Jesus Christ and the Holy Spirit being two poles of an objectivity and subjectivity in God's revelation—it remains to be seen how Barth can relate this reality to the relativities of creaturely life. He certainly says that 'the Word and therefore God . . . enters the mode of being of nature and history, our own mode of being'.[76] However, this will need to be spelled out in greater detail if

---

74. Barth, *Schicksal und Idee in der Theologie,* 61; author's translation.
75. *Ibid,* 70.
76. *Ibid,* 65: author's translation.

the perennial appeal of theological realism is to be averted. This will not be achieved simply by emphasising the truth of God's existence in terms of the objectivity and subjectivity of God's own inner triune life. It needs to be shown how the historical relativities of earthly existence in the humanity of the Son of God may be shown to have theological relevance to Barth's understanding of revelation and its trinitarian structure.

The other pole of human thought with which theology concerns itself takes its point of departure in the question of the correlation between the outward and inward givenness of existence. It asks the question, 'what is truth?'[77] This question presupposes the central concern of those theologies which find classical expression in the *via negativa* of Thomas Aquinas. The attempt is made to abstract from the individual entity to the idea of being itself. Wherever the idea of God is entertained there will be a legitimate attempt to distinguish between the givenness of God and that of all other being. In comparison to God, all other being must be described as non-being.[78]

Idealism in Barth's terms means emphasising the fact that, though the Word became flesh, the flesh did not become the Word. It ensures the aspect of veiling in the act of God's self-unveiling. Idealism does not deny the givenness of historical reality as revelation,

> but it wishes to understand it as transparent so that the truth may shine through it, without which it would not be the reality of God.[79]

Barth's criticism of theological idealism is that it often sidesteps the particularity of God's self-disclosure. It opts instead, on its own authority, for a general openness of the creature to the truth of God.[80]

> We have to consider revelation not as a general possibility of man, but as a special possibility of God: and as Christian theology, the possibility of God in Christ that is given in the witness to Christ in the Bible and the Church.[81]

---

77.  *Ibid*, 72.
78.  *Ibid*, 73, 74.
79.  *Ibid*, 76, 77; author's translation.
80.  *Ibid*, 78; author's translation.
81.  *Ibid*, 78.

Thus, genuine theological realism will recognise that the truth is established by God alone, 'not as an act of God *and* man, but as a deed of God alone'.[82] Knowledge of the truth thus entails acknowledgement. It means faith. Human reason allows that the truth of the matter is determined by that which is above it. 'To bring this Above, which we are to obey, back into the antithesis of spontaneity and receptivity would be meaningless.'[83] This antithesis, which has place in our knowledge of the truth of created things, has no place in the knowledge of faith. Reason must acknowledge that this antithesis is replaced in the knowledge of faith by a 'sphere of eternal relationships.'[84] It is just as disastrous for theology to identify human reason with God as it is for theological realism to identify God with created existence.

Barth rejects one sided realism and idealism, while recognising the legitimate claims of both ways to knowledge. Theology itself cannot achieve a synthesis in this matter of the structure of human knowledge, and use such a synthesis in its knowledge of God. Such attempts reveal the essential *hubris* of theology and exposure the contradiction in which the creature lives before God.[85] That theology can proceed with its work in the light of the contradictions of the human paths to knowledge is a possibility to be affirmed only on the basis of God's free grace. Only on that basis will God own the work of theology. 'This practical criterion of theological knowledge is the thought of *divine* election.'[86]

The epistemological relevance of election, in this context, means that both the speaking and the hearing of truth in theology is a matter of God's free decision to own that which the theologian offers. Theology will therefore be characterised by a certain humility in that its structures of thought will be open-ended, and in this way acknowledge that it serves an object (subject) which its thought cannot contain. This fact also entails that theology is a function of the church—there where the free unmerited approach of God to the creature is acknowledged. The practical implication of this is that theology is orientated towards Christology.[87]

In this emphasis, Barth signals an advance on the thought of revelation in *Die christliche Dogmatik*. There, the Trinity served to expound the sheer actuality

---

82.  *Ibid*, 80; author's translation; italics in the original.
83.  *Ibid*, 81.
84.  *Ibid*.
85.  *Ibid*, 86–87.
86.  *Ibid*, 90; author's translation; italics in the original.
87.  *Ibid*, 92.

of the event of revelation. The relationship of revelation to the situation of encounter could only be conceived in terms of an extreme dialectic grounded in a view of forensic justification: as a 'seeing' that was blind, an echo, an existence that could only be thought of as non-existence. He now stresses neither pure negation nor affirmation, but reconciliation in terms of the free election by God of the creature in its relationship to revelation. The 'spokenness of the Word and our hearing is always a matter of the free grace of God'.[88]

By locating the doctrine of election within the eternal relationships in which God exists as God, Barth has been able to make an advance in his understanding of the correspondence between the rationality of the creature and the actuality of revelation. He is able to establish a basis for the correlation between the rationality of the creature and the rationality of God, while still maintaining the Lordship of God in the event of revelation. Barth identifies the 'spokenness of the Word' with the election of God, implying thereby a correspondence between God's own self-affirmation as God and the event of revelation. Barth has thereby entered upon a way where it will be difficult to take into account the contingency and relativity of the life experience of Jesus as the Son of God in his developing understanding of the dogma of the Trinity. The life of Jesus is in danger of becoming merely illustrative of a pre-mundane divine decision. One is thus cautious of Barth's conclusion that

> to bring this Above, which we are to obey, back into the antithesis of spontaneity and receptivity would be meaningless. This antithesis has its place when we are dealing with recognition of *things. Here* we are speaking of the realm of eternal relationships.[89]

I would suggest that it is precisely because it is the place here described, with all its contradictions, that we cannot ask after an Above in which these contradictions find no place in determining the meaning of revelation as an event in human history.[90]

---

88.  *Ibid*; author's translation.
89.  Barth, *Schicksal und Idee in der Theologie*, 81; author's translation; italics are in the original.
90.  Cf HU von Balthasar, *Karl Barth: Darstellung*, 212–214, who speaks of a *'Punkt der höchsten Intensität'* in Barth which is a common feature of idealist theologies and philosophies. G Hendry, 'The Dogmatic Form of Barth's Theology', in *Theology Today* 13 (1956–1957): 300ff, 314, maintains that Barth should somehow combine the

## The influence St Anselm's theological method

To arrive at an understanding of the importance of St Anselm's thought on Barth's theological development, it will be necessary to assess the meaning of two of St Anselm's key theological concepts.

The concepts I have in mind are *veritas* (truth) and *rectitudo* (rightness). The discussion will focus on these as they relate to St Anselm's understanding of the part played by the humanity of the historical Jesus in God's act of reconciliation. As I have already noted, this is an area in the development of Barth's thought that has some questionable features. It is also the area that provides Barth with the greatest difficulties in assessing St Anselm's thought.[91]

For St Anselm, God is the Supreme Truth. 'There is truth in the essence of all that exists, because all things are what they are in the Supreme Truth.'[92] This Supreme Truth is the cause of all else that is said to be true, both propositions and states of affairs.

> Although all the different kinds of rightness . . . are what they are because the things they are in either are as they ought to be or else do what they ought to do, nevertheless the Supreme Truth is not rightness because it is under obligation. All things are obliged to it, and it is obliged to nothing else.[93]

St Anselm integrally relates truth to rightness. The two words signify the same reality.[94] Everything that is has a certain truth and rightness which makes it an integrated part of a complex of relationships. All things, even inanimate things which have no will, are under an obligation that is determined by its rightness. This obligation is specifically related to the Supreme Truth of all things.[95] This Truth, although it is itself not identical with any particular, is that which allows it to be said of this or that thing, state of affairs, etc, 'the

---

anthropological implications of the dialectic which he developed in his early work with the later intra-trinitarian dialectic in a 'higher synthesis'!

91. Barth, *CD* 4/1, 485ff.
92. St Anselm, *Concerning the Truth* (New York: Harper, 1967), chapter vii, 102.
93. *Ibid*, chapter x, 108. Cf chapters i and xii and St Anselm, *Proslogion*, chapter xiv, 21, 22.
94. *Ibid*, chapter xiii, 117 and chapter xii, 110, 111.
95. *Ibid*, chapter x,108. Cf St Anselm, *Monologion*, 38, 39.

truth of that thing'.[96] One can only come to an understanding of the truth and rightness of things when we understand in what relationship they stand to the Supreme Truth. St Anselm speaks, through the disciple, of things 'participating' *(participando)*[97] in the truth. The Platonic notion of participation should not be inferred from this. St Anselm makes the critical distinction between a thing's truth and that which is the *cause* of its truth. In concluding that truth is one in all things, St Anselm does not wish to suggest that all particular truth shares in a simple divine nature.[98]

St Anselm states emphatically that the Supreme Truth is radically different from any creaturely truth.[99] Truth and rightness with respect to God have a very specific meaning. The formula with which St Anselm conducts his celebrated proof of the existence of God—that God is a being 'than which nothing greater can be conceived'[100]—indicates the decisive importance St Anselm attaches to the ineffable nature of the Creator and Lord of all things visible and invisible. God is not to be measured by or conceived to be dependent upon anything apart from God.[101] The eternal Son is the truth of all created things not because he corresponds to the world but because he is its truth.[102]

The necessary reasons that serve as premises, by which St Anselm demonstrates his arguments, signify aspects of the exalted Truth, which remains beyond the grasp of the human intellect.[103] Therefore, St Anselm's demonstrations of the various articles of faith make more than simple logical connections between premise and conclusion. In each case, cohesion is achieved by presupposing factors, which cannot be contained in the connections within

---

96.  *Ibid*, chapter xii, 120.
97.  St Anselm, *Dialogus de Veritate*, Migne L Tomus clviii, Caput ii, Col 469: 'nihil est verum, nisi participando veritatum.'
98.  St Anselm, *Concerning the Truth*, chapter x, 109. Cf Monologion, chapter lxv.
99.  *Ibid*, 108.
100. St Anselm, *Proslogion*, chapter ii, 7ff.
101. St Anselm, *Monologion*, chapter v, 45ff; *Proslogion*, chapter xii.
102. *Ibid*, chapters xxxiii, 95ff; xlvii, 111ff; *Proslogion*, chapter xxiii, 28, 29.
103. I cannot accept Prenter's criticism of St Anselm that he is too indebted to St Augustine's Platonism and that his distinction between faith and understanding leads to neglect of the creaturely objectivity of the event of revelation. See Prenter, 'Glauben und Erkennen bei Karl Barth', in *Kerygma und Dogma* 2 (1956): 176ff, and 'Die Einheit von Schöpfung und Erlösung', in *Theologische Zeitschrift* 2 (1946): 161ff.

the logical demonstration. Propositions and concepts are not the cause of truth.[104] Propositions and concepts become true as they express the truth or rightness of things or states of affairs in their proper order established by their obligation to the Supreme Truth. St Anselm consequently left indeterminate the exact character of the relationship between created truth and the Supreme Truth. One may come to recognise that a thing or state of affairs exists in truth, but cannot describe or picture exactly the nature of the right relationship involved. The truth of the ineffable Creator and sustainer of all things can be partially perceived through created truth; it is God's truth that is perceived if only partially.[105] The 'fool' who denies the existence of God perceives truth entirely in terms of the definitions of words and concepts irrespective of their relationship to the reality to which they refer.[106] For St Anselm, on the other hand, the truth is directly related to the nature of the objective reality to which the words and concepts refer. The indeterminacy of St Anselm's method of understanding this relationship between things, states, and affairs that are said to be true and the Supreme Truth, implies an openness to objective reality as the vehicle of truth that derives from his understanding of the ineffable nature of divine truth.[107]

I now take up the important question of how Barth deals with St Anselm's understanding of the relationship between the incarnation and the atonement. At issue, here, is the place Barth is able to give to the relativities of the human decisions and purpose entailed in Christ's obedience to the Father's will. The question relates to the place of the historical relativities of the experience of Jesus determining the meaning of God's self-revelation, and consequently the structure of the Trinity. Barth's difficulty with St Anselm's understanding of the relationship between the incarnation and the atonement is expressed in his interpretation of St Anselm's *Cur Deus Homo*. This discussion will also indicate the central questions which will also occur in Barth's interpretation of the *Proslogion*, and which of course are of critical importance in determining the place of the Trinity in Barth's mature theological reflections in the *Church Dogmatics*.

Barth discusses St Anselm's position in the light of his understanding of revelation. In the doctrine of reconciliation,[108] which is structured according to

---

104. St Anselm, *Concerning the Truth*, chapter x, 108, 109.
105. St Anselm, *Proslogion*, chapter xiv, 22, 23.
106. *Ibid*, chapter vi, 9, 10.
107. Cf TF Torrance, *Theological Science*, 273.
108. Barth, *CD* 4/1–4.

the view of Lordship described in the doctrine of revelation,[109] Lordship means that God is revealed as the Lord who is a servant, the servant who is Lord, and the Lord who is the true witness. The unity of God's act of reconciliation is structured according to the unity of God's Lordship as revealed in the life and death, cross and resurrection of Jesus Christ.[110] Barth maintains that the divine forgiveness entailed in this event reveals human sin as

> the fact that man is God's debtor. He is a debtor who cannot pay. God has to excuse him . . . Indeed, when we see what the debt is, we see that no other reaction to it is adequate but the divine forgiveness.[111]

Since the creatures' debt is of such a nature that it cannot be repaid, it must be concluded that God forgives the debtor 'primarily and decisively because His forgiveness alone is the restitution of the right which has been broken by the sin of man.'[112] Barth therefore agrees with St Anselm's definition of sin as debt toward God. He finds St Anselm's presentation of the matter 'very accurate and complete',[113] but insists that the matter warrants closer examination.[114] By this he means that the creatures' guilt is both revealed and removed in God's act of pardon. God's forgiveness

> makes good our repudiation and failure and thus overcomes the hurt we do to God . . . His forgiveness repels chaos.[115]

Barth thus rejects St Anselm's exposition of the matter in this regard since he

> makes the remarkable assertion that it is not worthy of God to forgive man his sin *sola misericordia,* and therefore purely and absolutely and unconditionally. The divine forgiveness has to be

---

109. *CD* 1/1.
110. See G Watson, 'Karl Barth and St Anselm's Theological Programme', in *Scottish Journal of Theology* 30/1 (1977): 44, 45.
111. Barth, *CD* 4/1, 484.
112. *Ibid,*
113. *Ibid,* 485.
114. *Ibid,* 486.
115. *Ibid.*

thought of as conditioned by a prior satisfaction . . . the restitution of that which man has stolen from God.[116]

Barth sees a threat in St Anselm's view of a split between God's act of mercy and the creatures' pardon, since there can be no quantitative distinction between God's revelation of sin in Jesus Christ and its removal. Such a view would presuppose in the creature a freedom for God that is not presupposed by God's act of mercy; God's act of revelation as the act of reconciliation cannot be divided. Can there be any event

> more serious or incisive or effective than that in which God forgives man all his sins? And does not the recognition of the divine decision in this event depend upon the fact that it is understood as pure and free forgiveness?[117]

The prior condition to which Barth takes exception is St Anselm's emphasis on the importance of the personal choice of the man Jesus in the fulfilment of God's will in the divine act of pardon. I contend that Barth's rejection of St Anselm's exposition at this crucial point also raises doubts about his understanding of St Anselm's theological method in his critical study of the *Proslogion*. This will have serious implications for Barth's subsequent development of the dogma of the Trinity in the *Church Dogmatics*.

To appreciate the significance of St Anselm's position it must be understood that, prior to the chapter[118] in which Barth finds his evidence for the view that St Anselm construes the divine act of pardon as 'having to be conditioned before it can be accepted as a serious divine action', St Anselm had set about proving that Christ's death was not the result of a direct divine command but a free self-offering of the Son to the Father.

> The Father did not compel him to suffer death, or even allow him to be slain, against his will, but of his own accord he endured death for the sake of men.[119]

---

116. Barth, *CD* 4/1, 486; words italicised in the original.
117. *Ibid*, 487.
118. St Anselm, *Cur Deus Homo*, chapter xii, 230ff.
119. *Ibid*, book 1, chapter viii, 191.

Death could not be demanded of one who was as purely good as our Lord if he was unwilling to die,[120] since death was God's judgment upon the creature in its turning away from God: away from the truth and rightness of its created being in relationship to the Supreme Truth. Since the Son of God was without sin, no such judgment was upon him. If in fact the Son of God dies, it must be understood as a voluntary obedience of Christ to the Father in behalf of the creature. For God wills that, just as the creature came under judgment by an act of voluntary disobedience, so too the creature can only be pardoned by a voluntary act of obedience to God. The only sense in which one could say that the Father willed the death of the Son is that the Father willed that the creature should not be pardoned except through a voluntary act of obedience. To leave disobedience unpunished would be to recognise sin as under no obligation to the Supreme Truth of all things, that is to make sin equal to God, under no obligation at all. This would be impossible. Thus, the Son may say the Father desires his death in so far as the Son wills to suffer rather than that the whole human race should perish.[121]

We see that St Anselm is just as concerned as Barth is to understand sin and its removal as an act in which God alone pardons the creature. The difference between them concerns the nature of that divine *decision*. St Anselm, on the one hand, is concerned to emphasise the reality of the human struggle, the voluntary obedience of the incarnate Son of God. Barth, on the other hand, sees such an emphasis as compromising the freedom and therefore the unity of the divine decision of pardon.

St Anselm reflects upon the way the Son of God actually went in his obedience to the Father *a posteriori*. Barth appears to neglect the significance of the human struggle by an *a priori* view of what is possible as a divine decision. Any event postulated as an act of God concludes every aspect of God's relationship to the creature under the rubric of such an event presupposing a freedom of God for the creature. Any event in history that is not understood in this sense, as it relates to God, is excluded by definition from being involved in God's action in history.

However, it is the voluntary nature of the Son's self-offering as a human being that interests St Anselm, as distinct from the consideration of a divine decision which includes both the aspect of a divine command and the congruent human obedience. As if to emphasise this very point, St Anselm takes the issue up

---

120. *Ibid*, chapter ix, 193ff.
121. St Anselm, *Cur Deus Homo*, 196.

in the chapter following this initial discussion.[122] Here he expounds a series of texts that seem to implicate the Father in the death of the Son in such a manner as to preclude the Son's voluntary obedience. He concludes that

> whatsoever things are said of Him, similar to these which have been mentioned, they are all to be explained in accordance with the belief that He died not by compulsion but by free choice.[123]

This is the background against which St Anselm's view of the 'fittingness'[124] of the Son's death is to be understood. It is this idea, which in chapter xii gives rise to the view that God could not forgive by compassion alone, to which Barth takes such strong exception. Between chapters x and xii St Anselm deals with the problem of human sin as a debt which stands in need of satisfaction. This exposition, we have already noted, Barth finds 'very accurate and complete'.

It will be recalled that St Anselm's understanding of the 'truth' and 'rightness' of persons and things asserted that they fulfilled an obligation or debt to that which they were in the Supreme Truth. We see a link here between this understanding of the ordering of creation by the Supreme Truth and his view of the Son's voluntary obedience in the matter of God's pardon of humanity. For St Anselm, the only entity in which it was possible to conceive of sin as a failure in obligation was a creature. God, as the Supreme Truth, was under obligation to no one. If human sin was to be dealt with by God, the Son 'must' assume the being of a creature and as a creature fulfil the obligation of the creature in its relationship to God as a creature, and therefore in its relationships with other creatures.[125] St Anselm's notion of sin as debt, with which Barth agrees, is integrally related to his understanding of the voluntary obedience of the Son as a creature, which 'condition' Barth believes impugns the freedom and thus the Lordship of God in the event of revelation.

---

122. *Ibid*, 197.
123. *Ibid*, 199.
124. *Ibid*, 205, 206. In this connection see CRP Anstey, 'St Anselm Demythologised', in *Theology* 64 (1961): 17ff.
125. I suspect this is the reason why TF Torrance, *Space Time and Incarnation*, 56, finds it difficult to understand why there is not a closer link in Barth's theological work between creaturely thought forms and the conceptuality of theological formulations, given Barth's Christological concentration. See also the important article by the same author, 'The Ethical Implications of St Anselm's *De Veritate*', in *Theologische Zeitschrift* 24 (1968): 309–319.

In the argument about the nature of Barth's misunderstanding of St Anselm, in respect of the critical importance of the freely offered obedience of the man Jesus as an essential aspect of the divine act of reconciliation, is supported further when Barth deals with the objection Boso brings against St Anselm's argument.

> For since God is free as to be subject to no law, and to the judgment of no one, and is so merciful as that nothing more merciful can be conceived; and nothing is right or fit save as he wills; it seems a strange thing to say that he is wholly unwilling or unable to put away an injury done to himself, when we are wont to apply to him for indulgence with regard to those offences which we commit against others.[126]

Barth believes that St Anselm wrongly thinks he can overcome this objection, which is similar to his own, by asserting that

> the freedom of God is inwardly conditioned by that *quod expedit aut quod decet, nec benignitas dicenda est, quae aliquid Deo indecens operatur.* A god who willed to lie would not be God. Nor would a god who willed to forgive without the prior fulfilment of this condition.[127]

However, it must be realised that the fittingness of which St Anselm speaks expresses the actual way God has taken in the obedience freely willed by the incarnate Son of God. This is why there is no liberty *quod expedit aut quod decet.* This is how in fact it stands in the act of divine pardon revealed in Jesus Christ. Since this is so, it is impossible to say that God can lie, that is, allow sin to be subject to no law, as is the case with God.[128] The basis of this impossibility is not some abstract theory about what God can or cannot do, but what in fact God has done in the incarnate Jesus. To say that God cannot lie is the same as saying, in the context of St Anselm's argument, that Jesus was truly man. This

126.  St Anselm, *Cur Deus Homo,* 204, 205.
127.  Barth, *CD* 4/1, 486.
128.  St Anselm, *Cur Deus Homo,* 205, 206.

we take to be the substance of St Anselm's reply, which Barth believes is a piece of abstract theorising.[129]

In our examination of Barth's theological development in *Die christliche Dogmatik* and *Schicksal und Idee in der Theologie*, I have shown that Barth has real difficulty, in terms of his theological presuppositions related to his understanding of the event of revelation, in appreciating the relationship between God and the relativities of creaturely existence involved in that event. Now, in a consideration of Barth's relationship to St Anselm in the vital area of the doctrine of reconciliation, we can see a similar problem. It remains now to be seen, in a study of Barth's relationship to St Anselm, if this question determines his understanding of St Anselm's *Proslogion*, which was so decisive for his theological development.

> In those years I had to rid myself of the last vestiges of a philosophical or anthropological foundation and explanation of Christian doctrine. The essential document of this departure is not the much-read little book 'No', against Emil Brunner of 1934, but the book of 1931 about the proofs of God of Anselm of Canterbury, which I believe, of all my books, I wrote with the greatest love. Yet in America it is not read at all and in Europe the least of all my books.
>
> What was positively new is this: I had to learn in those years that Christian doctrine in all its expressions must be exclusively and consistently doctrine of Jesus Christ as the living Word of God spoken to us, if it is to deserve its name . . .[130]

## Barth and St Anselm's proof of the existence of God

We have seen how Barth attempted to understand the polarity of human thought reflected in theological realism and idealism by concentrating attention on the importance of God's free self-affirming election in the act of relationship with the creature. Barth saw this as an answer to the dialectic in the fundamental structure of human thought about the world and God by offering a theological realism tempered by an understanding of the central epistemological importance of the doctrine of election as part of the doctrine of God.

---

129. Barth, *CD* 4/1, 486, 487.
130. Barth, 'Parergon', in *Evangelische Theologie*, 8 (1948): 172; author's translation.

When Barth's work on St Anselm's *Proslogion* appeared, the apparent novelty of his exposition caused both philosophers and theologians to take sides on the question of Barth's exegesis.[131] Catholic critics were concerned to establish that St Anselm's proof was applicable to human reason apart from faith.[132] For his part, Barth argued that the proof must be understood in the context of St Anselm's specific theological scheme.[133]

Barth contends that St Anselm does not attempt to demonstrate by means of an independent 'proof' any article of the *Credo* that he affirms to be true in faith, but by means of the 'proof' demonstrates how such affirmations are true. Such understanding as is achieved by this means is interpreted in the context of faith: it is an attempt to understand what already is affirmed to be true. Thus the 'proofs' cannot be understood as arising out of philosophic doubt or any human idea of the divine.[134]

By means of the idea of *ratio*, St Anselm establishes the proper relationship between the human capacity to know and the reality of things that are known, above all between the human capacity to know and the reality of the object/subject of theological knowledge. This relationship in a theological context is called the *ratio fidei*.[135] In correlation to his doctrine of 'truth',[136] St Anselm understands the relationships between all the different *rationes* conditioned by the fact of the Word of God being *ratio veritatis*.[137] A direct result of this ensemble of relationships is the dependence of the noetic and ontic *rationes* on the *ratio veritatis*. As distinct from ontic and noetic *rationes*, the *ratio veritatis* is true not because it is *ratio* but because it is Truth.

---

131. Barth, *Fides quaerens intellectum;* see E Gilson, 'Sens et Nature de l'Argument de Saint Anselm', in *Archives d'Historie Doctrinale et litteraire du Moyen Age* 9 (1934): 5–51.
132. Gilson, *Sens et Nature*, 46.
133. Barth, *Fides quaerens intellectum*,15–59. Cf H Bouillard, *Karl Barth: Genese et Evolution de la Theologie Dialectique, Part 2. Parole de Dieu et Existence Humaine* (Paris: F Aubier, 1957), 146: 'Ce nom de Dieu est la donne, empruntee au Credo, grace a laquelle L'existence de Dieu posse comme X, doit se transformer de grandeur inconnue (quoique crue) en une grandeur connue.'
134. Barth, *Fides quaerens intellectum*, 96, 97.
135. *Ibid*, 44, 45.
136. See above, 21–23.
137. Barth, *Fides quaerens intellectum*, 45.

> The following holds good only of all those other *rationes* with
> which the *ratio Dei* is not identical but which as the *ratio* of his
> creation participate in the *ratio Dei:* Truth is not bound to it but it
> is bound to Truth.[138]

*Ratio* as such, either as noetic or ontic, is never higher than the truth, but
truth itself is the master of all *rationes*: beyond the contrast between ontic and
noetic, deciding for itself here and there what is true.[139] Human reason becomes
*vera ratio* when it is configured by the *ratio* of faith. This is the only possible
rational attitude it can assume before the authority of the believed but hidden
*ratio* of the object of faith.

> The antithesis between *auctoritas* and *ratio* does not coincide with
> the antithesis between God and man but represents the distinction
> between two stages of the one divine road along which man first
> attains faith and then on the basis of faith (but now *sola ratione*)
> attains knowledge.[140]

The necessity of faith's search for understanding, *fides quaerens intellectum*,
resides in the nature of the *ratio* of the object of faith, not in the inquiring intellect
of the creature. Faith and understanding could, therefore, never be opposed
to each other in St Anselm's thought, or conceived in terms of a higher and
lower form of knowledge.[141] This brings us to the point that is of fundamental
importance for Barth's understanding of St Anselm's theological method. It is
not a striving of the human intellect towards God, but 'a striving of the human
will into God'.[142] Faith and understanding presuppose the gracious approach of
God to the creature. It is this free approach that necessitates faith as the beginning
point of rationality for Christian faith; it is the anthropological correlate of
God's grace. The phenomenon of the 'fool' who denies God's existence poses

---

138. *Ibid*, 46. The emphasis here placed by Barth on the idea of participation seems
  heavier than justified by our idea of St Anselms doctrine of Truth. The original text
  of Barth reads, „aber als die seines Geschöpfs an ihr teilnehmende ratio'; Barth, Anselms
  *Beweis der Existenz Gottes im Zusammenhang seines theologischen Programs*, 44.
139. *Ibid*, 47.
140. *Ibid*, 48.
141. In opposition to the view of Prenter; see note 103.
142. Barth, *Fides quaerens intellectum*, 17.

the question of how such a situation is possible in the light of the object of faith. It can only witness to the fact that, while faith as a necessary description of the relationship of the creaturely *ratio* to the truth, it does describe a general human possibility. The truth must give itself to be known.[143] This possibility arises through the preaching of the church.[144] It is this aspect of St Anselm's thought that explains why the study of theology is directly related to prayer.

> Everything depends not only on the fact that God grants him [the believer] grace to think correctly about him, but also on the fact that God himself comes within his system as the object of his thinking.[145]

The possibility of the 'fool' misunderstanding and misreading a reality that applies to believer and fool alike explains the fool's existence but does not justify the fool. The fool's position must be regarded as absurd and cannot be taken seriously, but with a 'certain sense of humour'. There is no other way but to regard the existence of the fool as a sinner who is reckoned not to have sinned.[146]

## Barth's exposition of St Anselm's proof of the existence of God

Barth interprets St Anselm's proof of the existence of God in the context of the self-grounded nature of the *summa veritas* and its relationship to *fides, ratio* and *intelligere*, which I have already explained. The formula, 'that than which nothing greater can be conceived', draws attention to this critical unexpressed condition. This condition is the freedom of God: God's Lordship in the event of the creature's knowledge of God.[147] Thus, the name of God is deliberately chosen in order that 'the object which it describes emerges as something completely independent of whether men in actual fact conceive it or can conceive it'.[148]

The name of God can thus only be understood as a noetic rule since 'it contains nothing in the way of statements about the existence or about the nature of the

---

143. *Ibid*, 160. Cf H Bouillard, *Genese et* Evolution, 161ff.
144. *Ibid*, 22; cf 18ff.
145. *Ibid*, 39. This must happen if the '*intelligere* [of faith] is not to be a delusion'; 39, 40.
146. *Ibid*, 70.
147. Barth, *Fides quaerens intellectum*, 123.
148. *Ibid*, 74.

object described'.[149] This point is rather crucial to Barth's interpretation of St Anselm's proof, in particular of the relationship between chapters xi and cxi of the *Proslogion*. By interpreting the name as a noetic rule, Barth indicates two aspects of his subsequent theological development.

Firstly, it will be deduced that, since the divine name is a strict noetic rule, the existence of God cannot be derived from his nature. God is known in the event of revelation or not at all, since God is who God is in that event. This notion will be seen to be critical in Barth's analysis of revelation in terms of God's 'Lordship'.[150] It is from Barth's analysis of God's Lordship that he develops the root of the dogma of the Trinity.[151]

Secondly, as a consequence of the notion of revelation being defined in terms of God's Lordship, precisely congruent with Barth's understanding of St Anselm's name of God as strict noetic rule, the historical relativities involved in the event of revelation do not, as such, enter into the definition of the meaning of revelation and therefore the Trinity's relationship to the creation. The historical distinctions in the event of revelation derive their meaning from their relationship to the *summa veritas*, not vice versa. The name of God can only establish a 'strong and discernable connection' with the revelation and existence of God. God is not a content of human thought at all.[152]

The objection which may be brought against St Anselm's name, that it is an expression of an arbitrary human desire to express the inexpressible and therefore has no more meaning than that,[153] misses the point of the 'proof'. The absence of noetic content in the name brings to expression the truth that the incomprehensibility of God is defined by God's revelation alone. The whole point of the proof is to raise this incomprehensibility of God from being an article of faith to the level of understanding its necessity in terms of the object of theological knowledge.[154]

It is with respect to this characteristic of God's name that Barth understands the 'proof' offered in the *Proslogion* to be superior to that offered by St Anselm

---

149. *Ibid*, 75.
150. Barth, *CD* 1/1, 339ff.
151. *Ibid*, 349ff.
152. Barth, *Fides quaerens intellectum*, 76. Cf J Paliard, 'Priere et Dialectique: Meditation sur le Proslogion de Saint Anselme', in *Dieu Vivant* 6 (1946): 55.
153. St Anselm, *Apologetic in Reply to Gaunilons' Answer in Behalf of the Fool*, chapters iv and v, 159ff, 161ff.
154. Barth, *Fides quaerens* intellectum, 79ff.

in the *Monologion*.[155] In the *Monologion*, St Anselm had arrived at the formula which he expresses in different ways but means that God is that which is greater than all.[156] Such a formula was incapable of rigorous demonstration because it presupposed a relationship between God and contingent existence. This meant that the formula left open the possibility of the factual non-existence of God. In contrast, the formula offered in the *Proslogion*, precisely because of its strict noetic character, excludes dependence on the existence of things in general and is therefore intelligible only as its truth is determined by the object of faith. This exclusion of ontic content from the 'proof' corresponds to the fact that St Anselm demonstrates the existence of One who freely stoops to reveal God's truth to the creature. This change in the structure of the 'proof' in the *Proslogion* entails that there is no separation between *essentia* and *esse*, between potentiality and actuality, in God's existence.

> God is all that he is, not through participation in certain potentialities not identical with his actual Power; all his potentialities do not first require to be actualized in the reality of his Power, but he is himself what he ever is and what he ever is, he is himself. His Potentiality and his Reality are identical.[157]

Likewise, in chapter xi of *Proslogion*, the revealed name of God indicates that humans, in their acquaintance with things, have an assurance that they do not exist only in the mind but also in reality. However, the 'proof' does not have the power to forbid us thinking of the hypothetical non-existence of God. The 'proof' in *Proslogion* cxi has this specific power, which the 'proof' in

---

155. *Ibid*, 84, 86–88.

156. *Ibid*, 84, note 4.

157. *Ibid*, 94. This aspect of Barth's understanding of St Anselm's proof was to have decisive influence on Barth's doctrine of God and was to prove determinative in his attitude to natural theology. Barth understood natural theology to be an attempt to divide God's potentiality from God's actuality. Cf Barth, *CD* 2/1, 63ff, 85ff. This aspect of Barth's thought has not been widely understood. See *Natural Theology: Comprising 'Nature and Grace' by Professor Dr Emil Brunner and the Reply 'No!' by Dr Karl Barth* (London: G Bless, 1946); P Lehmann, 'Barth and Brunner: The Dilemma of the Protestant Mind', in *Journal of Religion* 20 (1940): 124ff; J Baillie, *Our Knowledge of God*, 17–34. The same kind of considerations are the basis of the distinction Barth makes between the 'proofs' offered by St Anselm in the *Proslogion* chapters xi and cxi. See Barth, *Fides quaerens intellectum*, 100, 123–128.

*Proslogion* xi lacked.[158] Thus, there is in *Proslogion* cxi no statement about God's existence in terms of the existence of things in general, including the creature's own conception of itself as existing. St Anselm is not Descartes.[159] By what the revealed name of God forbids, God is distinguished from all things whose existence can possibly be conceived as non-existent. The proof can only be understood as the means by which

> an article of faith, fixed in itself as such, has been proved in such a way that the opposite statement would be reduced *ad absurdum* by means of the statement of the Name of God ... *Intelligere* means to see into the noetic rationality and therefore into the noetic necessity of the statements that are revealed, on the basis that they possess ontic rationality and necessity as revealed statements, prior to all *intelligere*, to all 'proof' and therefore not based on proof.[160]

The view that St Anselm constructs his 'proof' in such a unique manner is supported, according to Barth, by the fact that it is in the form of a prayer. God stands over against the one who seeks understanding of God by means of the 'proof', 'not as an "it", not even as "he", but as "thou", as the unmediated "thou" of the Lord.'[161] This context conditions the believer's thinking about all created reality as well. Together with an understanding of who God is, the believer 'also has his thinking about existence, its values and its degrees, all entirely from the Creator'.[162] The 'fool' who fails to achieve understanding, by means of the revealed name of God, is considered neither as a rational or moral defective, but simply a fool. The 'fool' accomplishes that which, in the light of God's unique existence, it is forbidden to attempt. This attempt has its theological parallel in the sinner's attempt to justify the self apart from the grace of God in Jesus Christ.[163] Barth sees a direct connection between St Anselm's 'proof' in *Proslogion*

---

158. *Ibid*, 132, 133.
159. *Ibid*, 139.
160. *Ibid*, 143, 144.
161. *Ibid*, 151.
162. *Ibid*, 152.
163. *Ibid*, 160. The connection which Barth makes here between the existence of the 'fool' and his view of evil has ramifications for the *Church Dogmatics* where evil is described as '*das Nichtige*'; see *CD* 3/3, 327ff. Criticism of the universalist implications of Barth's understanding of the ontology of sin has generally not taken into account that it derives from his doctrine of God! Cf H Hartwell, *The Theology of*

cxi and the unconditional grace of God which makes the sinner righteous. This epistemological implication of God's revelation has the ethical implication that

> it is only by the grace of God that Anselm's solidarity with him [the fool] has been ended. The *insipiens* thinks and speaks as one who is not saved by the grace of God. That is the reason for his perversity, and why he can say, *Deus non est.*[164]

The proof of *Proslogion* cxi, which lacks reference to ontic factors, to created reality, takes cognisance of the implications in the sphere of epistemology of Barth's view that the doctrine of election is an integral part of the doctrine of God.[165] The proof offered in *Proslogion* cxi, precisely because it is a strict noetic rule, refers to no created existence; it thus coheres with—because it presupposes God's unconditional freedom—the grace of God's movement towards the creature. The creature's thinking and willing is unconditionally determined by the unconditional freedom of God to be the God of the creature. The only rational response in this context is one in which reason

> assents to that name of God as an article of faith and presupposes it for all that follows—it is able to illumine the noetic necessity of faith . . . by the roundabout route of ontic necessity which is inseparable from ontic rationality. Thus theology can know what is believed, that is, prove it.[166]

## Assessment of Barth's interpretation of St Anselm's proofs

I now take up the question of the validity of Barth's interpretation of St Anselm's theological program. This issue derives its importance in so far as it is conceded[167] that this study had a significant, if not decisive, influence on the mature form of Barth's thought achieved in the *Church Dogmatics*. Our point of departure is the relationship Barth establishes between *Proslogion* xi and cxi. The basis of Barth's distinction between the 'proofs' offered is on the grounds that the 'proof' in chapter cxi, in contrast to chapter xi, lacked any reference to a

---

*Karl Barth: An Introduction*, 186, 187.

164. *Ibid*, 160.

165. *Ibid*, 158–161. Cf Barth, *CD* 2/2, 76ff.

166. Barth, *Fides quaerens intellectum*, 83, 84.

167. See above, 29.

relationship between the existence of God and creaturely existence, which was not presupposed by the event of God's revelation.

> By the mere fact that God exists in just the same way as any other object, the problem of his existence is still not answered as far as Anselm is concerned (unlike Gaunilo).[168]

Barth's view is that the 'proof' of *Proslogion* xi concludes in a negative statement to the effect that, if God exists, it could not be in thought alone. The positive statement upon which this negative statement rests, which refers to God's unique existence, does not have its origin in this general 'proof'.[169]

However, H Bouillard, in an analysis of St Anselm's proofs,[170] concedes Barth's general point that St Anselm proceeds negatively and indirectly by way of reduction to the absurd in *Proslogion* xi. However, Bouillard insists that although St Anselm's 'proof' in *Proslogion* xi is limited to showing the internal contradiction involved in denying existence to a Being such that no greater could be conceived, he wishes to derive a positive conclusion. This is the real extra-mental existence of God, albeit in a negative form.

Bouillard insists that the 'fool' understands the formula expressing the divine name in *Proslogion* xi. This possibility is open to anyone who reflects upon the temporal and supra-temporal nature of contingent reality.[171] St Anselm thus argues that it is incumbent on the unbeliever to show that the propositions of faith are meaningless. The unbeliever needs to show that it is not merely within our experience that we do not compare things absolutely, as greater or more perfect, but that necessarily it is the case that things are not greater or more perfect. He needs to demonstrate that the things within our experience are necessarily the only things, and that therefore the notion of God is meaningless by definition.[172] Barth has methodological reservations that preclude him from appreciating this aspect of St Anselm's argument.[173] In this respect, Barth's

---

168. Barth, *Fides quaerens intellectum*, 130.
169. *Ibid*, 128, 129, 132, 133.
170. H Bouillard, *Parole*, 158ff, and *The Knowledge of God*.
171. St Anselm, *Apologetic on behalf of the fool*, chapter viii, 161ff. Here St Anselm's reply to Gaunilo stresses the fact of the meaningfullness of the formula in *Proslogion* xi by relating it to reflection upon things which are more or less good.
172. JN Findlay, 'Can God's Existence be Disproved?', in *New Essays in Philosophical Theology*, edited by A Flew and A MacIntyre (London: SCM, 1965), 55.
173. See TF Torrance, 'The Problem of Natural Theology in the Thought of Karl Barth',

understanding of St Anselm's 'proofs' express the same reservations regarding St Anselm's theology, which we have already encountered in Barth's exposition of his soteriology. There, it took the form of Barth's rejection of St Anselm's view that the freely willed obedience of a human being in relation to God could condition the act of God's forgiveness in Christ. Such a 'precondition' called into question the maxim that all the creature's relationship with God must be understood as presupposing the freedom of God in the event of God's self revelation to the creature.

Here, the position Barth takes up with respect to St Anselm's proofs implies a structural hiddenness in the event of God's self-revelation, which has methodological implications for Barth's theology. It entails that the rationality of human thought-forms and language is dependent upon their correspondence with the structure of the event of God's revelation. All distinctions and relationships presupposed by this event's occurrence in human history, the history of creation, these distinctions and relationships with which human rationality has to do are understood by Barth exclusively within the context of the event of revelation. Since this revelation is not a state of revealedness, speech and thought about God cannot be separated from the event of revelation, in which God's existence and nature coincide. Therefore, 'the man outside the church, the man who is without revelation and faith, knows nothing in actual practice of him who bears the Name'.[174]

However, given the event of revelation there is actualised in the church a possibility, which though open to all people, is hidden from them by the fall and the concrete mystery of God's election.[175] Barth is able on this basis to distinguish between knowledge of God that is validly an inference from the worldly nature of the event of revelation, as the believer seeks to understand what is believed, and that which is invalid. This applies also to the creature's knowledge of the creature, since the worldly form of revelation is understood in terms of it being presupposed by the freedom of God to be the God who is thus revealed.[176]

---

in *Religious Studies* 6/2 (1970): 121ff.

174. Barth, *Fides quaerens intellectum*, 116, 117.

175. *Ibid*, 117.

176. *Ibid*, See E Jüngel, *Gottes Sein Ist im Werden*, 6, 7. Cf H Gollwitzer, *The Existence of God as Confessed by Faith*, 186, 187; Barth, *How My Mind Has Changed*, edited by J Godsey (Virginia: John Knox Press, 1966), 82.

Consequently, it should be noted that when Barth set about eliminating what he perceived to be the weaknesses of his first systematic attempts at a Christian *Dogmatik* in the *Church Dogmatics*, we find substituted for the analysis of the situation of the preacher and the hearer, an analysis of the nature of the Word of God as the point of departure for understanding God's revelation. Barth relates the determination of the ontic forms of revelation, that is, the event nature of revelation, Scripture, proclamation, and the noetic determination of the creature as the recipient of revelation to the nature of the Word of God. Thus section 5 of the first volume, 'The nature of the Word of God', is the link between sections 3-4 and 5-6. As this analysis of the 'nature of the Word of God' serves as the basis of Barth's understanding of God's revelation, it is also the basis also of the dogma of the Trinity.[177]

Our study of Barth's presentation of the theology of St Anselm, in respect to his arguments concerning God's pardon of humankind and God's existence, reveals a consistent inability to appreciate the fundamental importance in the structure of St Anselm's argument of the relativities of creaturely existence and rationality. This inability will have serious consequences for Barth's understanding of the place and the meaning of the dogma of the Trinity that becomes, as a result of his Anselm book, the framework and foundation of the *Church Dogmatics*.

## The place of the Trinity in the *Church Dogmatics*

Congruent with the way in which Barth conceives the unique existence of God and thus the peculiar method of theology, as it seeks understanding of its unique Object, is the particularity of the sphere in which this activity takes place. This sphere is the church. Here, on the authority of past revelation, human words are used to speak the Word of God.[178] The possibility of putting the question of truth to this human undertaking cannot be separated from the context in which the reality of God's present self-witness puts this question of truth. Dogmatics inquires into the *summa veritas*, the *ratio* which grounds both the ontic and the noetic necessity and rationality of Scripture and proclamation. Dogmatics can thus only give an account of itself as a churchly undertaking, since it can only occur within the context of the revealed but hidden truth which the church is

---

177. Barth, *CD* 1/1, 51ff, 98ff, 141ff, 162ff, 184ff, 213ff, 284ff.
178. *Ibid*, ix, 46, 47, 57, 91, 92.

given. It describes the reality that posits the possibility and validates the truth of the worldly forms of revelation.

It is this understanding of dogmatics, derived directly from Barth's understanding of St Anselm's 'proof' of God's existence in *Proslogion cxi*, which leads to the view that the dogma of the Trinity is to be understood, in the context of the prolegomena of dogmatics, as the 'proof' of God's unique Lordship present in the event of revelation.[179] As distinct from the procedure Barth adopted in his previous attempts at systematic presentation of his thought, now, in the *Church Dogmatics*, Barth relates the determination of the ontic forms of revelation, that is, the event nature of revelation, Scripture, proclamation, and the noetic determination of the creature as the recipient of revelation, to the nature of the Word of God.

Barth divides his exposition of the nature of the Word of God into three major aspects, 'The Word of God as God's Language', 'God's Language as God's Act', and 'God's Language as God's Mystery'.[180] God's Word is God's *self-communication*. As opposed to all irrationalism and mystical approaches, which seek an otherworldly reality above or beside the verbal character of language, the Word of God is to be understood as supremely rational. Corresponding to God's unique existence is God's unique address. This speech does not derive its character from the structure of human language but from God's own self address.[181] This effective barrier which prevents God's speech being reduced to a syntactical system or an irrational communication is the equation, grounded in God's own being: 'God's Word is God's Son.'[182] The *wörtliche* character of God's speech is determined in both its verbal and rational nature by the fact that God is 'lord of the verbal character of His Word. He is not bound to it, but it is bound to Him.'[183]

From the nature of God's address to the creature Barth deduces, understands, 'proves' in the Anselmian sense, that God is Creator, Reconciler and Redeemer.[184] He thus avoids the critical flaw of his previous attempt at a systematic presentation of his thought in *Die christliche Dogmatik*. There it was left open, through a consideration of the nature of the Word of God in relation

---

179. *CD* 1/1, 16, 58, 163, 339ff, 369, 384.
180. *Ibid*, 150ff, 162ff, 184ff.
181. *Ibid*, 153.
182. *Ibid*, 156
183. *Ibid*, 157.
184. *Ibid*, 162.

to the structure of the preacher and the hearer, whether the Word of God was 'proved' in such a manner as to preclude its nature determining the ontic and noetic conditions of its being the revelation of God. The possibility remained of considering the possibility of revelation apart from its reality. This is to divide God's essence from God's existence. It is to do what natural theology at all times does. It is to repeat the problematic of Schleiermacher's theology and that of Kierkegaard. [185]

When Barth further clarifies the nature of God's Word as God's language, which is also God's act and God's mystery, he is not adding to what he has already said about God's speech and its *wörtliche* nature. He is viewing the same reality from a different perspective. This further analysis does not introduce any new possibilities that are not present in the reality of revelation as God's personal presence. [186]

To speak of the Word of God as God's act is to refer to that specific act in which God speaks God's Word. God's being as personal defines the *wörtliche* nature of God's being .

> It is the divine Person, the Person of the Lord of history whose self utterance as such is an alteration and an absolute alteration of the world, whose *passio* in history is as such an *actio*.[187]

This entails that to understand God's Word as historical we must not assume its meaning from an understanding of historicity derived from a view of what is possible as an historical event in general. The distinctions involved in the manner of God's speech considered as historical phenomena—the act of God's self-revelation, Scripture, and church proclamation—cannot, as such, be the ground for understanding God's Word. However seriously we may take such distinctions, 'the differences inherent in history are not sufficient to justify a serious use of the concept "Word of God".'[188] Knowledge of the Word of God as God's act has nothing to do with the problem of historical understanding of events such as the act of God's self-revelation, Scripture, and church proclamation, since the

---

185. See above, 8–15..
186. Barth, *CD* 1/1, 150, 151.
187. *Ibid*, 164.
188. *Ibid*, 167.

the varying position in God's order distinguishes these three times in a way not otherwise characteristic of man's times, a way in which they differ only here, in which only the times of the Word of God differ.[189]

Corresponding to the unique freedom of God's Word as God's act, which itself makes history, is the epistemology that is appropriate to such an event. God's Word as God's act does not confront the creature with an either or, a possibility which may be accepted or rejected. By its nature, God's Word as God's act is a 'transposition of man into a wholly new position' in the creature's relationship to God and the world.[190] This entails that the world cannot be taken seriously in its godlessness![191]

From the way in which Barth understands God's Word as God's act, it is obvious that this act cannot be understood from its aspect as an historical event. The historicity of God's Word as God's act is grounded in the historicity of God's being. God's being is in his act. In this act, God determines God's being as *wortlich*. As such, God is God's Word as revealed. The historicity of God's being as God's act presupposes God's ineffable freedom to choose God's self as the God of the creature. This means that God's aseity must not be understood as a kind of metaphysical hinterground predicated on the idea of God's unknowability. [192] God's aseity is identical with God's ineffable act in which God chooses God's self as God. Thus, revelation of God's Lordship in God's Word is identical with God's nature.[193]

It is to bring out the unique nature of the Word of God as God's language and God's act that Barth treats of the language of God as God's mystery. [194] The distinction between the Word of God as God's language, expressing its personal and rational nature, and the decision of God which grounds the Word of God in the freedom of God's act to be the God that God is, would still not complete or 'prove' God's existence as the Lord in the revelation of God's self. It would still be possible, on Barth's view, to understand these basic features of God's being in a dialectical relationship, as if the one implied the other. It must be made

---

189. *Ibid*, 165. Cf 167, 168.
190. *Ibid*, 173.
191. *Ibid*, 176.
192. *Ibid*, 179.
193. *Ibid*.
194. *Ibid*, 184–187.

clear that revelation's personal character and its worldly form as event are in no way conditional upon the being of the creature that is implied by the form of revelation and its being an event in history.

This is a very similar situation to the one I encountered in Barth's analysis of the relationships between St Anselm's proofs in *Proslogion* xi and cxi. There, it was noted that though the existence of God was 'proved' within the context of faith in *Proslogion* xi, it was however possible to conceive of the factual non-existence of God because the 'proof' assumed a relationship between the existence of God and the existence of the creature.[195] Barth saw the 'proof' of *Proslogion* cxi to be a superior 'proof' precisely because it did not assume such a relationship.

It is to ensure that such a situation obtains also in his understanding of the event in which God Lordship is revealed that Barth emphasises the unique nature of the Word of God as God's language and act, and that he treats of the language of God as God's mystery.[196] The relationship between the Word of God as God's language and the Word of God as God's act cannot be explained in terms of some dialectic that presupposes the existence of the creature in any way. The relationship between the Word of God as language and event is the mystery in which God determines God's self to be God. This impenetrable mystery is the mystery of God's own eternal being, but at the same time it is the basis of all our knowledge of God's self-revelation, of God's relationship to the creature and the creature' relationship to other creatures. This twofold aspect of the mystery of God, the mystery of God's being the God that God is and the mystery whereby God's language and act correspond in our knowledge of God's Word, can only be understood as the being of the person of the Holy Spirit.[197]

In this exposition of the nature of the Word of God under a threefold aspect, Barth has already indicated the basis upon which he will later 'prove' the dogma of the Trinity. The central significance and strategic importance of this analysis of the Word of God cannot be over estimated in understanding the development of Barth's theological method. This analysis of the nature of the Word of God is placed between the material of dogmatics, the church's preaching, the basis of this preaching in the threefold form of the Word of God, and the epistemological

---

195. See above 22.
196. Barth, CD 1/1, 184–187.
197. *Ibid*, 207; cf 200. See also Barth, 'A Theological Dialogue', in *Theology Today* 19/2 (1962–1963): 175.

relevance of the Word of God—sections 3–4 and 6–7, respectively. This forms the substance of chapter one of the *Dogmatics*. It reveals that the lessons Barth learned in his exposition of St Anselm's 'proofs' have had a decisive influence of the structure of Barth's mature thought. The dogma of the Trinity will be expounded with this specific context as part of the doctrine of revelation of the Word of God.

## Barth's starting point and the development of the dogma of the Trinity

Barth's strategy in understanding the ontic and noetic forms of revelation by means of an analysis of the nature of the Word of God, we have contended, derives from his interpretation of St Anselm's theological program. It derives from St Anselm's view of the unique existence of God and what this unique existence implies for the mode of rationality appropriate to it on the part of the creature.

Barth's analysis makes it clear that the only rational way the creature can achieve understanding of God's revelation, its content and form, is by way of *a posteriori* questioning of the reality and possibility this event presupposes in the Subject[198] of revelation: God. Thus in the rest of the volume 1 of the *Church Dogmatics*, Barth simply sets forth the exegetical basis of the dogma of the Trinity which his analysis of the Word of God, the mode of God's Lordship presupposed by the Word of God considered as God's language, act and mystery, makes plain. In this sense,

> propositions about the Trinity of God, of course, claim to be, not directly but indirectly, identical with the propositions about revelation.[199]

---

198. Barth, *CD* 1/1, 339: 'Revelation absolutely insists on being regarded from the side of its subject, God.' Cf Barth's attitude to Calvin: Calvin, *Institutes of the Christian religion*, Book 1, chapter 13, secs 1ff; Barth, *CD* 2/2, 41, 65ff; 4/1, 367; W Niesel, *The Theology of Calvin*, translated by H Knight (Philadelphia: Westminster, 1956), 54. For an approach to the dogma of the Trinity similar to that of Calvin see, JS Whale, *Christian doctrine* (Cambridge University Press, 1941), 107, 108, and L Hodgson, *The Doctrine of the Trinity* (London: Nisbet, 1943), 98ff. On the rise of trinitarian thought in the church see GL Prestige, *God in Patristic thought* (London: SPCK, 1956), 76ff.
199. *Ibid*, 335.

This intimate connection between revelation and the dogma of the Trinity gives Barth's exposition of the dogma a distinctive character. He differs, for example, from John Calvin's presentation in his *Institutes*, where the doctrine of the Trinity only arises 'after discussing how we come to know God'. Then the question is asked about the content of such knowledge. For Barth, such a separation between the form and content of theological knowledge of the self-revealing God is impossible. This is the whole problem with 'natural theology' and neo-Protestantism evinced in Schleiermacher. It was to eliminate such co-positing of God and the creature apart from the event of God's self disclosure that Barth has edged his way through the *Göttingen Dogmatics, Die christliche Dogmatik*, to the *Church Dogmatics*. The development of Barth's theology to this point has shown an ever increasing concentration on the central importance of an appropriate theological method which takes account of the *being* of God in the act which constitutes God's being, and the *act* in which God constitutes God's being as God of the creature. This concentration has the effect of methodologically excluding a consideration of the dogma of the Trinity as being determined in any significant degree by the relativities and contingencies of the historical form of the humanity of Christ in relationship to God. It also excludes the experience of salvation, celebrated by the creature within the context of the church's liturgy, as bearing on the shape of the dogma. It is in this regard that I will raise serious questions as to the validity of Barth's exposition of the Trinity on the basis of his analysis of God's Lordship in God's self-revelation.

The haunting emptiness which lies at the heart of Barth's trinitarian doctrine results directly from his methodological refusal to relate the event of revelation to the historical nexus in which it is found. In giving the dogma a unique dynamic configuration—grounding it in the act of God whose being is constituted by God's personal choice to be the God of the creature in the event of God's self revelation—Barth has sacrificed an essential element of trinitarian doctrine. This is its relationship to, and expression of, the experience of the creatures' new life celebrated in the church's liturgy.

# Chapter Two

# The Doctrine of the Trinity and its Relationship to Christology

We have seen how, for Barth, it would not be a genuine interpretation of the ontic and noetic aspects of the event of revelation if it did not throw light on their reality and possibility presupposed in the nature of the Word of God. The ontic and noetic aspects of revelation are understood when they are seen as answers to the question of their reality and possibility in the Word of God. If this is the case, the theologian must allow that the question to which revelation is the answer is the theologian's too. *Credere* by its very nature must become *intelligere*. If this does not happen then, as Barth discovered with the publication of *Die christliche Dogmatik*, the possibility of understanding the noetic and ontic forms of revelation is sought either idealistically or realistically in the structure of creaturely existence.[1] It is this that leads Barth to place under the ban of the holiness of God any attempt to understand revelation in terms of the humanity of the historical Jesus.[2]

---

1. Barth, *CD* 1/2, 9, 10. Barth indicates that in his first attempt at a theological prolegomena, in 1927, he sought to ground the necessity of God's hiddenness in revelation in the nature of the historical forms of revelation. Cf, in this connection, R Bultmann's positing of the Christian doctrine of creation in the structure of human existence in 'The Meaning of the Christian Faith in Creation', in SM Ogden editor, *Existence and Faith*, 218, 219, 221. On the same issue, see D Bonhoeffer, *Act and Being*, transl by B Noble (London: Colllins, 1962), 74ff: H Ott, 'Objectification and Existentialism', in HW Bartsch, *Kerygma and Myth*, volume 2, 312ff. For the logical outcome of the Christian faith being understood on the basis of the structures of human existence see S Ogden, *Christ without Myth* (London: Collins, 1962), 126ff, 137.

2. Barth, *CD* 1/1, 369-372. Here Barth insists that 'the *humanitas Christi* comes under the reservation of God's holiness, i.e., the power and continuity in which the man Jesus of Nazareth . . . was in fact the revealed word, consisted here also in the power and continuity of the divine action in this form and not in the continuity of this form as such' (371). Compare Barth's attitude to his teacher W Herrmann's attempt to emphasis the significance of the humanity of Jesus as the essential condition of real encounter with God. Barth labels such an attempt to objectivise the being of God in the human sphere as 'Monophysite'. See Barth, *Theology and Church*, 238ff,

The question of the extent to which God is Lord in the forms of revelation is what posits the possibility of the dogma of the Trinity. How far is God, in the inconceivable freedom in which God exists, both subject and object in the event of God's self-revelation?[3] This question takes the form of asking after the possibility in God, which posits the ontic and noetic rationality of these forms. It also entails that no distinction can be made between God's freedom to be who God is in God's own self, and who God wills to be for the creature in God's self-revelation.[4] Thus, the historical figure of Jesus of Nazareth is considered in direct relationship to the event that this figure presupposes: this is the inconceivable event in which God constitutes God's self as Lord of the creature.

Consistent with his analysis of the Word of God, Barth understands the question of the *creature's* knowledge of this event as a possibility posed by the reality of the unity of the event of God's self-revelation—that is, the unity of the Subjective and Objective reality of this event. In Barth's analysis of the nature of the Word of God, this aspect was understood as the language of God as God's mystery, the inconceivable unity of God's decision to be both One and Another as the Lord of the creature. Here, he expounds the doctrine of revelation under this aspect as 'The Outpouring of the Holy Spirit'.[5] Already here, it is obvious that Barth's defence of the *filioque* clause will be of fundamental importance for his understanding of the Trinity.[6] The origin of the *hypostasis* of the Holy Spirit will be understood in terms of Barth's view that the being of the Spirit is the mystery of God's realisation of unity as God. Consequently, both the object and subject in the event of revelation will exclude reference to any ontic factor not presupposed by the nature of this event of revelation. Barth understands the Eastern church's rejection of the *filioque* to be tantamount to tritheism![7] The East, of course, understands the Holy Spirit's *hypostasis* in relationship to the economy of salvation where the contingencies and relativities of history are not related to the inconceivable intra-trinitarian relationships of the event in which God posits God's self as God. On the contrary, the *hypostasis* of the Spirit

---

　　　264.
3.　　　Barth, *CD* 1/1, *The Revelation of God*, Pt 1, 'The Triune God', 339ff.
4.　　　*Ibid*, 349–359. Cf E Jüngel, *Gottes Sein ist im Werden*, 6 (note 18), 27ff.
5　　　Barth, *CD* 1/2, 203ff.
6.　　　*CD* 1/1, 556. See also G Watson, 'The Filioque: Opportunity for Debate?' in *Scottish Journal of Theology* 41/3 (1988): 313–330.
7.　　　*Ibid*, 551ff.

is understood in terms of an ineffable voluntary condescension in which God *becomes* a creature for the sake of the renewal of the creature.[8]

For Barth, revelation means *Dei loquentis persona*, and this means that its truth is 'wholly and in every respect, that is, ontically and noetically, within itself'.[9] Thus, the form of revelation can have no independent meaning; it cannot be regarded as the 'root' of the doctrine of the Trinity in the various distinctions, which the forms of revelation have in history. These distinctions, as worldly forms, 'cannot be applied to the biblical concept of revelation'.[10] The distinctions that Barth of course makes between Scripture and proclamation, on the one hand, and revelation on the other, or the distinctions between Jesus of Nazareth and the disciples and Jesus the ascended Lord and the apostles, are all understood in the light of what they presuppose in the divine freedom whereby God determines God's self to be God in the event of revelation.[11] It is in this context that the statement, 'God reveals Himself as the Lord', is to be understood as the analytical root of the doctrine of the Trinity.[12] There is, however, a 'narrower' root of the doctrine of the Trinity. This is brought to understanding as one asks after the reality, which posits the possibility of the revelation of God's Lordship in the person of Jesus Christ. This is the question of the divinity of Jesus Christ. It is this that is 'the real theme of the Biblical witness'.[13]

## The 'root' of the doctrine of the Trinity and the divinity of Jesus Christ

It is true that, historically, the figure of Jesus Christ confronts us with the question of revelation,[14] and true that when the Bible speaks of revelation it narrates a story the content of which it assumes to be the revelation of God. It is nevertheless also true that the self-unveiling of God presupposed by these

---

8.  See G Watson, 'The *Filioque:* Opportunity for Debate?; K Rahner, *The Trinity*, 18ff.; N Nissiotis, 'The Importance of the Doctrine of the Trinity for Church Life and Theology', in A Philippou, editor, *The Orthodox Ethos*, 32ff.

9.  Barth, *CD* 1/1, 335.

10. *Ibid*, 351.

11. The question of the meaning of time as the form of these relationships will be considered as we look at Barth's exposition of the christological dogma. See *CD* 1/2: 'The time of revelation', 45ff.

12. *CD* 1/1, 352.

13. *Ibid*, 361.

14. See R Bultmann, *Theology of the New Testament*, volume 1, 43: 'Jesus' call to decision implies a Christology.'

phenomena cannot be considered as the 'logically material' centre of these stories.[15] The self-unveiling involved in these accounts is related to the fact that the God who is unveiled cannot be unveiled by the content of these accounts considered as part of the historical process. The fact that God exists for the people of the Bible,

> as Esau existed for Jacob, as Mount Horeb or the ark of the covenant for the people of Israel, John for Peter or Paul for his Church . . . can be explained by or derived from neither the will and act of man nor the rest of the world's course.[16]

Consequently, the self-unveiling of God in the event of revelation is not something to be considered in terms of the factuality or contingent nature of the event, for what is at stake is the ability of God

> to distinguish Himself from Himself, i.e., in Himself and hiddenly to be God yet at the same time in quite another way, namely manifestly, i.e., in the form of something He Himself is not, to be God a second time.[17]

The secret of the 'narrower root' of the doctrine of the Trinity, the form of God's self revelation in Jesus Christ, the fact of Him being a creature in creaturely history, being 'objective' and sharing the creature's contingency and relativity as a creature, rests on the possibility of God being objective to God's self.[18] The veiling in the self-unveiling of God in the event of revelation is a direct result of the fact that, since God is who God is in the revelation of God's Name, the objectivity of Jesus Christ is as inconceivable as the objectivity of God who determines God's own being as both One and Another. It is for this reason, and not on the basis of some dialectic associated with the structure of human existence or the situation of the preacher and hearer of the Word of God, that Barth says, 'it is the *Deus revelatus* who is the *Deus absconditus.*'[19]

---

15.    Barth, *CD* 1/1, 362.
16.    *Ibid*, 363.
17.    *Ibid*, 363.
18.    Barth, *CD* 2/1, 16ff. Cf TF Torrance, *Theological Science*, 43ff.
19.    Barth, *CD* 1/1, 368.

From this consideration of God's Lordship, Barth 'proves' that the reality and possibility of revelation coincide with God's freedom to distinguish God from God. God as unveiled is the Son as veiled is the Father.[20] Before we show how Barth establishes that God is yet God in a third way of being God, we take a step forward and examine the manner in which Barth 'proves' the divinity of the Son in terms of God's veiling and unveiling in the event of God's self-revelation. It is in the divinity of the Son that Barth locates the 'narrower root' of the doctrine of the Trinity.[21] This narrower root, located in the divinity of the Son, again emphasises what became apparent in the analysis of Barth's understanding of the event of revelation in terms of the concept of God's Lordship. This is that the ontic content, the humanity of Jesus as such, does not enter into the definition of who God is in the revelation of God's name. Jesus as the revelation of God is known 'absolutely in the death of man, at the end of his existence'.[22] The life and death of Jesus as such can only be understood as the revelation of God beyond the negative limit of human existence, from a point of view that presupposes the resurrection of the dead. Since this event coincides with the inconceivable event in which God posits God's self as God, in which God distinguishes God from God, it cannot be thought that the revelation of God, God unveiled, is dialectically related to the limit of human existence. The revelation of God

> enters the life of man, not identically with death, nor yet merely in the manner of death, but really along with death, executing death upon man, impressing the signs of death upon man . . . The life that His will creates [ie, the self-unveiling of God] will be a life that has passed through death, risen from death, eternal life, a really new birth.[23]

The continuity between the life of the earthly Jesus and the life of the risen Christ is a continuity posited in the inconceivably free act in which God posits God's self as God.[24]

---

20.   *Ibid*, 372, 373.
21.   *Ibid*, 361.
22.   *Ibid*, 465.
23.   *Ibid*, 445; brackets are author's..
24.   *Ibid*, 446–450. This relationship between the life of Jesus and his being as the resurrected Lord, by which Barth establishes the 'narrower root' of the doctrine

Barth gives further clarification of his understanding of the 'narrower root' of the doctrine of the Trinity, in terms of the deity of the Son revealed in the resurrection, by an exposition of the relevant section of the *Nicaeno-Constantinopolitanum* Creed.[25] I simply draw attention to one aspect of this exposition, which reiterates, in another way, my understanding of Barth's position vis-à-vis the significance of the humanity of Jesus as entering into the definition of God's self-revelation.

The Symbol states that the Son is 'begotten of the Father before all time'. Barth insists that in order to understand the 'time' referred to here one must see this time as an aspect of the event in which God distinguishes God's self from God's self. So the meaning of these words must be seen not to

> exclude time, either the *illic et tunc* of revelation as it is attested in Scripture, or the *hic et nunc* in which it is to become revelation for us. It does not exclude, it includes time (concretely, this time, the time of revelation); and so with history. But this very fact that time (time of our time, the sinful creature's time and history, which is also the time and history of revelation) is included in a divine 'before all time', this does not go without saying, this is a grace, a mystery, a foundation to be recognised in the fear of God.[26]

While it is true that the event of revelation is marked by its relation to the process of human history and its relative time scales, 'this marked nature which

---

of the Trinity, is also of decisive epistemological significance for the creature's knowledge not only of God but, for that very reason, of the creature as well. The Son's divinity is established as he reveals the Father beyond the negative limit of human existence in his resurrection from the dead, a distinction that corresponds to the distinction in which God posits God's self as both one and another. This entails that the creature who is represented as a creature in its relationship to God and other creatures in the humanity of Jesus becomes as inconceivable to itself as the inconceivability of God's own self-positing as God. There can be no Christian anthropology based on deductions made, or 'read off', from the humanity of Jesus considered as a historical phenomenon. Christian anthropology presupposes a faith that is necessitated by the establishment of God's relationship to the creature, and the *creature's* relationship to God and other creatures, beyond the negative limit of human existence by God's action in the resurrection of Jesus from the dead. See Barth, CD 3/1, 13–15, 18, 19, 24ff, 31, 32; 3/2, 47–52, 55ff, 132ff, 152ff.

25. Barth, *CD* 1/1, 484.
26. *Ibid*, 487, 488.

they have does not itself originate and proceed from time'.[27] If this were not the case and understanding of the event of revelation was to assume the 'marked' nature of, say, the humanity of Jesus in its relation to other historical events and persons as being that which characterises the nature of this event as an event in time, it would entail that the event as an event in which God reveals God's self would 'only be relatively marked . . . of which there are many others of the kind.'[28]

This method of understanding the temporal nature of the event of revelation will also characterise Barth's understanding the distinctions between the trinitarian hypostases in terms of the time-conditioned aspects of the economy of salvation in history. What Barth classifies here as the 'marked' nature of the historical events of the event of revelation will become, in the exposition of the Trinity, an emphasis on the doctrine of appropriations as defining the distinctness of the hypostases in relationship to each other.[29]

## The Holy Spirit and the 'root' of the doctrine of the Trinity

The question involved in the relationship between the narrower 'root' of the doctrine of the Trinity and the Holy Spirit is that the biblical view of revelation presupposes that it is historical; it reaches human beings. 'Historical' here has a very specific meaning.

> We should have once more to discard all that was previously said about the mystery in revelation, did we wish now to describe just a single one of the events of revelation narrated in the Bible as 'historical', i.e., as apprehensible by a neutral observer . . . What the neutral observer of these events might apprehend or may have apprehended of these events was the form of revelation.[30]

The important thing about the historicity of the events of revelation is not the more or less correct content of the statements that refer to them but 'the

---

27. *Ibid.*
28. *Ibid.*
29. The problem ( as will be seen), with this method of understanding the distinctions involved in the dogma of the Trinity is that it will be difficult to see how one is able to determine which of the hypostases is incarnate! Cf K Rahner, *The Trinity*, 24–30.
30. Barth, *CD* 1/1, 373.

fact of them'.[31] The factuality of the events of revelation corresponds to, as it presupposes, the fact that the God who is revealed cannot be revealed by the relative nature of the forms of revelation. As the life of Jesus is concluded under the *Deus absconditus*, so that Jesus' revelation of the Father is beyond the negative limit of human existence in death by the resurrection as the *Deus revelatus*; the event of revelation is to be considered 'a fact as it takes place, vertically from heaven'.[32] If this 'factuality' of the event of revelation in which God is 'veiled' is to reach the creature to whom it is directed, then 'we mean nothing but Pentecost, the outpouring of the Holy Spirit'.[33] But this one who unites the event in which God is both the *Deus absconditus* and the *Deus revelatus* must be God too.

> The fact of His doing this, this third thing also—which does not follow obviously from the first and second, as surely as there is nothing, absolutely nothing, obvious in their existence and co-existence either—that there is such a manifestation of the Father and the Son, is what we mean when we say that He reveals Himself as the Lord.[34]

Barth 'proves' the Lordship of the Holy Spirit, in so far as the event of revelation is understood, as a unity in which God is present for the creature. However, God's being present for and to the creature in the unity of the event of revelation is such that nothing is added to or subtracted from the being of God. God is Lord of the creature from the side of the *creature's* presence with God precisely because God is present to God's self in this relationship. The Holy Spirit is the reality of God

> subjectively present to men not only from without, not only from above, but also from within, from beneath. It is reality, therefore,

---

31.　*Ibid.*

32.　*Ibid*, 378–379. Cf Kierkegaard, *Philosophical Fragments*, 89ff, and 104: 'Even if the contemporary generation had not left anything behind except these words, "we have believed that in such and such a year the god appeared in the humble form of a servant, lived and taught amongst us, and then died"—this is more than enough.' See also H Deim, *Kierkegaard's Dialectic of Existence* (Edinburgh: Oliver and Boyd, 1959), 60ff.

33.　Barth, *CD* 1/1, 380.

34.　*Ibid*, 381, 382.

by God not only coming to man, but meeting Himself from man's end.[35]

It is for this reason that Barth has doubts about the manner in which St Athanasius posits the 'conceivability' of the Spirit in his defence of the deity of the Spirit.[36] Barth interprets any attempt to posit the person of the Holy Spirit in terms of an aspect of the worldly form of revelation, apart from considering the event of revelation as presupposing the inconceivable event of God's own self-positing, as an attempt to presuppose the existence of God by some aspect of creaturely existence. This is to turn God into a creature![37] For if the Holy Spirit is the One in whom God realises God's existence as both One and Another, in terms of the event of revelation, that is as the *Deus absconditus* and the *Deus revelatus* (the Father and the Son), then the Spirit's existence cannot be understood apart from this inconceivable event in which God realises God's self as God. To imagine that the creature can presuppose this event with an aspect of its existence is to turn the creature into God and God into a creature. It is for this reason that Barth sees his defence of the Western addition to the creed of the *filioque* as 'no less than the entire statement of our view . . . of the doctrine of the Holy Spirit and of the Trinity in general.' That to which the *filioque* draws

---

35.  *Ibid*, 516. Thus 'the Spirit is less the reality in which God makes us sure of Him, as on the contrary the reality in which He makes Himself sure of us, in which by His immediate presence He makes good and executes His claim as Lord upon us'; 520.

36.  *Ibid*, 529; cf 526–529. St Athanasius develops his account of the deity of the Spirit by taking full account of the humanity of Jesus and its significance for understanding the ontological renewal of the creature celebrated in the Eucharist. The appropriatess of such a context for understanding the Spirit's deity is called into question by Barth's insistence that the conceivability of the *creature's* presence with God in the event of revelation coincides with the conceivability of the unique existence of God. For St Athanasius's arguments see *Select Library of Nicene and Post Nicene Fathers*, volume 4, 'Four discourses against the Arians', Discourse 1, chapter 9, sec 39, 329; secs 43–45, 331ff; Discourse 2, chapter 14, secs 9ff, 353ff; chapter 21, secs 62ff, 382ff; Discourse 3, chapter 26, secs 29ff, 409ff; St Athanasius, *The Incarnation of the Word* (London: Mowbray, 1953), secs 4–9, 38–41, secs 42–45, 59–61; St Athanasius, *Letters concerning the Holy Spirit*, translated by CRB Shapland (London: Epworth, 1951),Epistle 1, sec 25, 128–129; sec 29, 136–139; sec 9, 80–84 (see note 13, 82); secs 22-23, pp 120–124; Epistle 3, secs1–7, 169–178.

37.  Barth, *CD* 1/1, 532.

attention in understanding the being of God in the event of God's self-unveiling is that

> there exists not only for us, but exists in God Himself no possibility
> of an opening and readiness and capacity in men for God.[38]

The *filioque* is a 'proof' for Barth of his method of understanding God in the event of revelation in which the presence of the creature at revelation, or in revelation, is posited on the presupposition of the inconceivable relationship between the *Deus absconditus* and the *Deus revelatus*.[39]

Barth rejects any modification of the *filioque* in terms of understanding the phrase as meaning 'through the Son'.[40] This modification disputes the *relatio originis* between the Son and the Spirit, so that the Spirit can be called the Spirit of the Son only improperly. The basis upon which Barth mounts this argument is his view of the unity of the event of the self-revealing God—precisely the same as that by which he established the deity of the Spirit.

The interpretation 'through the Son' presupposes a distinction between the self-revealing God and God in and for God's self apart from the event of God's revelation. To relegate the *relatio originis* to some other realm, apart from the event in which God reveals God's self, is to assume a distinction between God and God's self-revelation which is not included in that revelation; this is impossible. It is consequently in the interests of God's tri-unity that Barth adheres to the *filioque* and rejects 'the curious juxtaposition of the Father and the Son with respect to the Spirit', implicit in the Eastern doctrine of procession from the Father alone.[41]

The positive significance of the Western addition is the particular emphasis it places on the manner and extent to which God is free for the creature. It brings to understanding that what God is in God's self, God is in relationship to the creature.

---

38.   *Ibid*, 548, 549.
39.   For the following see also G Watson, 'The Filioque: Opportunity for Debate?', in *Scottish Journal of Theology*, 41/3 (1988): 313–330.
40    Barth, *CD* 1/1, 543.
41.   *Ibid*, 552. Cf V Lossky, *The Mystical Theology of the Eastern Church*, 54–57, 62, 157, 158.

> By being the Father who brings forth the Son, He brings forth the Spirit of love; for, by bringing forth the Son, God already negates in Himself, from all eternity, in His utter simplicity, existence in loneliness . . . God is directed toward the Other . . . will only possess Himself, by possessing Himself along with the Other, in fact in the Other.

With respect to the creature, this means that in its very different 'otherness' from God it presupposes, in this relationship, the relationship in which God negates loneliness in God's self. Its distinction from and relationship to God presuppose the relationship and distinction in which God possesses God's own life as both One and Another.

> In the Son of His love, i.e., in the Son in and with whom he brings Himself forth as love, He then brings forth also in the *opus ad extra*; in creation the creaturely reality distinct from Himself, and in revelation reconciliation and peace for the creature that had fallen away from Him. The Love which meets us in reconciliation and, looking backwards from that, in creation, is therefore and thereby Love, the highest law and ultimate reality, because God is Love antecedently in Himself . . . But He is Love antecedently in Himself, by positing Himself as the Father of the Son. This is the interpretation and proof of the *qui procedit Patre*.[42]

Barth also rejects the interpretation of the *filioque* which would suggest that there needs to be also considered a *spirituque*, a corresponding procession of the Son from the Father and the Spirit to complement the procession of the Spirit from the Father and the Son.[43] There are, Barth admits, certain exegetical reasons why the question should be raised. There is also a systematic argument, which may be used to defend the possibility of a *spirituque*. It runs like this:

---

42. *Ibid*, 553; cf also 548.
43. Barth, *CD* 1/1, 554. For a description of the problem of a *spirituque,* see GS Hendry, 'From the Father and the Son: the Filioque after nine hundred years', *Theology Today*, 11/4 (1954–1955): 449–459, and by the same author, *The Holy Spirit and Christian theology,* rev ed (London: SCM, 1965), 41–52, 109–117. Also see J McIntyre, 'The Holy Spirit in Greek Patristic Thought', in *Scottish Journal of Theology* 7/4 (1954): 353, 371–375.

If we apply our rule here also, that dogmatic pronouncements upon the immanent Trinity can and must be read off according to content from the determinations about God's modes of existence in revelation, are we not in that case forced to assume also between the Spirit and the Son an original relationship, which in that case would be neither generation nor breathing but a third thing? And . . . that only then is the circle of mutual relations, in which God is One in three modes of existence, a complete and self enclosed one, and that already for that reason such an origin of the Son from the Father and the Spirit is to be postulated.[44]

This systematic argument may 'at once be dismissed'.[45] If the argument is to be complete, an origin of the Father from the Son and the Spirit would have to be postulated. However, the relations of the intra-trinitarian being of God are not such as to involve origins as such, but are to be understood as modes of existence of the one God.[46] We may allow the postulate of this systematic argument in the sense that it is

a further description of the *homoousia* of the Father, Son and Spirit, but with begetting and breathing in themselves it has nothing to do, and so moreover does not require any completions in this direction.[47]

Yet the question immediately arises, if the unity of God, of which Barth allows the systematic argument to be a 'further description', is conceived in terms of the unique act in which God posits God's self as Lord, why shouldn't the argument apply to the 'origins' as well as the 'modes' of God's existence? In principle, it is difficult to see how Barth can distinguish between modes of existence and the way in which God posits God's self as God. Barth uses a distinction necessary for his argument, but for which there are no grounds in his exposition of the nature of the event of revelation.[48]

---

44.   Barth, *CD* 1/1, 555.

45.   *Ibid*

46.   *Ibid*, 554.

47.   *Ibid*, 555.

48.   Hendry, 'From the Father and the Son', 454: 'The argument with which Barth follows the tradition of Western theology in resisting this inference is singularly

This weakness in Barth's defence, in respect of an issue he regards as of critical significance for his whole doctrine of the Trinity, [49] is compounded when he considers the exegetical material he associates with the suggested *spirituque.* In considering the question, it must be borne in mind

> that the work of the Holy Spirit regarding the Son in revelation . . . is not the sort of thing that might be described as commensurable with the eternal generation of the Son through the Father or with the eternal breathing of the Spirit through Father and Son, so that from it a further eternal relation of origin might possibly or necessarily be read off. [50]

For Barth's argument to be cogent, he must assume a distinction between the forms of revelation to which the texts bear witness, for example the relationship between the Holy Spirit and the child in Mary's womb, and the question of the hypostatic origin of the Holy Spirit. However, such a distinction is completely out of the question in terms of Barth's methodology. The worldly form of revelation is concluded under the *Deus absconditus* in Barth's analysis of the event of God's self-revelation. To assume a distinction in the worldly form of revelation, between its content and the hypostatic origin of the Spirit, is on Barth's own analysis excluded. The distinctions of hypostatic origin cannot be related to distinctions in the worldly forms of revelation. These cannot be understood unless they are seen as grounded in God's own act of self-positing which is revealed in the *Deus revelatus,* beyond the negative limit of human existence in the resurrection of Jesus Christ from the dead. Barth is caught here in a conflict between the systematic implications of his doctrine of revelation in which is to be found his exposition of the Trinity and the contingent activity of God in the history of salvation, witnessed to in the biblical record.

Another form of the dilemma, in which Barth finds himself at this point, is reflected in his assertion that the work of the Spirit in the incarnation is 'prototypical' of the Spirit's activity in being the One in whom human beings become children of God, as distinct from the Spirit's 'ectypical' work in the relation between the Father and the Son.

---

unconvincing.' Cf RD Williams, 'Barth on the Triune God', in *Karl Barth: Studies of his Theological Method,* edited by SW Sykes (Oxford: Clarendon, 1979), 170ff.

49. See footnote 38.
50. Barth, *CD* 1/1, 555.

> What is ascribed to the Holy Spirit in the birth of Christ is the
> assumption of human-ness in the Virgin Mary into unity with
> God in the Logos mode of existence . . . This work of the Spirit
> is proto-typical of the work of the Spirit in the *becoming* of the
> children of God . . . But that work of the Spirit is not ectypical of
> a work of the Spirit upon the Son of God himself . . . So that what
> is to be inferred from these passages for the understanding of the
> eternal Trinity, has nothing to do with an origin in God. [51]

We see again, from a different perspective, how Barth's methodological presuppositions in respect to his understanding of the event nature of revelation in terms of the inconceivable freedom in which God posits God's self as God, create difficulty in giving significance to the relative and contingent aspects of the event of revelation considered as a worldly event.

## Barth's doctrine of God's three-in-oneness

We have already seen that Barth's understanding of the 'narrower root' of the doctrine of the Trinity in the deity of the Son entailed that the form of revelation, the humanity of Jesus, was understood in terms of the event structure of revelation. This presupposes the inconceivable freedom of God in God's positing God's self as both One and Another in the unity of a third. Therefore, since God's essence and his operation are not to be distinguished in terms of the worldly forms of revelation, those activities of God attributable to differing modes of God's existence can only be understood in direct relation

---

51.   *Ibid*, 556. Cf K Schilder, *Zur Begriffsgeschichte des 'Paradoxon' mit besonderer Berücksichtigung Calvins und des nach-Kierkegaardschen 'Paradoxon'* (Kampen: BJ Kok, 1933), 338. Schilder indicates that the reason Barth has this problem is that he detaches the paradox involved with understanding the event of revelation from the relationship between the communication and the receiver in order to make it an attribute of the communication. See also FG Downing, *Has Christianity a Revelation?* (London: SCM, 1964), 171, 227, 228, and HM Kuitert, *Gott in Menschengestalt: eine dogmatisch-hermeneutische Studie über die Anthropomorphismen der Bibel* (München: Kaiser, 1967), 101–107. Certain catholic writers have taken Barth's distinction between the proto- and ectypical work of the Spirit in revelation and accused him of ecclesiological Nestorianism. By this they mean there is an inconsistency in Barth's refusal to allow the same relationship to apply to the church as to the humanity of Jesus in the Spirit's work in the incarnation of the Word. See C O'Grady, *The Church in the Theology of Karl Barth* (London: G Chapman, 1968), volume 2, 264ff.

to the act in which God posits God's self as God. In revealing God's self, God also interprets God's self. Yet it is important to distinguish God's essence from God's operations *ad extra*.[52] The importance of this distinction derives from the fact that God's operation *ad extra* is not necessary to God's essence.[53]

It is through God's operation that we come to know God's threeness, and God is who God is in the revelation of God. Consequently, the forms of revelation considered in themselves cannot be the distinctions posited by the freedom of God in which God both distinguishes God's self from God's operation and distinguishes God's self from God's self in being who God is. The conceivability of the scriptural witness to the distinctions in the forms of revelation, in relation to these distinctions, is 'absolutely separate'.[54] That God is known in God's threeness and unity in the forms of revelation depends upon the freedom in which God distinguishes God's self from God's operation, and God's self from God's self, becoming the conceivability of these other 'absolutely separate' distinctions. This seeming contradiction is explained when it is realised that, in our conceiving of the distinctions involved in the forms of revelation, 'we do not conceive the distinctions in the divine modes of existence'.[55] If we conceive that which by definition cannot be conceived, and name the distinctions in terms of a doctrine of the Trinity, it must be the case that God 'goes bail' for the truth of the distinctions involved in the forms of revelation and their ability 'to make us aware of the distinctions in the divine modes of existence'.[56] If this proviso were not made, and we sought our knowledge of the distinctions in God in the forms of revelation,

> we should be assuming three gods or a tripartite essence of God . . . Thus, we must believe that those distinctions in the operation of God really take place within the sphere and limits of our conceivability, but that even here they neither properly nor primarily signify the last word in the hidden essence of God, that in these distinctions cannot rest the distinctions in God Himself.[57]

---

52. Barth, *CD* 1/1, 426.
53. *Ibid*.
54. *Ibid*.
55. *Ibid*, 427.
56. *Ibid*.
57. *Ibid*.

We see here, from another perspective, how Barth's view of the threeness of God's mode of being in relation to the creaturely forms of revelation emphasises the same relationship as was discussed previously in terms of the humanity of the Son with reference to his deity as the 'narrower root' of the doctrine of the Trinity. In both cases, he interprets the forms of revelation as serving the question of their reality and possibility in the unique act in which God determines God's self for the creature and the creature for God. It is therefore quite consistent that Barth should elaborate his view of the conceivability posited by the forms of revelation by means of the doctrine of appropriations.[58]

Barth finds a 'hint' of the doctrine of appropriations as the means by which the distinctions in the forms of revelation and the act in which God distinguishes God's self from God's self can be conceived. It is a 'hint' which recognises 'the unattainability of the thing itself',[59] an unattainability which has nothing to do with a puzzle which in principle is soluble, since this 'hint' can only be understood in terms of the inconceivably free act of God's self-positing which it presupposes. This exposition by Barth, of course, draws attention to the systemic problem with his methodology we have indicated. The concrete worldly forms of revelation are presupposed in their conceivability by the inconceivable act in which God posits God's self. They thus become inconceivable in terms of their worldly form as the means by which God's self-interpretation in the event of revelation is understood.[60]

---

58.   Barth, *CD* 1/1, 428. In respect of the conceivability posited by the forms of revelation and its relationship to the conceivability posited by the distinctions in which God posits God's own existence, I found myself in agreement with E Jüngel, *Gottes Sein ist im Werden*, 49, 50. Jüngel sees the relationship between the two kinds of conceivability in terms of Barth's idea of the essence of God consisting in the reality and possibility inherent in God's own self-positing. Since in God's self-positing God distinguishes between God's essence and God's operations, the relationship between the two conceivabilities alluded to above is to be understood as that which exists between the doctrine of appropriations and *perichoresis*. The former gives expression to the concreteness in which God *posits* God's self. The latter brings to expression that it is *God* who posits God's self in the event of God's self-interpretation in revelation. See also Barth, *CD* 1/1, 427–431, and 3/2, 65ff.

59.   *Ibid*, 428.

60.   See on this issue Paul D Molnar, *Divine Freedom and the Doctrine of the Immanent Trinity: in Dialogue with Karl Barth and Contemporary Theology* (Edinburgh: T & T Clark, 2002); also KW Hector, 'God's Triunity and Self-Determination: a Conversation with Karl Barth, Brucer McCormack and Paul Molnar', in *International Journal of Systematic Theology* 7/3 (July 2005): 246ff. In this debate between Professors B

One can only conclude with K Rahner that such an interpretation of the doctrine of appropriations, as the means whereby God's threeness is to be understood in terms of the trinitarian dogma, cannot easily identify which of the *hypostases* is incarnate or sent. If the concrete distinctions involved in the forms of revelation are not allowed to speak in their contingent and relative character of the God who is present with and for the creature in the revelation of God's name, then it would appear to be immaterial which of the divine persons is involved.[61] Further, such an understanding of God's self-revelation becomes impersonal because is it impossible to tell which of the divine persons is revealed, and also because revelation itself is reduced to the realm of an all encompassing idea. Barth combines the doctrine of *perichoresis* with that of

---

McCormack and P Molnar on the nature of Karl Barth's doctrine of election within the doctrine of God, the same issues that we are concerned with in respect of the contingency of the events of revelation in relation to understanding the doctrine of the Trinity arise. 'Though McCormack and Molnar agree with Karl Barth's insistence that God's immanent triunity is known only by way of God's economic triunity, they disagree sharply in regard to its implications. What, for instance, is the relationship between God's triunity and God's self-determination to be God-with-us? What does "freedom" mean when predicated of God? What is the identity of the *logos asarkos*?' (see Hector, 246) In this debate, both McCormack and Molnar find evidence in Barth for their respective positions on the nature of God's freedom in the relation between the doctrine of election and the doctrine of God, but appear to fail to appreciate the importance to both their positions of Barth's understanding of the relationship between the doctrines appropriations and *perichoresis* for his view of God's trinitarian freedom. As stated above in respect of the conceivability posited by the forms of revelation and its relationship to the conceivability posited by the distinctions in which God posits God's own existence, we find ourselves in agreement with Jüngel (*Gottes Sein*, 49, 50) who sees the relationship between the two kinds of conceivability in terms of Barth's idea of the essence of God consisting in the reality and possibility inherent in God's own self-positing. Since in God's self-positing God distinguishes between God's essence and God's operations, the relationship between the two conceivabilities alluded to is to be understood as that which exists between the trinitarian doctrines of appropriations and *perichoresis*. The former gives expression to the concreteness in which God *posits* God's self. The latter brings to expression that it is *God* who posits God's self in absolute freedom in the event of God's self-interpretation in revelation.

61.   K Rahner, *The* Trinity, 14, 15, 23ff. Cf St Cyril of Alexandria's criticism of Nestorius on the same issue in 'Five Tome Contradiction of the Blasphemies of Nestorius', *A Library of the Fathers of the Holy Catholic Church* (Oxford: Parker & Rivingtons, 1881), Tome 1, 34. Cf 16, 18–19, 35.

appropriations in order to combine, in a dialectical fashion, both the freedom
and the concreteness of the divine self-positing by God, of God's threeness and
oneness. However, it does nothing to alleviate this problem. Whilst in Barth's
terms it may indicate the 'dialectical completion of the concept of three-in-
oneness',[62] it only emphasises the inconceivability of the forms of revelation in
their worldly forms as the means of God's self-communication.

## God's one-in-threeness

The unity of God, that to which the doctrine of *perichoresis* drew attention as one
part of the dialectic just mentioned, is understood by Barth under the concept
of Lordship. This means 'the divine *essentia, natura or substantia*'.[63] If we ask
after the basis upon which Barth establishes this view of the unity of God, then
reference is made to the 'concept of the Lordship of God, with which we found
the whole Biblical concept of revelation to be related'.[64]

  As was made clear in the doctrine of revelation in respect of the 'nature of
the Word of God', and in the doctrine of the Trinity in respect of the part played
by the forms of revelation in understanding God's threeness, so here Barth is
careful to point out that

---

62.   Barth, *CD* 1/1, 431. GS Hendry, '*From the Father and the Son: the Filioque after Nine
      Hundred Years*, 458: 'The external operations of the Trinity are not only undivided,
      they have become indistinguishable.'

63.   Barth, *CD* 1/1, 401. It is of importance to note that Barth takes his bearings for
      understanding the meaning of *perichoresis* from John of Damascus (ibid, 425): one
      of the divine modes of existence is invariably in the other two modes of existence,
      as also the two are in the one. However, the original meaning of the term was
      related to Christology. See GL Prestige, *God in Patristic Thought*, 291ff. Here the
      relationship to which *perichoresis* referred is one which, on the one hand, involved
      all persons of the Trinity and, on the other hand, that which is not God, that is the
      human nature of our Lord. Thus the relationship was conceived as *perichoresis* 'to'
      (εις) or (προσ), not *perichoresis* 'in' (εν) or 'through' one another. It is not surprising
      that Barth is glad to be reminded by the Western interpretation of the doctrine of
      *perichoresis* of the inappropriateness of the Eastern interpretation which still clings
      to the idea of *temporal successiveness*. This, of course, was the original intention of
      the doctrine in respect to the relationship between God and the human nature of
      our Lord. See Barth, *ibid*, 425.

64.   *Ibid*.

the concept of the revealed unity of the revealed God . . . does not exclude but includes a distinction (*distinctio* or *discretio*), an arrangement (*dispositio* or *oeconomia*) in the essence of God.[65]

Thus, we must understand God's unity apart from the forms of revelation and any aspect of creaturely being which may be related to them. Rather, God's unity is expressed in terms of the way in which God posits God's self in an ineffable freedom, which includes the manner in which God's threeness is expressed. This aspect of Barth's thought is emphasised in his choice of the idea of 'mode of being' over 'person' to express the distinctions in the way in which God posits God's self as triune.

In a sympathetic analysis of St Thomas' modification of the Aristotelian-Boethian definition of person as *naturae rationabilis individua substantia*,[66] Barth draws attention to only two elements in his exposition that prove tenable. These are the ideas of *subsistere* and *incommunicabilitas* in respect of the hypostases of the Trinity. Since St Thomas does not give his definition of these terms by means of the concept *persona*, but by means of the concept of relation, Barth feels free to abandon the term 'person', though it is hallowed by traditional usage.[67]

Barth prefers the term 'mode of being' to express the kind of distinction to which we have already drawn attention in his understanding of the relationship between God's unity and threefoldedness. This unity and threefoldedness are understood in terms of the idea of God's positing God's existence in an inconceivable freedom, to which the forms of revelation bear little relationship.[68]

Barth's emphasis on the element of *subsistere* in the traditional analysis of *persona* defines what he means by mode of being as it relates to the *act* in which God posits God's self as God. We may recall a similar conclusion reached by Barth in terms of his understanding of the dialectical relationship between the unity and threefoldedness of God, as between the doctrines of *perichoresis* and appropriations. The former refers to the unity of God in terms of the inconceivable act of God's self-existence.

---

65. *Ibid*, 407.
66. *Ibid*, 409.
67. *Ibid*, 410.
68. See above, 12, 13 with footnote 60.

The other element Barth sees as tenable in St Thomas' interpretation of the traditional concept of *persona* is that of *incommunicabilitas*.[69] We take this to be a parallel to Barth's understanding of the doctrine of appropriations. *Incommunicabilitas* does not refer to any distinctions read off, as it were, from the forms of revelation, but is to be understood in terms of the Lordship of God in God's operations *ad extra*.

> Thus, distinct from the First there is, as the Second, Revelation itself, as the event of the manifestation of what was previously hidden. And as the common result of these two elements, constituting the Third, a Revealedness. [On the basis of these] regularly recurring mutual relations is founded God's threeness in oneness.[70]

The concept of 'mode of being' brings to understanding how the oneness and threeness of God's being are related to the way in which, in inconceivable freedom, God posits God's self as the creature's Lord. In this way, God is able to be for the creature what God is in God's being in and for God's self, without at the same time compromising the inconceivable freedom in which God exists.

## The Trinity and Christology

The comprehensive answer to the question Barth puts to the biblical witness to revelation, 'Who is the self-revealing God?' is 'that we are impelled to consider the Three-in-oneness of God'.[71] In this way, Barth sought to develop the doctrine of the Trinity in answer to the question of the way in which the self-revealing God is Lord in the event of God's self-disclosure. Barth proceeds by asking how God is Lord in this event. The various answers he has given are along the lines that God is Lord through and by God's self. Thus, the worldly forms of revelation are brought to understanding by asking after their meaning in that which they presuppose: that is, the actuality and freedom of this self-revealing God. The christological question can only be understood as a variant

---

69.   Barth, *CD* 1/1, 414.

70.   *Ibid*, 417, 418. See the criticism of Barth by Rahner, *The Trinity*, 14, 15, 24ff, 73ff, 110ff, and Jüngel's defence of Barth, *Gottes Sein ist im Werden*, 50, 51.

71.   *Ibid*, 348.

of that which raised to understanding the doctrine of the Trinity in terms of the Lordship of God.

This question, which raised to understanding the doctrine of the Trinity, obviously presupposed that 'we had before us the further question about what God does for us and what God does in us'.[72] This question is not put in a way that contradicts the self-enclosed circle of knowledge of God, which Barth has expounded in the doctrine of the Trinity in terms of God's Lordship. It is a matter of seeing

> how far God in His revelation is free for us, i.e., free to reveal Himself to us, free to be our God without at the same time ceasing to be the Lord.[73]

Barth's doctrine of the Trinity has given him the answer to the question as to who the self-revealing God of the Bible is in terms of an analysis of the event of revelation. Now, Barth seeks to understand the factuality of this event in the context of that answer. Thus the factuality of the event of revelation, the man Jesus, cannot be understood as a historical figure amongst other historical figures, such as Peter and John or Pilate, and the intra-mundane possibilities which presuppose their existence in history. We cannot understand the man Jesus apart from the freedom in which God determines God's self as Lord of the creature. Thus,

> it would not be a genuine interpretation of the reality that is there, if it did not at the same time throw light upon its possibility as well. We have not genuinely let ourselves be told, if we cannot also as a result tell ourselves what has been told us . . . It would not be a serious awareness of this reality [i.e., the human Jesus] were it not immediately to turn to understanding also. That would not be a *credere*, which did not force its way through to an *intelligere*.[74]

If the question as to the existence and meaning of the man Jesus does not issue in an interpretation that is conditioned by the question as to the extent to which God in freedom is the creature's Lord, then the question of fact has been

---

72.   Barth, *CD* 1/2, 2.
73.   *Ibid*
74.   *Ibid*, 26.

put wrongly. In the first edition of the Prolegomena, Barth himself was guilty of just such an error. There he attempted to prove

> that if the Triune God wished to reveal Himself to man He would have to become man, because only as a man could He be at once hidden and manifest.[75]

Barth realised he was seeking after a possibility which did not reside in the reality of revelation. Any attempt to interpret the possibility of the existence of the man Jesus prior to the fact of his being who he is, is not thought which seeks understanding in terms of the reality and possibility posited by the Object (subject) of faith, and is thus theologically irrational.[76]

Another way in which Barth's method configures our understanding of the person of Jesus Christ is that he develops a particular view of the time of revelation, which coincides, with nature of the God who is revealed in Jesus Christ. Consequently, the time we think we possess as we reflect upon our experience of existence cannot be considered as the time that presupposes the event of revelation, the time of the man Jesus Christ. The relationship between our time and the time God has for us in Jesus Christ is precisely the same as that which Barth propounded in his analysis of the forms of revelation in terms of the nature of the Word of God. There we noted that the forms of revelation were brought to understanding by considering them in relation to the nature of the Word of God as God's language, God's act and God's mystery. This issued in an understanding of the event nature of God's revelation as presupposing God's Lordship. The event of revelation thus understood was seen as presupposing a relationship between the *Deus absconditus* and the *Deus revelatus*. In respect to our time and the time of revelation, the time that presupposes the person of Jesus Christ and his existence in time, we are faced with the same hiddenness. The time of revelation is hidden from us not in the sense that some day it may be found, but hidden as something can only be hidden which presupposes the inconceivable freedom in which God posits God's self as Lord of the creature.[77] Consequently, the time form of revelation in its christological aspect involves the consideration that

---

75.  *CD* 1/2, 9–10.
76.  See on this aspect of Barth's thought, TF Torrance, *Space, Time and Incarnation*, 54, 55.
77.  Barth, *CD* 1/2, 47.

the Word spoken from eternity raises the time into which it is uttered (without dissolving it as time) up into His own eternity as now His own time, and gives it part in the existence of God which is alone real.[78]

Nevertheless, without our having knowledge of it, given the presupposition upon which it is reality, the time which God has for us in Jesus Christ is a time which coincides with 'God's inconceivable freeness and so His existence for us'.[79] The possibility of distinguishing this time from the time of the creature is not inherent in the creature's-self understanding of its temporality. This is a distinction only God can make since it involves the exercise of God's Lordship, and thus presupposes God's freedom to be Lord of the creature.[80]

Barth applies this dogmatic concept of time to the question of the relationship of the time of the apostles and prophets to the time of revelation. The relationship of the 'previousness' of the prophets' witness and that of the apostles to the 'pastness' of revelation does not emanate from their historical difference.

---

78. *Ibid*, 52. Time considered in this sense may thus be seen as 'God's being in its concrete act of actualisation'; Jüngel, *Gottes sein ist im Werden*, 51; author's translation.
79. *CD* 1/2, 55. Cf 64.
80. Consequently, Barth rejects the question of the relationship between revelation and history as it has been raised consequent upon the nineteenth century's concentration of attention on it. He thus rejects R Bultmann's understanding of the event nature of the resurrection in terms of the creature's understanding of its temporality. See Barth, *CD* 3/2, 442ff, and, 'Rudolf Bultmann—An Attempt to Understand Him', in HW Bartsch editor, *Kerygma and Myth*, volume 2, 83ff, 94ff, 109ff, 116–119. The same arguments are used aginst the validity of Lessing's question concerning contingent historical facts and necessay truth. See Barth, *CD* 4/1, 287ff, 290, and on the same issue, H Ott, 'Der Gedanke der Souveranität Gottes in der Theologie Karl Barths', *Theologische Zeitschrift* 12 (1956): 409ff. There are, of course, those who have interpreted Barth's position as a flight from history. All historical distinctions are referred to the structure of the event of revelation and thus have no independent meaning.See W Pannenberg, 'Redemptive Event and History', in C Westermann editor, *Essays on Old Testament Interpretation* (London: SCM, 1963), 314ff; Richard Niebuhr, *Resurrection and Historical Reason* (New York: Scribners, 1957), 42–51, 84–89, 178, 179.; AM Fairweather, *The Word as Truth: a Critical Examination of the Christian Doctrine of Revelation in the Writings of Thomas Aquinas and Karl* Barth (London: Lutterworth, 1944), 75–86,124.

> Where expectation is genuine, 'previously' does not mean 'not
> yet'; just as, where recollection is genuine, 'subsequently' does
> not mean 'no longer'. Genuine expectation and recollection .
> . . are different, but one in their content, in their object, in the
> thing attested, and also one in that for them this thing attested is
> neither merely future nor merely past; as 'future' and as 'past' it
> is present.[81]

Hence genuine expectation and recollection, considered as a phenomenon of
history, are hidden in a similar way as revelation itself is hidden. As the historical
form of revelation in the humanity of Jesus was brought to understanding
by seeing it as presupposing the *Deus absconditus* and the *Deus revelatus*, so
also genuine expectation and recollection can only be understood as they
presupposes this non-cognisable dialectic which involves the act in which God
reveals God's self as Lord.[82] It is this relationship between the 'hiddenness' of
the expectation and recollection of the witnesses to revelation, that makes it
possible to posit the Subject of the expectation and revelation to be the same,
and therefore genuine expectation. In this sense,

> Christ was indeed suffering Israel, the suffering prophet, the
> suffering righteous man. Not an idea of Christ, but the real
> historical Christ *qui passus est sub Pilato*.[83]

If the time of expectation of revelation is considered apart from the relationship
it has with the hiddenness of revelation, then it becomes a 'Jewish abstraction.'[84]
Similar considerations are brought to bear on the nature of the New Testament
witnesses. So the time, which is subsequent to the event of revelation, 'as little
coincides with the time *post Christum natum* as preceding time does with the
time *ante Christum natum*.'[85]

It is just as hard and just as easy to understand the relationship between the
time of the apostolic witness to revelation and the time of revelation as it is with
respect to the prophetic witness to revelation. The difference between the Old

---

81.   Barth, *CD* 1/2, 70–71.
82.   *Ibid*, 72. Cf Barth, *The Word of God and the Word of Man*, 28ff.
83.   *Ibid*, 89.
84.   *Ibid*.
85.   *Ibid*, 101.

and New Testaments is not to be sought in the time differences of the respective witnesses, considered as historically prior or subsequent to the historical figure of Jesus. The differences and connections between the two are to be understood by their relationship to the hiddenness of God common to both witnesses.

> The No of the New Testament, its witness to the hiddenness of God, is no less than the demonstration of the manifest glory of the Son of God. If the same is said also of the No of the Old Testament—as it must and can be said—it is because we are taught to say it by the New Testament.[86]

Barth achieves understanding of the time form of revelation's witnesses in the same way as he achieved understanding of the reality and possibility posited by the earthly historical form of revelation itself, in considering the question of the deity of Jesus Christ as the 'root' of the doctrine of the Trinity. There the form of revelation, considered as a historical phenomenon, was understood in terms of the hiddenness of God, the *Deus absconditus*, which presupposed the revelation of God beyond the negative limit of human existence in death through the resurrection of the man Jesus, the *Deus revelatus*. Here, too, when it is a question of understanding the meaning of the christological question in relation to the time form presupposed by the worldly witnesses to that revelation—the prophets and the apostles—it is a matter of achieving understanding as an answer that presupposes the structure of the revelatory event in which God is inconceivably free for the creature in the event of God's self-positing.

### The christological problem and the confession: 'Jesus Christ, very God very Man'

Congruent with previous considerations regarding the form of revelation and its relationship to the time of its witnesses, Barth insists that christological dogma can only be considered as an inquiry into 'the presuppositions of this work and event, hidden in the life and passion of Christ and revealed in His resurrection.' The dogmatic formulae of the church 'fix the fact regarding the subject active in revelation'.[87]

---

86.  *Ibid*, 112.
87.  Barth, *CD* 1/2, 122, 126.

Thus, the person of Jesus Christ will be considered within the context of the dialectic that presupposes revelation as of the *Deus absconditus* and the *Deus revelatus*, the unity of which is in the mystery of Pentecost. This focuses the christological question on the manner in which the 'and' in the confession, 'Jesus Christ, very God *and* very man', finds its rationality and necessity as the church's confession in the inconceivable freedom in which God is Lord of the creature.[88] The practical application of this mode of christological thought may best be illustrated in Barth's doctrine of reconciliation.[89] Here Barth achieves understanding of Christ's work of reconciliation in terms of Christ's person. His being is shown to be a history in terms of the event in which God constitutes God's self as Lord. His being as God and man consists in this deed, this action, this history.[90] The contents of the movement which make up Christ's history, and so his person, is humiliation and exaltation. God humbles God's self to the creature who by and in this action is exalted to be one with God. These two movements, through which Christ's being is constituted in the act of God's self-positing, *are* the two natures of Christ. The doctrine of the two 'states' of Christ, his being as exalted in unity with the Father as the eternal Son and his lowly being as the Son of Mary, are consequently identical with his person.[91] The two states are but two aspects of the one reality of who Christ is. Christ's deity is identical with God's work of reconciliation, his humanity with the creature in its relationship to the reconciling God. Christ's existence as God and man is precisely the unity in which these histories occur.[92]

---

88.  *Ibid* 132ff, 147ff, 159ff.

89.  Barth, *CD* 4/1, 122ff,133ff.

90.  *Ibid*, 138–140, 126–128.

91.  *Ibid*, 145ff, 132ff. Hence the structure of Barth's doctrine of reconciliation follows this exposition of the being of God in the act in which God determines God's self for the creature and the creature for God in the person of the Son of God. Hence, volume 4/1 concerns the condescension of Jesus Christ: 'The Lord as servant',159ff. volume 4/2 expresses the exaltation of the creature which takes place concurrently with the condescension of the Son of God. Jesus Christ is 'The servant as Lord', 3ff. volume 4.3 expresses the unity of this movement of condescension and exaltation in the Son of God's self-revelation as the truth of God and the creature. Jesus Christ is 'The true witness', 3ff. There is here an unmistakeable structural relationship between Barth's doctrine of reconciliation and his doctrine of revelation in which is found his doctrine of the Trinity.

92.  Barth, *CD* 4/3, Part 1, 10, 11.

The unity of this act, in which Christ's deity and humanity is understood, is the unity of the being of God in the act of God's self-positing, in which revelation is the self-interpretation of God, the revelation of who God *is*. Barth understands the words of St John 1:14 in terms of the subject of revelation assuming flesh.[93]

> His becoming is not an event which in any sense befalls Him, in which in any sense He is determined from without by something else.[94]

Enlarging his interpretation of this aspect of the christological problem, Barth uses the doctrines of *an-* and *en-hypostasis*. The mystery of the unity of the act, in which the Word *became* flesh as coincident with the unity of the being of God, can be expressed by these traditional doctrines.

> [T]he event of the incarnation of the Word, of the *unio hypostatica*, has to be understood as a *completed* event, but also as a completed *event*.[95]

The former, the *anhypostatic* reference, emphasises that aspect which finds characteristic expression in traditional Lutheran Christology. This states that the Word,

---

93. Barth, *CD* 1/2, 160.

94. *Ibid.* Cf the comment of F Godet, *Commentary on the Gospel of St John*, translated by F Crombie and M Cusin (Edinburgh: T&T Clark, 1876), 362: It is a curious fact that Protestant orthodoxy, whether Lutheran or Reformed, has also refused till now to accept the meaning of the word 'become' in all its strictness. It is evaded in the former case by means of the theory of *communicatio idiomatum*, in virtue of which the divine subject, the Word, chose somehow at will, and at every moment, between the two modes of divine and human existence, transferring alternatively to the one the attributes of the other; in the latter case, by asserting more strictly the distinctions between the two modes of being . . . Neither the one nor the other of these views . . . corresponds to the real meaning of the word to 'become'. The proposition: 'The Word became flesh', can only, as it seems to me, signify one thing, viz, that the divine subject entered into the human mode of being at the cost of renouncing His divine mode of being.

95. *CD* 1/2, 165. Cf 161–162, 167–170. On the doctrines of *an-* and *en-hypostasis* see AB Bruce, *The Humiliation of Christ* (Edinburgh: T&T Clark, 1881), 82ff, and M Hoogland, *Calvin's Perspective On the Exaltation of Christ* (Kampen: J Kok, 1966), 2, 3.

without becoming unlike Himself assumed His likeness to us,
and that now He is to be sought and found of us here, namely,
in His human being. There is no other form or manifestation in
heaven or on earth save the one child in the stable, the one Man
on the cross.[96]

For Barth, this aspect of Christology brings to attention its 'static ontic'
character. Its danger is that revelation will be dealt with as a 'state' rather than
an event. A *perichoresis* is maintained between the Word of God and the human
nature such that, 'as humanity only has reality through the Word, so too the
Word has reality through and in the humanity'.[97] This incorrectly implies a
mutual conditioning between God and the creature, which distorts the meaning
of the *anhypostasis*. It is meant to explain the event of the incarnation in terms of
the sole initiative of God as a *completed* event. It is this that gives the incarnation
its 'ontological reference'.[98]

Since the objectivity of the *completed* event is the objectivity of an act of
God, and since the Lutheran emphasis needs to be counterbalanced, this ontic
aspect must be seen in relation to the counteremphasis of the *enhypostasis*. This
draws attention to the fact that we must understand the objectivity of the event
of revelation as a completed *event*. In bringing this aspect of Christology to
understanding, theology must travel 'the inconceivable path that is trodden
again from the closed to the open mystery, from the cross to the resurrection.'[99]
By seeing the event of revelation from this perspective, we visualise 'the
dynamic element in the εγενετο', and as such it 'preserves the noetic interest of
Christology'.[100]

However, as with the *anhypostatic* emphasis, this *enhypostatic* aspect of
Christology can be distorted. The distinction between the Word who assumed
and the flesh assumed holds the seeds of an incipient Nestorianism which
obscures the end for which the εγενετο stands; this is the unity of both. To speak
with clarity, Barth suggests that all reflection on the way to this end should be
dropped.[101]

---

96.    *Ibid,* 165; cf 166.
97.    *CD* 1/2, 166.
98.    *Ibid,*165.
99.    *Ibid,*168.
100.  *Ibid,* 170.
101.  *Ibid.*

As Barth points out, his discussion of the significance of the doctrine of *enhypostasis* is related to what became known in the Reformed tradition as the *extra Calvinisticum.*[102] Barth understands the concern of Calvin at this point to mean that the

> λογος ασαρκος [is] to be regarded equally seriously as the *terminus a quo*, as the λογος ενσαρκος was regarded as the *terminus ad quem* of the incarnation.[103]

Barth attempts to interpret the doctrines of *an-* and *enhypostasis*, in terms of his view of the relationship between the form of revelation and the inconceivable act in which God determines God's self for the creature and the creature for God in Jesus Christ. However, this appears to changes the meaning of the *enhypostatic* doctrine and its relation to what Calvin's *extra Calvinisticum* signified. Barth views both of these as visualising what he calls the dynamic noetic aspect of Christology. We take this to mean that aspect of Barth's interpretation of the event of revelation, in which the event is considered as presupposing the mystery of the unity of the *Deus absconditus* and the *Deus revelatus*. In the doctrine of the Trinity, this mystery was associated with the person of the Holy Spirit whose mode of being corresponded to the reciprocity of the act in which the Father determined himself for the Son and the Son for the Father. I doubt that this is what the doctrines of *enhypostasis* and the *extra Calvinisticum* mean!

Calvin's concern was to concentrate attention on the factuality of Christ's historical humanity in terms of what he understood God willed him to be for us as the Mediator of creation and reconciliation. This led him to distinguish between God's incomprehensible essence—what and who God is in and for God's self—and God's will expressed to the creature in Christ. This distinction presupposes that the nature of God's condescension in Christ the Mediator is one which is not understood in terms of God's incomprehensible essence, in Barth's terms, the inconceivable freedom in which God posits God's self as God. Rather, it is to be understood in terms of the relativity of Christ's earthly humanity in its contingency. It was Calvin's insistence on this point that brought him into conflict with the Lutheran theologian Osiander. Osiander attempted to draw a structural relationship between God's being and the event

---

102.  *Ibid*, 168ff; cf 4/1, 52, 53,180ff.
103.  Barth, *CD* 1/2,169.

of the incarnation. Calvin refused to see the event of the incarnation as entailed by the act of creation. It is his distinction between the role of the Son of God as Mediator of creation and redemption, on the basis of the specific form of revelation considered as an historical event, that principally led to the Lutheran branding of Calvin's Christology as implying an 'extra' of the being of the Son of God which was not completely included in the incarnate humanity. It implied that, in one real sense, the Son of God never left heaven when he was born of the Virgin and lay in her lap. That is to say, God's being cannot be understood as added to or subtracted from. Thus, the distinction between the *Logos ensarkos* and the *Logos asarkos* does not entail 'something' of the Son of God's person not being included in the incarnate Son. The incarnation does not take place so that the inner essence of God may be revealed, but that the creature *qua* creature may be renewed as a creature in its relationship to God. The revelation of God in God's condescension to the creature has its foundation and scope in God's will toward the creature as distinct from it being understood as a disclosure of the incomprehensible being of God to the creature.[104]

Historically, the doctrine of *enhypostasis* has been associated with Leontius of Byzantium (c 485–543). It sought to emphasise the reality of the particularity of the humanity of Jesus against interpretations of the Chalcedonian decree that tended to absorb the human nature into the divine nature. The over-riding interest was the fact that 'the human nature is personalised in the Divine Logos which assumes it, and is thus not impersonal (*anhypostatos*) but inpersonal (*enhypostatos*)'.[105]

On both counts, in respect of the *extra Calvinisticum* and the doctrine of *enhypostasis*, there does not appear to be any connection with Barth's view

---

104. See J Calvin, *Institutes of the Christian religion*, book 2, chapter 12, secs 4–7, and the important study, ED Willis, *Calvin's Catholic Christology: The Role of the So Called 'Extra-Calvinisticum' in Calvin's Theology* (Leiden: EJ Brill, 1966), 70, 71, 79ff; M Hoogland, *Calvin's Perspective*, 50ff, 168–188,192ff. A co-lateral consideration which bears on Barth's misunderstanding of Calvin's purpose with respect to the *extra Calvinisticum* is his rejection of Calvin's openness to the issue of 'natural theology', since Calvin does not consider the question of revelation from the point of view of it presupposing the inconceivable event in which God posits God's self as God. See Barth, *CD* 2/1, 127ff; 2/2, 106–112, 166ff; 4/1, 366, 367; TF Torrance, *Calvin's Doctrine of Man*, 13ff, 30, 31, 39, 40, 59–61, 63, 64.

105. D Baillie, *God Was in Christ* (London: Faber, 1961), 90. See also TF Torrance, 'The Atonement and the Oneness of the Church', in *Scottish Journal of Theology*, 7/3 (1954): 248ff.

that these doctrines concentrate attention on what he calls the dynamic noetic aspect of Christology. The emphasis appears in both cases to be on the empirical humanity of Christ as decisive in understanding God's relationship with the world, that form of revelation which Barth concludes under the rubric of the *Deus absconditus*. Barth understands the humanity of Jesus by bringing it into direct connection with the inconceivable freedom in which God posits God's self as God. The hiddenness of revelation is commensurate with the inconceivability of this event in human terms. Thus, the humanity of Jesus can only be understood beyond the negative limit of human existence in death through the resurrection of Jesus, the *Deus revelatus*. However, both doctrines in question pursue a different agenda that, in terms of Barth's method, is excluded. Both the *extra Calvinisticum* and the doctrine of *enhypostasis* see the humanity of Christ in its historical particularity as playing a decisive role in defining the place of God's transcendence and immanence. This is a role that, given Barth's method, one could only understand as presupposing a freedom of the creature for God which is not presupposed by God's freedom for the creature. It would thus divide God's revelation, call into question the unity of God's self-revelation as God's self-interpretation and hence either divinise the creature or divide the Godhead. This is the cul-de-sac into which one is driven if one assumes with Barth that the issue of the unity of God's self-revelation in respect of the humanity of Jesus Christ is to be understood as presupposing the inconceivable event in which God posits God's self for the creature and the creature for God in the person of Jesus Christ.

We encounter the same issue from a different perspective when the question of the relationship between the Word's conception by the Holy Spirit and his birth of the Virgin Mary is considered. As with the meaning of the doctrines of *an-* and *enhypostasis* and the *extra Calvinisticum,* this relationship is considered by means of the non-cognisable dialectic in which God determines God's self as both One and Another in the mystery of God's unifying act. This presupposition of the unity of the person of the one who is incarnate, in terms of his conception by the Holy Spirit and his birth of the Virgin Mary, is consistent with Barth's vigorous defence of the *filioque*.[106] The dogma of Christ's conception by the Holy Spirit and birth of the Virgin mother of God cannot be understood in terms of the historical form presupposed by the New Testament witness. The only

---

106. See above, 55–60.

question which can be legitimately raised against those who deny the dogma is whether they can still acknowledge

> that in His revelation to us . . . to our measureless astonishment and in measureless hiddenness the initiative is wholly with God . . . May it not be the case that the only one who hears the witness of the thing is the one who keeps to the sign by which the witness has actually signified it?[107]

Paradoxically, the sign only becomes a sign in terms of its historical characteristics in virtue of the fact that they confront us with the measureless hiddenness of God. To know the signs as signs one must presuppose the thing signified as the inconceivable freedom and mystery of the act in which God determines God's self as God's Lord.

For this reason, Barth rejects E Brunner's interpretation of the Virgin Birth as a biological miracle. For Brunner, the fact that the Virgin Birth is a biological miracle indicates its non-necessity as a Christian dogma. Barth rejects this proposal, not because he wants to assert the importance of the biological aspects of the dogma as important for the dogma but because Brunner's rejection presupposes an illegitimate question. This is that God is verifiable in terms of historical facts.[108] For Barth, the figure of Mary is representational rather than that of a particular human being. Mary's actual virginity has no systematic connection with the meaning of the dogma of the Virgin Birth. Mary is a sign of measureless hiddenness. Her existence presupposes the same inconceivable freedom that presupposes the revelation of the *Deus absconditus*.

> [I]n the birth without previous sexual union of man and woman . . . man is . . . involved only in the form of the *virgo Maria*, i.e., only in the form of non-willing, non-achieving, non-creative, non-sovereign man, only in the form of man who can merely receive, merely be ready, merely let something be done to and with himself . . . It is not as if virginity as a human possibility constitutes the point of connexion for the divine grace.[109]

---

107. Barth, *CD* 1/2, 180.
108. *Ibid,* 185, 186.
109. *Ibid,* 191–192; cf 193ff.

Whilst the figure of the Virgin Mother of God cannot be understood in terms of a repetition of the explication of the *vere Deus* and the *vere Homo*, 'in its own way it expresses, explains and throws light upon it'.[110] The dogma of the Virgin Birth can thus be understood as an aspect of the unity of the event in which the self-revealing God posits God's own existence. It is an aspect of the unity of the person of Jesus Christ. It indicates the way, the manner, in which God is free for the creature.

The full picture of the meaning of the Virgin Birth can thus only be gained in terms of the *conceptus de Spiritu sancto*. In this context, the relationship between the sign of the Virgin Birth and the thing signified comes into 'full view'.[111] Since it is in the Holy Spirit that God is present to God's self as the Father and the Son, it is uniquely in the Holy Spirit that the creature is present with God. So, as God is antecedently in God's self what God is in revelation,

> only through the Holy Spirit can man be there for God, be free for God's work in him, believe, be a recipient of His revelation, the object of the divine reconciliation.[112]

## Conclusion

I have so far been concerned to understand the relationship Barth establishes between the doctrine of the Trinity found within the doctrine of revelation and the doctrine of Christology. The reason for this interest is that I want to understand the relationship, posited by Barth's doctrine of creation, between the trinitarian God of the doctrine of revelation and the creature. However, the being of the creature is already presupposed by the unity between God and the creature, which we have met in Barth's understanding of the event of revelation. This unity is grounded in, and coincides with, the person of Jesus Christ. His being in relation to the Father in the Spirit is identical with the inconceivable act in which God's posits God's self as the creature's Lord: as 'event, act, life'.[113] It is this dynamic being of God that gives rise to Barth's reinterpretation of the traditional formulae in which the christological doctrines have been expressed.

---

110.  *Ibid*, 177.
111.  *Ibid*, 197.
112.  *Ibid*, 198. Cf 200.
113.  Barth, *CD* 1/2, 294, 296, 262–264.

# Chapter Three

# The Relationship in the Dogma of the Trinity with the Doctrine of Creation
## Part One

**The orientation of the doctrine of creation within the structure of Barth's thought**

It is important for understanding the doctrine of creation, within the trinitarian perspective developed by Barth in the doctrine of revelation, to indicate how his central concerns in expounding the doctrine of the Trinity condition the structure of the doctrine of creation. In this we will see the inner consistency of Barth's thought and how he 'proves' the existence of the creature, in the Anselmian sense.[1]

The first consideration in coming to terms with the orientation of the doctrine of creation within the structure of Barth's dogmatics is the fact that the doctrine of God is interposed between the doctrine of revelation and the doctrine of creation. This fact is critical for understanding the doctrine of creation in the sense that 'the concept of "presupposition" is of paramount importance in coming to terms with the central questions in Barth's theology'.[2] With respect to the place of the doctrine of God in the structure of the dogmatics, we are to understand that if the self-revealing God is the Lord in the unique way in which Barth has developed this idea in the doctrines of the Trinity and Christology within the doctrine of revelation, then it must be seen that God is Lord of the transcendent relationship in which God stands as Lord of the creature in the event of God's self-revelation. But

> God is also the One who is event, act and life in His own way, as distinct from everything that He is not Himself, even though at the same time He is its source, reconciliation and goal. God is not

---

1.   See above 21–29.
2.   HU von Balthasar, Karl Barth: *Darstellung und Deutung seiner Theologie*, 129. Cf R Jenson, *Alpha and Omega: A Study in the Theology of Karl Barth* (Edinburgh: Nelson, 1963), 65ff.

merely differentiated from all other actuality as actuality generally and as such, or as its essence and principle, so that, while He is differentiated from all other actuality, He is still connected to it . . . He is, of course, differentiated from it in this way too . . . But the particularity of His working and therefore His being as God is not exhausted by this dialectical transcendence which, however strictly it may be understood, must always be understood with equal strictness as immanence. On the contrary, without prejudice to and yet without dependence upon this relationship to what is event, act and life outside Him, God is in Himself free event, free act, and free life.[3]

It is this aspect of God's primary positing of God's being in freedom and love that Barth considers in the doctrine of God, after the doctrine of revelation. This primary positing of God's being emphasises God's Lordship over against any idealist or realist attempt to correlate God's being with aspects of the subject-object relationship inherent in understanding the event of God's self-revelation. The consideration of the doctrine of God after the doctrine of revelation and before the doctrine of creation makes this point quite clear. For it brings to understanding the 'depth' of the Lordship of God Barth intends to be understood in the relationship between the doctrine of revelation and the doctrine of God.[4]

---

3.      Barth, *CD* 2/1, 264.

4.      Both E Jüngel, *Gottes Sein ist im Werden*, 78–86, 93, 94, 115, 116, and, *Reformation Old and New: A Tribute to Karl Barth*, edited by FW Camfield (London: Lutterworth, 1947), 52, 53, 60ff, emphasise this aspect of Barth's thought. It should be noted that the distinction which Barth draws, on the basis of God's self-revelation, between the event or act in which God posits God's self in inconceivable freedom and the event or act in which God reveals God's self, is related to Barth's understanding of 'person' in the doctrine of the Trinity. The distinction thus posited by Barth entails that the nature of the event character of revelation is grounded in the self-constituting act in which God posits God's self as God. Barth's understanding of 'person' is that dialectical relationship between the doctrines of *perichoresis* and appropriations (see chapter 2 above) as that which presupposes the inconceivable freedom in which God posits God's self as God. 'Person' is that which refers to the divine unity: the 'I' of the divine being. Cf *CD* 2/1, 265–272; J Moltmann, *The Trinity and the Kingdom of God* (London: SCM, 1981), 63, 172ff.

The distinction that Barth emphasises—one established between God and the creature—is grounded in the nature of God's self-positing. Its characteristics are that God *posits* God's self. But God also posits God's *self*. The former characteristic specifies the *particular* nature of God's self-revelation, while the latter specifies that God is *free* in relation to the transcendent relationship God establishes with that which is not God's self. These two characteristics are not considered in a random order. The particularity of God being who God is must be understood as defining God's freedom and not vice versa. Consequently, Barth considers the being of God in the act of self-positing as God being 'the One who loves'.[5] Barth turns to the other aspect which has to be taken into account; the fact that God *posits* God's self presupposes that God posits God's *self*. In this aspect Barth sees 'the mystery of His [God's] freedom'.[6]

It is because God's being as love has this 'depth', in which God *posits* God's being as love, that the creature to whom God relates is not swallowed up in God's absoluteness. Since God is free in relation to God's own being who God is, the transcendent relationship God establishes with the creature can include God's being with and for the creature without the creature being called into question as a creature. This entails that God's transcendence cannot be understood in terms of the transcendence posited by the event, or form, of revelation considered as a worldly event in which God acts. For,

> the freedom of God is primarily and fundamentally defined as God's freedom in Himself, and only from that point of view understood as His independence of the world, and therefore His absoluteness in the usual sense of the term.[7]

It is the freedom and transcendence of God in relation to God's self and the relationship God posits within God's self to the creature that presuppose the transcendence and immanence of the relationship God establishes between God's self and the creature. Consequently, the being of the creature in relation to God will be considered in precisely the same terms as the event nature of the form of revelation.

Thus, the doctrine of God is of decisive importance in understanding the way in which Barth establishes the relationship between God and the creature

---

5.　　Barth, *CD* 2/1, 273ff.

6.　　*Ibid*, 284.

7.　　*Ibid*, 309.

in the doctrine of creation. When Barth considers the doctrine of election as part of the doctrine of God, he lays the foundation for the key concept by which he will bring to understanding the reality of the creature in relationship to God. This concept is that of the covenant. The distinction to which we have alluded is one in which God's *positing* of God's *self* establishes the basis for God's transcendent relation to the creature and the creature's relationship to God as a creature, without at the same time calling into question God's 'Godness' and the creature's creatureliness. But this distinction is no abstract notion; it is a distinction the unity of which is none other than the person of Jesus Christ. It is in him and through him that God is God in the heights, in the freedom presupposed by the fact that God posits God's *self*. He is also the One in whom God *posits* God's self in the depths as the God who *loves* in freedom.[8] 'In him God has loved himself from all eternity. In him he has loved the world.'[9] Jesus Christ is the centre in whom must be understood the primary and secondary ways in which God is present to God's self and to the creature. He is

> not merely the focus and the crown of all relationship and fellowship between God and the world, but also their basic principle, their possibility and presupposition in the life of the Godhead.[10]

Thus the unity of God and the creature in the doctrine of creation presupposes the unity of God in the event of God's self-revelation. This unity becomes, in the doctrine of God, the being of God who *loves* in *freedom*, who *posits* God's *self*. For if God's freedom and love both in and for God's self and for the creature is identical with Jesus Christ, then it is proper, from Barth's perspective, that the relationship between God and the creature should already be considered in the doctrine of God as the doctrine of election. This is consistent with the fact with which Barth begins his doctrine of revelation where the doctrine of the Trinity has its place. There Barth understands the event of revelation in terms of an analysis of the concept of the Lordship of the self-revealing God. The God who begins with God's self in relation to the creature is its Lord, just as the one who posits God's self in freedom and love, begins with God's self in relation to God's self. The fact that God is the self-revealing God entails that

---

8.    Barth, *CD* 2/1, 317.
9.    *Ibid*, 321.
10.    *Ibid*, 317, 318.

God is the self-electing God. It would be an abstraction if the doctrine of God were developed apart from the relationship that is presupposed by the event of revelation.

> It is not as though God is forced into this relationship [with the creature]. It is not as though He is in any way constrained or compelled by this other . . . God is love. But He is also perfect freedom . . . Even if there were no other outside Him, He would still be love. But positively, in the free decision of His love, God is God in the very fact, and in such a way, that He does stand in this relationship, in a definite relationship with the other. We cannot go back on this decision, if we would know God and speak accurately of God.[11]

The reality of God's self-determination for the creature is part of the doctrine of God in so far as this relationship is the way in which God *posits* God's self. The distinction which Barth makes between the existence of God in this relationship with the other, and God's existence in and for God's self, is not posited on the basis of some dialectic between two kinds of God: one who is revealed and the other not. The distinction is drawn on the basis that God not only *posits* God's self; God also posits God's *self*. God is Lord of God's being in so far as God's being includes this relationship with the other, the creature.

However, given this fact, the relationship with the creature, whilst not impinging upon God's freedom, makes the creature inconceivable in terms of its creaturely being in relation to God. This is the case since the creature's relationship to God is brought into direct connection with the inconceivable freedom in which God posits God's self as God.[12]

## Jesus Christ: electing God *and* elected Man

Barth's insistence that the doctrine of election is part of the doctrine of God brings to fruition the twin concepts that have guided his consideration of the being of God in view of the event of God's self-revelation. God in being Lord of the creature, as Father of the Son in the unity of the Spirit is, God who *posits*

---

11.   *CD* 2/2, 6.

12.   Cf Jüngel, *Gottes Sein ist im Werden*, 114, 115: 'Gottes Für-uns-Sein ist ebensowenig von sich selbst wie es ein Zu-sich-selbst-Kommen Gottes ist.'

God's *self*. As has just been pointed out, this self-affirming decision in which God is the God of the creature is not a synthetic dialectic between two aspects of God's Godness, one in relation to the world and one in relation to God's self. No, in

> the primal and basic decision in which He wills to be and actually is God, in the mystery of what takes place from and to all eternity within Himself, within His true being, God is none other than the One who in His Son or Word elects Himself, and in and with Himself elects His people.[13]

We must understand this double election or predestination in which God determines God's self as God to be coincidental with the existence of the Son of God, Jesus Christ. The latter is not only one with the Father and the Spirit as the electing God, the God who in love and freedom posits God's self as God for the creature. Jesus Christ is also the one who, in and with this inconceivable freedom of God's choice of God's self as the Lord of the creature, is determined by this act of election as the creature![14]

As one with the Father and the Spirit, and therefore very God Himself, Jesus Christ may be said to be 'at the beginning of God's dealings with the reality that is distinct from Himself.' However, as such he may not be said to be 'at the beginning of God, for God has indeed no beginning.'[15] This seemingly strange juxtaposition is a direct result of Barth's view of the nature of God's inconceivably free act of *self*-positing. Jesus Christ as one with the Father and the Spirit can be said to be at the beginning of all God's ways and works toward the creature; but, precisely because he is this, his determination as this one cannot be identified with the 'beginning' of God. For God is inconceivable free love. The relationship God establishes with the creature cannot be correlated with any aspect of the being of God or the creature.

Another way of putting the same thing is that Jesus Christ is not only electing God, in unity with the Father and the Spirit, he is also the object of this election. He is elected Man. However, in being the object of God's election, an election in which God chooses God's own life as well as that of the creature in the person

---

13.    Barth, *CD* 2/2, 76.

14.    *Ibid*, 94ff.

15.    *Ibid*, 102.

of God's Son,[16] Jesus Christ must never be abstracted from the inconceivable freedom in which he posits *himself* with the Father and the Spirit as God in the divine freedom in which God loves.[17]

In this analysis we should note the correspondence with the foregoing exposition of the doctrine of the Trinity and its relationship to Christology.[18] There we saw that the *hypostasis* of the Son as incarnate was understood in terms of the unity of God's essential being as God. We now see that the unity of God and the creature in Jesus Christ presupposes the inconceivable love and freedom in which God posits God's self. Consequently, the historical form of Jesus Christ, the God-Man, presupposes the being of God that is

> a divine activity in the form of history, encounter and decision between God and man . . . God does not therefore become the living God when He works or decides to work *ad extra*—in His being *ad extra* He is, of course, the living God in a different way—but His being and activity *ad extra* is merely an overflowing of His inward activity and being, of the inward vitality which He has in Himself. It is a proclamation of the decision in which in Himself He is who He is.[19]

This 'overflow' of the 'history', in which God is who God is, presupposes the creature in its existence as a creature in distinction from and in relationship to God, and the creature's existence in relationship with other creatures. Hence,

> Christology . . . must always constitute the basis and criterion for the apprehension and interpretation of the freedom of God in His immanence. The legitimacy of every theory concerning the relationship of God and man or God and the world can be tested by considering whether it can be understood also as an interpretation of the relationship created and sustained in Jesus Christ.[20]

---

16.   For discussion on this issue see footnote 60 in chapter 2, see above 62.
17.   *Ibid*; cf 105.
18.   See chapter 2 above, 47–49.
19.   Barth, *CD* 2/2, 175.
20.   *CD* 2/1, 320; cf 2/2, 177, 178.

What are meant are relationships and decision between God and the creature in the eternal being of God. In Jesus Christ, God and the creature meet in an event which is the origin and type of all other history.[21]

## The doctrine of creation and the covenant

The event to which I have been referring is the substance of the doctrine of election within the doctrine of God, in which Barth sees the origin of all God's ways and works *ad extra*. This is the decision of God to be who God is in the event of God's self-revelation in Jesus Christ. It is this decision Barth describes as the original covenant.[22] This decision and resolve of God is the essential historicality in which God exists in Jesus Christ. This decision stands in fundamental relationship to all history of the creature in relationship to God and other creatures. This is *Urgeschichte,* primal history. It presupposes all events in time and space; it is the law of all other history.[23]

The connection between the doctrine of the Trinity and the doctrine of creation is to be understood in terms of this essentially historical nature of God which Barth has expounded in the doctrine of revelation in terms of the doctrine of the Trinity, and in the doctrine of God. God is in God's self both one and another in the unity of the act in which God is who God is. It is thus appropriate but not necessary that such a God be the God of the creature. It can be said, given the precondition that God in inconceivable freedom posits God's *self*, that 'we can see how far it was not only appropriate and worthy but necessary that God should be the Creator'.[24] Creation is presupposed in its existence and goodness in him in whom God posits God's self, Jesus Christ electing God and elected Man. The act in which this positing of God is consummated, and therefore the eternity of God becomes 'historical', is the Spirit understood as the relationship between the Father and the Son. So it may be said,

> it is in the Holy Spirit that the mystery of God's trinitarian essence attains its full profundity and clarity . . . It is in the Holy Spirit that the commission of the Father and the obedience of the  Son

---

21.    *CD* 2/2, 177, 180, 184, 194, 197, 202.
22.    *Ibid*, 157.
23.    *Ibid,*  202ff, 184ff.
24.    *CD* 3/1, 51.

. . . coincide in the decree which is the intra-divine beginning of all things.[25]

Thus the Trinity will be the means by which Barth achieves understanding of the creature in relationship to God.

> The recognition of the unity of the divine being and its particularity as Father, Son and Holy Spirit will prove effective . . . for the recognition not only of the interconnections but also the variations in the relation between creation and covenant.[26]

Because the Spirit is the mutuality of the bond in which the decision of God in Jesus Christ to be with and for the creature is actual, the Spirit may be said to be the one in whom 'the creature as such pre-exists'.[27]

## Creation as the external basis of the covenant

Barth understands the being of God—presupposing the event nature of God's self-revelation under the twin aspects of God who *posits* God's self and God who posits God's *self*—as the God who loves in freedom. This is further refined in terms of God's self-revelation as focussing on Jesus Christ the electing God and the elected Man. So, too, the compact between God and the creature must bring to expression the truth of this reality of God's being who God is in God's self-revelation.

Precisely because God posits God's *self*, the relationship between God and the creature must be one in which God is transcendent of the relationship between God and the creature. This safeguards the creature as a creature in relationship to God, and at the same time ensures that there is nothing in God or the creature that makes the relationship between them necessary. On the other hand, God is a God who *posits* God's self, actualising God's existence as the God that God is. Thus the creature in relation to God derives its particularity as a creature from the fact that its existence presupposes the particularity of Jesus Christ as electing God and elected Man: an eternal covenant.

---

25.  *CD* 3/1, 56.
26.  *Ibid*, 48, 49.
27.  *Ibid*, 56.

Thus, the creature's existence does not presuppose any neutral ontology which can be understood apart from the decision and act of God in which God determines God's existence as God for the creature and the creature for God in Jesus Christ. The creature's existence can only be understood in terms of the fact that

> the love of God could not be satisfied with the eternal covenant as such; as it willed to execute it and give it form outside the divine sphere, it made itself this external ground of the covenant, i.e., it made necessary the existence and being of the creature and therefore of creation.[28]

Since the being of the creature presupposes the eternal and particular compact in which God determines God's self for the creature and the creature for God in Jesus Christ, it follows that knowledge of the creature, like knowledge of God, can only be understood in faith. Faith is necessitated by the fact that knowledge of the being of the creature is configured by the inconceivable act in which God posits God's self as God. The knowledge of faith, then, is the only 'rational' way in which the creature can be understood.

> As everything which exists outside the Creator owes its existence to Him and to Him alone, so any knowledge of existence which arises outside Him can only come to be because He does not conceal but reveals His infallible knowledge of His own existence (which is the ground of all other existence). This self disclosure of the Creator, i.e., this revelation of His own infallible knowledge of His existence (the ground of all else that exists) is the living confrontation which meets the creaturely consciousness and in virtue of which knowledge of existence, reality and being is possible and real even outside God.[29]

The noetic determination of the creature corresponds to its ontic reality as the external basis of the eternal covenant; it is the covenant's 'technical possibility'

---

28.   *CD* 3/1, 97. For Barth's understanding of the creature's actualisation, its particularity in respect of God's particularity, see 344–365.

29.   *Ibid*, 348, 349; see 120, 121, 126ff on the creation of light and time and their inter-relationship.

in time and space.[30] This distinction between covenant and creation corresponds to and presupposes the distinction in the way God's being is posited by God. It is the basic distinction that we have already encountered in the doctrine of God following the doctrine of revelation, where the doctrine of the Trinity finds its place.[31] The being of the creature as the 'technical possibility' of the revelation of the covenant, which is identical with the being of Jesus Christ, the electing God and the elected Man, is to be understood as

> one long preparation, and therefore the being and existence of the creature one long readiness, for what God will intend to do with it in the history of the covenant. Its nature is simply its equipment for grace. Its creatureliness is pure promise, expectation and prophecy . . . In this way creation is the road to the covenant, its external power and external basis . . .[32]

An illustration of this argument from the mass of biblical material, which Barth assembles to expound his position on this matter of the relationship between creation and the covenant, is the bi-sexual nature of the human creature considered as the image of God.[33] As distinct from all other creatures who share this sexual determination, the human creature alone has this characteristic as that which defines its creatureliness. The image of God is not some ontological addition to the creature as a creature.

> There is no point in asking in which of man's peculiar attributes and attitudes it [that is, the image of God] consists. It does not consist in anything that man is or does. It consists as man himself

---

30.   *Ibid*, 97. Cf E Jüngel, 'Die Möglichkeit theologischer Anthropologie auf dem Grunde der Analogie: eine Untersuchung zum Analogieverständnis Karl Barths', in *Evangelische Theologie* 22 (1962): 535ff. Jüngel correctly relates the relationship between the covenant as the inner ground of creation and creation as the outer ground of the covenant to Barth's understanding of analogia relationis. It is this analogy which provides the basis for Barth's exposition of human and creaturely existence.

31.   See above chapter 2, 2, 3.

32.   Barth, *CD* 3/1, 231; cf 219.

33.   *Ibid*, 184. Cf the discussion of this aspect of Barth's thought in A Come, *An Introduction to Barth's Dogmatics for Preachers* (London: SCM, 1963), 146ff.

consists as the creature of God . . . He is the image of God in the fact that he is man.[34]

The basis of this understanding of the creature as the image of God is the inconceivable act in which the self-revealing and thus the self-electing God determines God's self to be both One and Another.

The *tertium comparationis*, the analogy between God and man is simply the existence of the I and the Thou in confrontation. This is first constitutive for God, and then for man created by God.[35]

It is because of this ontological determination of the creature as the external basis of the covenant which is identical with the eternal compact in which God determines God's self for the creature and the creature for God in Jesus Christ, that the image of God cannot be something in addition to the creatureliness of the human creature as man and woman. If such were, *per impossible*, the case then an aspect of the creature would not be presupposed by the nature of the act in which God determines God's self to be the creature's Lord.[36] The creature's being the image of God is thus not dependent upon the attitude of the creature to God. The human creature remains the image of God precisely because God remains its Lord, and is faithful to God's self and thus to the creature in Jesus Christ.

This view of the basis of anthropology, the creature's ontological determination as the external basis of the covenant, has important implication for Barth's understanding of the importance of the relativities of ethical judgments. Since no human judgment or action can impugn the goodness of creation in virtue of its determination by and for the covenant, the judgments the creature makes cease to have significance for the creature's relationship as a creature to God. This is particularly the case in the sphere of social and political ethics, where the relativities inherent in any analysis of historical circumstance

---

34.   Barth, *CD* 3/1, 184.

35.   *Ibid*, 185.

36.   As C O'Grady indicates, *The Church in the Theology of Karl Barth*, volume 1, 90ff, this view of the image of God which Barth propounds in *CD* 3/1 differs from that advanced in 1/1, 273ff. There Barth puts forward the view that the image of God consists in the creature's original righteousness which was lost in the fall. Cf also GC Berkouwer, *Man: the Image of God* (Grand Rapids: Eerdmans, 1954), 92ff, 100f.

cease to have meaning in terms of the creature's relationship to God. Since Jesus Christ is the beginning before which there is no other beginning, and since the creature's existence presupposes and is determined by and for the covenant which he is, there can *be* no demonic states or political structures. Charles West, who cannot be considered an unsympathetic commentator on Barth's theology, opines that this seeming indifference in Barth's approach to the relativities of historical decision-making processes derives from the notion of 'all-embracing grace'.[37]

The fact that the human creature is determined by and for Jesus Christ does not mean that this determination is some immanent characteristic of the creature's being. Both aspects of the covenant of which it is an image as the 'technical possibility' of the revelation of the covenant, presuppose the ineffable freedom in which God posits God's self as God. This is because the covenant, of which the creature is the external basis, is identical with Jesus Christ who is God's being for the creature *and* the creature's being for God. Thus the empirical form the human creature can only be understood in faith which recognises the premundane divine presupposition of the creature's existence.

> According to 1 Cor. 11:7 there is a man who actually *is* the image and glory of God, and from this standpoint the same can be said of every man. And side by side with this man there is a woman who is His glory as He (the Head of the woman but not without her) is the glory of God, and from the standpoint of this woman, or rather of her Husband, the same can be said of every woman. This man together with this woman is the man who is the image of God, who *is* it and does not merely indicate it or establish its physical possibility, like Adam and Seth and all the subsequent members of the genealogical tree.[38]

---

37. C West, *Communism and the Theologians: Study of an Encounter* (London: SCM, 1958), 313. On the same issue see W Herberg, *The Social Philosophy of Karl Barth* (New York: Anchor Books, 1960), 29ff, 54ff, 64–67; HH Schrey, H Walz, and WA Whitehouse, *The Biblical Doctrine of Justice and Law* (London: SCM, 1955), 38ff, 170-183, 190–193; JC Bennett, 'Comment on "Letter to American Christians" by Karl Barth', in *Christendom* 8/4 (1943): 460ff.
38. Barth, *CD* 3/1, 203; italics are in the original.

This image of whom Adam and Seth and the rest of humankind are merely the physical possibility is the

> body of which Jesus Christ is the Head, the community of which
> He is Lord . . . It is with them that Jesus Christ is God's image.[39]

Precisely because it corresponds to and presupposes the inconceivable freedom and love in which God is Lord of the creature, the promise inherent in the teleology of human existence as I-Thou, as the external basis of the covenant, cannot be identified with any given actuality of creaturely existence. The equation which makes this characterisation of human existence the image of God must presuppose the reality of the *creature's* participation in the relationship between Jesus Christ and the church. It thus presupposes faith as the means of understanding.[40] In this, Barth is consistent in reaching understanding of the creature as the image of God according to the maxim he derived from his study of St Anselm: *fides quaerens intellectum*.[41] To posit any other basis for understanding the creature would be to attempt to look into the abyss of non-being excluded by God's choice of God's self for the creature and the creature for God's self in the freely determined act in which God posits God's own existence.[42] Creation, then, and the image of God in particular, can only be understood when seen in the context of the fact that it presupposes

> the divine meaning and necessity which . . . is God's free love, i.e.,
> the love of God in which He wills and posits another by Himself
> and is Himself for it—the free love in which He accomplishes
> this willing and this positing in His own power and by His own
> independent resolve. It is in the same free love that He Himself
> is God, i.e., the Father in the Son and the Son in the Father by the

---

39.  *Ibid*, 205.
40.  E Jüngel, 'Die Möglichkeit theologischer Anthropologie auf dem Grunde der Analogie: eine Untersuchung zum Analogieverständis Karl Barths', in *Evangelische Theologie* 22 (1962): 549. Jüngel is therefore quite correct when he posits the possibility of a theological anthropology on the basis of Barth's understanding of the *analogia relationis* based on the double predestination of God and the creature in Jesus Christ as the electing God and the elected Man, and in being this is thus, as God, *the* Human for other humans in the I-Thou relationship.
41.  *Ibid*, 553.
42.  Barth, *CD* 3/1, 333, 334, 340–344, 347–349, 363–365, 372–375, 387, 388.

Holy Spirit. Again, it is the same free love that He resolved in Himself from all eternity on fellowship with man in the person of His own Son. As this free love is revealed, i.e., made visible outside His own being, His hidden glory is revealed. And this is creation to the extent that it makes the creature the exponent, sign and witness of the divine meaning and necessity.[43]

## The covenant as the internal basis of creation

If consideration of the creature as the external basis of the covenant corresponds to the freedom in which God posits God's *self*, the understanding of the covenant as the internal basis of the creation corresponds to the love in which God *posits* God's self. This does not add to or subtract from what has already been said concerning creation as the external basis of the covenant. But

> the main interest now is not on how creation promises, proclaims and prophesies the covenant, but how it prefigures and to that extent anticipates it without being identical with it . . . not Jesus Christ as the goal, but Jesus Christ as the beginning (the beginning just because He is the goal) of creation.[44]

Barth is still moving within the bounds of his understanding of the unity of the Triune God, and of the unity of God and the creature, when he proceeds to discuss the ontological structure of the creature's existence. That the creature is one whose existence is not only determined *for* the covenant of grace, might suggest that the creature may be free for some other reality apart from the truth which presupposes its existence in the covenant. The creature must be understood as an existent which is actually free for the covenant. The ontology of the creature must reflect the fact that God's freedom is the actual freedom of God's self-positing to be the God of the creature in Jesus Christ, that God *posits* God's self. The creature *is* thus a *definite* creature as presupposing *this* choice of God. The covenant is thus

> not something which is added later to the reality of the creature, as though the history of creation might equally have been succeeded

---

43.    *Ibid*, 230.
44.    *Ibid*, 232.

by any other history. It [i.e., the covenant] already characterises creation itself and as such, and therefore the being and existence of the creature.[45]

In examining of this aspect of the creature's being, I again refer to Barth's exposition of the human as the image of God. We recall that Barth had previously identified and referred the I-Thou relationship of the creature in the form of man/woman to the existence of Jesus Christ and his Church. This reference of the I-Thou relationship to the being and existence of Jesus Christ and his Church meant that the creature presupposed the being and existence of God's self-positing and therefore, as such, could only be known in faith. The creature as the external basis of the covenant is essentially unknowable. This follows once the distinctions and connections of creaturely existence presuppose the distinctions and continuities in which God posits God's self.

We come to the same conclusion when we now proceed to examine Barth's exposition of the creature in the context of the covenant as the internal basis of creation. This conclusion is again supported by Barth's exegesis of the biblical text, in this case the second creation narrative of the Book of Genesis (2:4b–25).[46]

Barth sees the peculiarity of the second creation narrative to consist in its concern to express the creature who is the creature of the history of salvation. 'Gen. 1 tells the story of the natural, pagan man, and Gen. 2 that of the Jew, i.e., the man of the history of salvation.'[47] The human creature is configured by the fact that its being is grounded in the covenant that is the internal ground of creation. While it shares with all other creatures its earthly origin—this piece of dust as opposed to all other dust that is formed into a human creature distinct from the beast[48]—the human creature has a distinct characteristic that it does not share with any beast. In this characteristic 'we have a material parallel to what the first account called his divine likeness'.[49] As opposed to the beasts, the human becomes a living soul as God breathes into it the breath of life 'in a most direct and personal and most special act'.[50] This entails that the human has its existence as it proceeds

---

45.   *Ibid*, 231.
46.   *Ibid*, 232–240.
47.   *Ibid*, 240.
48.   *Ibid*, 236.
49.   *Ibid*.
50.   *Ibid*.

from death to life. But the realisation of this hope [presupposed by the creature's being a living soul] waits for man as the being which, earthy by nature, will triumph over the aridity, barrenness and deadness of the earth because God is his refuge and hope, because God has constituted Himself as such.[51]

And it is

Jesus Christ [who] is the man whose existence was necessary for the perfecting of the earth; for the redemption of its aridity, barrenness and death . . . He is the man taken from all creation, all humanity and all Israel, and yet belonging to them and a victim of their curse . . . The man of whom the saga spoke, objectively if not subjectively, is . . . this man Jesus.[52]

As with Barth's view of the image of God in the human creature, so here the human creature cannot be identified with the human whose existence is determined by the covenant as its internal ground. Precisely because the human creature proceeds from the Creator, its being is as immeasurably hidden from itself as the being of God is hidden from the creature. The covenant as the internal basis of the creature's existence presupposes the same inconceivable free act of love as that in which God posits God's self as God.

Thus we see the same considerations applying here as those with which we became familiar in the doctrine of revelation. There the form, the earthly content, of the event was understood in terms of the inconceivable act, which presupposed God being considered as the *Deus revelatus* and the *Deus absconditus* beyond the limits of creaturely existence in the resurrection of Jesus Christ from the dead. The unity of revelation and the unity of God and the creature were conceived in terms of a doctrine of the Trinity based on an analysis of God's Lordship in which God posited God's self as both One and Another in the unity of a Third. We now see, as we have also observed in our analysis of Barth's view of the person of Jesus Christ in his Christology, that the being of the creature is brought to understanding as it is seen to be constituted by the inconceivably free act in which God actualises God's own being as God. Thus, the creature is *essentially* hidden from itself—not accidentally, as it were, through its rebellion

---

51.   *Ibid*, 237.
52.   *Ibid*, 239.

against the truth of its life before God (for example, Romans 1:20–23), but essentially hidden as only that is hidden which presupposes the inconceivability of God's own act of self-positing.

Barth broadens and deepens his understanding of the second creation narrative by concentrating attention on the creation of woman and the fact that the woman is created out of the man.[53]

> The completion of all creation is described here, i.e., the completion of man by the creation of woman, is not only one secret but *the_*secret, the heart of all secrets of God the Creator . . . The preparation of his nature for God's grace, and the basis, concealed in his creaturely existence, of God's merciful good pleasure in him, is the secret of God. It is sufficient that man can say Yes to the result of this preparation and foundation and therefore to his own humanity and nature . . . But in the divine act which creates the presupposition for his knowledge and confession he does not participate either actively or consciously.[54]

Barth sees significance in the fact that God caused a deep sleep to fall upon Adam, during which God takes a rib from him and fashions it into woman whom God brings to the man who joyfully recognises her as the other granted to him by God. This means the intrinsic determination of the creature by the covenant as the internal basis of creation. This is the covenant in which Jesus Christ in his unity with the Father and the Spirit is God who posits God's self for the creature, and in his distinction from the Father and the Spirit is God who determines himself as Man for God.

> Why did the first man have to fall into that deep sleep when the work of God was done in which woman had her origin? . . . [B]ecause the church of Jesus Christ was to have its origin in His mortal sleep and to stand complete before Him in His resurrection.
>
> Why can man jubilantly exclaim: 'This is now . . . ?' Because the Church of Jesus Christ did not first recognise Him but was first

---

53.   Barth, *CD* 3/1, 289ff. Cf E Jüngel, *Gottes Sein ist im Werden*, 62, 118, 119. For Barth's exposition of faith and the creature's knowledge of its creaturely existence, see *CD* 4/1, 751ff.

54.   *Ibid*, 295.

recognised by Him, being created for Him by divine omnipotence in the power of His resurrection.[55]

Consequently, the noetic basis of the creature's existence before God is not exhausted in the mere fact of its existence, but in the fact that, as a creature, it is both one and another. The mystery of the person of the woman in relationship to the man is the mystery of Christ and his church. It is the mystery of grace.

> The account [Genesis 2] does not merely introduce woman . . . God Himself brings her to him [the man] . . . Without this link everything which precedes and follows is unthinkable . . . He creates not only the I and Thou, man and woman, but also their mutual relationship.[56]

Why must this be so? Because the creaturely ontology corresponds to the specific unity and diversity of the covenanting God who makes God's self the presupposition and the future of the creature's being as man and woman. As the God who is revealed by God's own self-revelation is understood as triune, the covenant that is the inner basis of the creature's existence, constituted by this divine unity and diversity, entails that creaturely existence corresponds to its inconceivable grace. God posits God's self as both One and Another in the inconceivable unity of a Third, in terms of the configuration of the event of God's self-revelation as the *Deus absconditus* and the *Deus revelatus*, in a unity beyond the negative limit of creaturely existence in the resurrection of Jesus Christ, actualised in the Spirit. In the same way, we must seek the truth of the creature's being and relationship as man and woman in the 'divine action, thus indicating that it escapes all observation and concepts'.[57]

Thus, from the complimentary point of view of the covenant as the internal basis of creation, Barth raises to understanding the being of the creature in relationship to God and itself as man and woman. All aspects of creaturely being which fall within the purview of Barth's theological method presuppose God as being the God who *posits* God's *self*. That is to say, the reality of creaturely being is determined by the fact that its existence presupposes that God is a God who actualises God's existence in a unique act. God posits God's *self*. God is so free as

---

55.   *Ibid*, 321, 322.
56.   *Ibid*, 298.
57.   *Ibid*, 297.

to allow the creature to be in relation to God's self without the creature ceasing to be a creature because God's being as such presupposes in its actualisation an inconceivable freedom, which expresses itself as love in the form of relationship to the Other. In this aspect, the creature was considered as being the external basis of the covenant, which is identical with who God determines God's self to be for the creature in Jesus Christ. But the being of the creature is determined as the specific creature that it is by the fact that, among the infinite possibilities for its form as a creature, its being is such as to be configured for the covenant. This presupposes the fact that God is the particular God who, grounded in God's infinite freedom, is God who *posits* God's self.

The unity and distinctions with which Barth delineates the structure of the human creature's existence for the covenant of grace, because it comes from the covenant of grace which is identical with God's decision to be the God of the creature in Jesus Christ, these distinctions and this unity are not dialectical concepts open to manipulation. They derive from, as they presuppose, the distinctions and unity of the creature's Lord. Barth remains profoundly consistent with his dogmatic method. The existence of the creature is raised to the level of understanding in terms of the meaning of the unique existence of the self-revealing God. This is achieved by means of questions which presuppose the principle of *fides quaerens intellectum*.[58]

The self-revealing God is 'proved' to be the trinitarian God in the doctrine of revelation, and the reality of the being of God is shown in the doctrine of God to be the God who posits God's self in the freedom of love. God is the self-electing God who, in choosing God's own being as God, also chooses the creature in relationship to God's self in the man Jesus Christ, the real man in relationship to God and in relationship to other human creatures. It is by means of this self-election that the covenant, which *is* this decision of God, becomes the means by which creation is shown to be both its external basis and internal purpose. For Barth, then, creation is 'intrinsically trinitarian in its ontology'.[59]

---

58.   See G Watson, 'Karl Barth and St Anselm's Theological Programme', in *Scottish Journal of Theology* 30/1 (1977): 31–45. On the issue of the 'new Barth' whereby it is suggested that somehow Barth underwent a change in his theological method consequent on the publication of his anthropology in *CD* 3/2, see Appendix 2.

59.   H Hartwell, *The Theology of Karl Barth: An Introduction*, 114.

## The relationship between knowledge of God and knowledge of the creature

To further clarify the relationship between God and the creature in Barth's trinitarian methodology, and at the same time to show the inner consistency of his arguments, we intend now to elucidate this relationship in terms of how it comes to expression in creaturely knowledge of God and creaturely knowledge of the creature. We will see here the inner connection between Barth's exposition of knowledge of God in the doctrine of God, which presupposes the doctrine of the Trinity based on the fact of the revelation of the self-revealing God, and knowledge of the creature in the doctrine of creation, which presupposes the self-electing God whose creation is the external possibility of the revelation of the covenant which is its internal reality. From this perspective we can appreciate how, through his theological epistemology, Barth understands the creature in relationship to God.

In the the chapter on the doctrine of revelation, Barth has shown[60] that God's Lordship in the event of revelation is such that God is known by and through God's self. We cannot by definition ask of the event of revelation, considered as a historical phenomenon, whether and how God is knowable without at the same time missing the point of who the God is who is revealed in God's self-revelation. God is God in God's self-revelation or God is not the God of the Bible and the church's confession of God as the Lord. Thus, where the actuality of God's revelation is, there and there only is the possibility of knowledge of God.

> The question (of the knowledge of God) cannot then be posed *in abstracto* but only *in concreto*; not *a priori* but only *a posteriori*, the *in abstracto* and *a priori* question of the possibility of the knowledge of God obviously presupposes the existence of a place outside the knowledge of God itself from which this knowledge can be judged . . . [But] just as the reality of the Word of God in Jesus Christ bears its possibility within itself, as does also the reality of the Holy Spirit, by whom the Word of God comes to man, so too the possibility of the knowledge of God and therefore the knowability of God cannot be questioned *in vacuo*, or by means of a general criterion of knowledge delimiting the knowledge

---

60.   See above 39–44.

of God from without, but only from within this real knowledge itself.[61]

In considering the question of the objectivity involved in the event of revelation being part of creaturely history, Barth distinguishes between the objectivity in which God knows God's self and the objectivity in which God is known in God's self-revelation: the event in which the creature is given to participate in God's own self-knowledge.

> If we ascribe objectivity to God (as we inevitably do when we speak of the knowledge of God) a distinction becomes unavoidable. As He most certainly knows Himself first of all, God is first and foremost objective to Himself . . . In His triune life as such, objectivity, and with it knowledge, is divine reality before creaturely objectivity and knowledge exist. We call this the primary objectivity of God, and distinguish it from the secondary, i.e., the objectivity which He has for us too in His revelation, in which He gives Himself to be known by us as He knows Himself.[62]

Consequently, the parameters of creaturely knowledge of God are not defined by creaturely knowledge or consciousness of lack of knowledge of that which is regarded as God. The limits of creaturely knowledge of God are presupposed in the distinctions by which God distinguishes God's self from God's self. These distinctions in which God posits God's self as God in the freedom of love are the reality which presupposes creaturely existence before and with God and, consequently, creaturely knowledge of God and creaturely knowledge of the creature as God's creation.

> What happens when God is known becomes clear and understandable to us, and visible to us as a form, when we know the *terminus a quo* and the *terminus ad quem* of this event, the point with which it begins and the point with which it ends.[63]

---

61.   Barth, *CD* 2/1, 5; author's brackets.
62.   *Ibid*, 16. Cf TF Torrance, *Theological Science*, 136ff.
63.   Barth, *CD* 2/2, 179.

Since the self-revealing God posits God's *self*, we must seek the *terminus a quo* of the knowledge of God in the hiddenness in which God posits God's self in inconceivable freedom. This has nothing to do with an arbitrary limit or the perceived inability of creaturely perception and discursive thought.[64] If we come to know the genuine *terminus a quo* of the knowledge of God, we can only confess that we do not come to know it of ourselves. But this judgment presupposes that we stand in the realm of the actual knowledge of God. For whilst 'the capacity to know God is taken away from us by revelation', it can only be 'ascribed to us again by revelation'.[65]

The *terminus ad quem* of the knowledge of God is grounded in the fact that the self-revealing God is the God who *posits* God's self in the particularity of God's life. While the *terminus a quo* is to be located in the freedom in which God posits God's *self*, the *terminus ad quem* is located in the event of God's self-*positing* as the God of the creature in the eternal Son, Jesus Christ. The *terminus ad quem* is the unity of Jesus Christ with the God who posits God's self as the God of the creature. So both the origin and goal of creaturely knowledge of God presuppose the unity of God's self-constituting act in which God is Lord of the creature.[66] It is precisely because this is the case that all creaturely knowledge of God and other creatures is christological knowledge. In Jesus Christ it is true for the creature that God is known within the genuine limits of creaturely knowledge of God.

> [I]t is because He is this place, but only because He is, that we too become and are this place. If we are this place it is only by faith in Him . . . In Him who is true God and true man it is true that in His true revelation God gives to man a part in the truth of His knowing, and therefore gives to man's knowing similarity with His own and therefore truth . . . It is not our knowledge of God, but the knowledge which is and will be present in this man Jesus, that we have described in our description of its reality, its possibility, and now finally its limits.[67]

---

64.  *Ibid*, 184. This entails that Barth rejects any argument against 'natural theology', since it is God's revelation alone which invalidates the creature's attempt to know God 'naturally'; cf 182.

65.  *Ibid*; cf 188, 190, 191.

66   *Ibid*, 210, 214, 215.

67.  *Ibid*, 252.

The justification of the use of analogical language to speak truly of God—since analogical speech presupposes neither a complete parity or a complete disparity as human speech—is to be sought in the correspondence posited by God between God's knowing of God's self and God's knowing of God as a creature in the man Jesus Christ. Human speech, thus authorised, entails that God 'takes to Himself something that belongs originally and properly to Him.'[68] This 'taking to Himself' of which Barth speaks assumes the freedom in which God, in electing God's self, elects Jesus Christ as man for God. Thus, in the *terminus ad quem* of creaturely knowledge of God we meet with the same Lordship as that which is found in its *terminus a quo*.

## Creaturely knowledge of God and creaturely knowledge of the creature

We have seen that Barth considers the actuality of the *creature's* existence in terms of the covenant as its internal ground, and its existence as the external basis of the covenant's actualisation. Creaturely knowledge of God consequently presupposes the inconceivable freedom and love of God that grounds the self-election and self-revelation of God. In this way, Barth shows how the reality of God's being who God is in the event of God's self-revelation is both the *terminus a quo* and the *terminus ad quem* of creaturely knowledge of God that presupposes the existence of the self-revealing, self-electing God. These limits are identical with the reality of God's self-election as God in Jesus Christ, who is both electing God and elected Man.

We now turn to see how the actuality of creaturely knowledge of God and creaturely knowledge of other creatures is realised in Jesus Christ. The first thing that must be said is that Barth considers this question from a specifically anthropological standpoint. The question can only be understood in terms of the human creature and not creatureliness in general or the relationship between God and the cosmos as such. The reason for this is that

> God's eternal Son and Logos did not will to be an angel or an animal but a man, and that this alone was the content of the eternal divine election . . . He (in His humanity) is the centre of all creation, of the reality of which the creed said that God created it.[69]

---

68.   *CD* 2/1, 228.
69.   Barth, *CD* 3/1, 18, 19; cf 25–29.

This fact entails that creaturely knowledge of the creature, its *terminus a quo* and also the *terminus ad quem*, is posited in and with the same inconceivable act which posits the limits of creaturely knowledge of God.

It is now a matter of explicating the nature of the creature's knowledge of itself in terms of the relationship between its being as determined by and for the covenant and the creature whose existence *is* the covenant. For in the man Jesus Christ we see 'the One in whose identity with Himself we must recognise at once the identity of God with Himself.' However, God does not

> infringe His own sovereignty. He does not lose Himself by being present and revealed in His existence . . . This Man is there in and by the sovereign being of God . . . Not two juxtaposed realities—a divine and then a human, or even less a human and then a divine— constitute the essence of man, this man, but one divine reality, in which as such the human is posited, contained and included . . . This is the distinction which is His and His alone.[70]

This Man is for God in such a way that he is identical with God's being for the human creature, he is envisaged by the creation saga in its account of the creature, and he exists for God and is God. Since this is so, the same distinctions posited in God's own being, by which God's being presupposes the creature's being, presuppose the distinctions between God and the creature. The humanity of the Man Jesus thus 'corresponds externally to the inner life of the Father, the Son, and the Holy Ghost.'[71]

Knowledge of the creature cannot, then, be simply a deduction from the humanity of Jesus in terms of a framework defined by a 'neutral' anthropology. This is of decisive importance in understanding Barth's anthropology, since

> we remember that between the man Jesus and ourselves as men stands not only the mystery of our sin, but primarily and decisively the mystery of His identity with God. It is impossible to understand Him even as man except in this identity. But it is impossible to understand ourselves in this identity. We are here confronted by the irremovable difference between Him and us.

---

70.   *CD* 3/2, 68, 69.
71.   *CD* 3/1, 16; cf 3/2, 10, 11, 15, 18.

There can be no question, therefore, of a direct knowledge of the nature of man in general from that of the man Jesus.[72]

A 'direct' knowledge of the humanity of the Man Jesus, that is, including Jesus' humanity with a general anthropology as the basis for understanding the creature in relationship to God and other creatures, would obviate the necessity of faith. Faith is presupposed as the way to knowledge in this case by the fact that this Man Jesus' existence is identical with the inconceivable freedom and love in which God posits God's self as Lord of the creature. We must therefore proceed to knowledge of the creature in precisely the same way that Barth answered the question as to the knowability of God.[73] This means that if we are to obtain true knowledge of the creature as a creature, then the path to be followed must ask after the knowability of the creature in terms of the freedom and love that presuppose the existence of this man Jesus among other men.

The first and primary fact about the creature, asking the question 'Who is the creature if this man Jesus is among them as the One He is?' is that the creature 'is something other than what he would have been if this One had not been man too'.[74] For,

> the man who is with Jesus—and this is man's ontological determination—is with God. If he denies God, he denies himself. He is then something which he cannot be in the Counterpart in which he is. He chooses his own impossibility.[75]

Thus, the *terminus a quo* of creaturely knowledge of the creature is established by the fact that, in Jesus Christ being amongst them as the one he is, human creatures can only begin to know who they are as their knowledge presupposes the inconceivable freedom and love in which he, in unity with the Father and the Holy Spirit, is God for them.

The *terminus ad quem* of creaturely knowledge of the creature is established by the existence of the man Jesus, being not only man who is for God but also man who exists under heaven upon earth as a cosmic being. He exists with other creatures. Since the being of the creature is determined ontologically by the fact

---

72.   *CD* 3/2, 71.
73.   See above 100–104.
74.   Barth, *CD* 3/2, 133.
75.   *Ibid*, 136.

of Jesus Christ being the man for God, the same conditions apply when it is a matter of understanding who the human creature is in relationship to other creatures. Jesus Christ is the man for others. This cosmic dimension of the being of Jesus Christ has an 'ontological' connection[76] with the primary determination of his being as the man for God, for Jesus being the man for others derives from and is grounded in His being Man for God.

> That His divinity has as its correlative in this form of His humanity, that it is 'human' in this specific sense, i.e., in address to other men, is not arbitrary or accidental . . . His orientation to others and reciprocal relationship with them are not accidental, external or subsequent, but primary, internal and necessary. It is on the basis of this eternal order that He shows Himself to be Neighbour.[77]

Hence, when it is a matter of establishing the other limit of creaturely knowledge of the creature, its *terminus ad quem*, we find—as with the source and foundation of creaturely knowledge of the creature in its *terminus a quo*— that we have to do with the same inconceivable freedom and love of God. In determining God's self for the creature and the creature for God's self in Jesus Christ, God also determines the creature to have its essential reality in being for and with other creatures. In these limits of creaturely knowledge of the creature, its *terminus a quo* and its *terminus ad quem*, we meet the same inconceivable freedom and love of God in which God posits God's own existence. For in this christological foundation of the creature's knowledge of other creatures, God

> repeats in this relationship *ad extra* a relationship proper to Himself in His inner divine essence. Entering into this relationship, He makes a copy of Himself . . . The humanity of Jesus, His fellow humanity, His being for man as a direct correlative of His being for God, indicates, attests and reveals this correspondence and similarity . . . It follows the essence, the inner being of God. It is this inner being which takes this form *ad extra* in the humanity of

---

76.   *Ibid*, 210.
77.   *Ibid*; cf 216, 217.

Jesus, and in this form, for all the disparity of sphere and object, remains true to itself and therefore reflects itself.[78]

Since the *terminus ad quem* of creaturely knowledge of the creature confronts us with the inconceivable freedom in which God posits God's existence, it follows that the truth of the *creature's* being who it is is hidden from itself apart from the faith that acknowledges this fact. So,

> even in respect of this natural correspondence [the I-Thou relationship] and similarity of human nature there is no natural knowledge of God. Even in this matter we are concealed from ourselves, and need  the Word of God to know ourselves. But . . . there is something in ourselves to know. In virtue of this correspondence and similarity, our humanity too has a real part in the mystery of faith.[79]

The only meaningful question, then, that proves or tests the foundation of Barth's theological anthropology in terms of his basic theological presuppositions, is how far human creatures can 'be represented by the man Jesus in His suffering and conquering. We have to ask what it is that makes them possible for the covenant which is revealed and operative for them in Him'.[80]

### Karl Barth's doctrine of analogy

Any discussion of the relationship between God and the creature, in terms of

---

78.    *Ibid*, 218–220; cf 4/2, 46, 47, 62ff, 84ff, 94, 101, 113, 114.
79.    Barth, *CD* 3/2, 207. Cf the debate between H Gollwitzer and E Jüngel with respect to the legitimacy and appropriateness of Barth's basing his theological anthropology on a repetition in the creaturely sphere in Jesus Christ of God's own inner essence, God's own self-positing; Jüngel, *Gottes Sein ist im Werden*, 113–116.
80.    Barth, *CD* 3/2, 223, 224; cf 225. For criticisms of this aspect of Barth's anthropology as compromising its creatureliness and becoming a pale reflection of the divine, see R Prenter, 'Dietrich Bonhoeffer and Karl Barth's Positivism of Revelation', in *World Come of Age: A Symposium on Dietrich Bonhoeffer*, edited by RG Smith (London: Collins, 1967), 93ff; R Prenter, Die Einheit von Schöpfung und Erlösung', in *Theologische Zeitschrift* 2 (1946): 161ff; G Rödding, 'Das Seinsproblem in der Schöpfungslehre Karl Barths', in *Kerygma und Dogma* 10 (1964): 1ff; JD Smart, *The Divided Mind of Modern Theology*, 149–151. But see E Jüngel, *Gottes Sein ist im Werden*, 114ff; R Jenson, *Alpha and Omega*, 84ff.

Barth's view of the relationship between knowledge of God and knowledge of the creature, would be incomplete without specific reference to the way in which Barth develops his method of understanding God and the creature by means of the doctrine of analogy. We have already examined how Barth understands the reality of creaturely knowledge of God on the basis of his understanding of the self-positing of the self-revealing Triune God who expresses the divine freedom of God's life in love. Barth defined this more closely in the doctrine of the creation. There, the biblical notion of the covenant brought to expression the being and life of the creature in relationship to God who in electing God's self elects the creature in relationship to God's self and other creatures in God's eternal Son Jesus Christ. It is this basic orientation of Barth's thought that is now to be examined in respect to the doctrine of analogy as an aspect of creaturely knowledge of God and other creatures.

In 1932 Barth wrote that, as part of his new attempt at a *Dogmatik* consequent on his dissatisfaction with previous efforts,[81] his purpose must be to purge his work of any suggestion that he sought to justify the Word of God in terms of a correlation with the structure of creaturely existence. Any such attempt could only lead to a compromise with the doctrine of *analogia entis*.

> I can see no third possibility between play with the *analogia entis*, legitimate only on Roman Catholic ground, between the greatness and the misery of a so called natural knowledge of God in the sense of the *Vaticanum*, and a Protestant theology self-nourished at its own source . . . I regard the *analogia entis* as the invention of Antichrist, and think that because of it one can not become a Catholic. Whereupon I at the same time allow myself to regard all other possible reasons for not becoming a Catholic, as short sighted and lacking seriousness.[82]

In 1940, after an examination of the doctrine of *analogia entis* by a Catholic scholar G Söhngen, Barth wrote,

---

81.   See above, 29–32.
82.   Barth, *CD* 1/1, x.

if this is the Roman Catholic doctrine of *analogia entis* then naturally I must withdraw my earlier statement that I regard the *analogia entis* as the 'invention of the Antichrist.'[83]

Some have used this apparent retraction by Barth to indicate a change in his basic theological orientation.[84] I believe that Barth should be taken quite seriously when he claims that

> in the twenty three years since I started this work I have found myself so held and directed that, as far as I can see, there have been no important breaks and contradictions in the presentation; no retractions have been necessary (except in detail) . . . That is how I myself see it . . . my contemporaries (and even perhaps successors) ought to speak more circumspectly when at this point or that they think they have discovered a 'new Barth' . . . [T]here is perhaps more inward and outward continuity in the matter than some hasty observers and rash interjectors can at first sight credit.[85]

I believe that Barth's own assessment of his thought is accurate, particularly in this matter, which he regarded as so central to his whole enterprise, the rejection of the doctrine of *analogia entis*. I propose now to indicate the correctness of Barth's opinion by examining it in the light of the correlations I have established in Barth's understanding of the bases of creaturely knowledge of God and creaturely knowledge of the creature in the unity and diversity of the self-revealing, self-electing triune God of the covenant.

Berkouwer's judgment is quite sound in advising that any interpretation of Barth's doctrine of analogy and his opposition to the *analogia entis* must take into account what Barth intends to achieve by this opposition.[86] As Barth sees it, the doctrine of *analogia entis*, as practiced in Roman Catholic theology, proposes a division between the knowledge of God and the being of God, the

---

83.   *CD* 2/1, 82; the English translation has no date. See Barth, *Die Kirchliche Dogmatik II, Erste Halband* (Zürich, 1940).

84.   See E Brunner, 'The New Barth', in *Scottish Journal of Theology* 4 (1951): 123ff, and Appendix 2 below.

85.   Barth, *CD* 4/2, xi.

86.   GC Berkouwer, *The Triumph of Grace in the Theology of Karl Barth*, 190.

self-revealing God of the Bible. It proposes 'a *posse* which is not included in and with . . . [the] divine encroachment.'[87] It makes

> a provisional division or partition in regard to the knowability of God, and this will inevitably lead to a partitioning of the one God as well . . . The primary reference of our contradiction is to this partition . . . We have taken the unity of God seriously, not only in theory but in practice. We have answered the question of the knowability of God in the light of this unity.[88]

From Barth's point of view, then, the doctrine of *analogia entis* proposes a freedom of the creature for God which is not presupposed by the actual freedom of God for the creature. In fact, it denies the revealed unity of the self revealing God. We have already seen how, for Barth, the revealed unity of God presupposes creaturely knowledge of God and creaturely knowledge of the creature; it is its *terminus a quo* and its *terminus ad quem*. These limits of creaturely knowledge are based in the inconceivable freedom in which God posits God's self as Lord of the creature, electing God's self for the creature and the creature for God's self in God's eternal Son Jesus Christ.

In discussing the appropriateness of analogical speech in relationship to God it can never, therefore, be the case that it is justified on the basis of some theory of human language and its appropriateness or otherwise in respect of speech about God. The necessity of analogical speech for Barth is to be found in the reasons why the doctrine of God follows the doctrine of revelation in the structure of Barth's dogmatic method. The God who reveals God's self and who starts with God's self in the revelation of God's name in the doctrine of

---

87.   Barth, *CD* 2/1, 79.
88.   *Ibid*, 84: 'The intolerable and unpardonable thing in Roman Catholic theology is . . . that there is this splitting up of the concept of God, and hand in hand with it the abstraction from the real work and activity of God in favour of a general being of God which he has in common with us and all being' . . . 'We reject this (doctrine of *analogia entis*) because it is a construct which obviously derives from an attempt to unite Yahweh with Baal, the Triune God of the Holy Scripture with the concept of being of Aristotelian and Stoic philosophy . . . We cannot, therefore, attack it in detail. For how can we attack it? We can only say Yes and Amen to it as far as it applies to the god, the false god, to whom it refers. It is in itself incorrigible. But we cannot allow that it says anything about God at all, or that it is one of the assertions that have to be made in the Christian doctrine of God.'

revelation, must be seen as starting with God's self in all God's relationships *ad extra* because that is the starting point *ad intra*. As the self-revealing God, God is the self-electing God. The relationship between God's being 'in-and-for-God's self' and God's 'being-for-us' is the basis for analogical speech, referring human language and concepts of this world to God.

> Between our views, concepts and words, and God as their object, there exists, on the basis of the revelation of God, the relationship of analogy, of similarity, of partial correspondence and agreement. On the basis of this similarity there is true knowledge of God and therefore the human knowledge of God reaches its goal. But how does this partial correspondence and agreement arise? . . . [We] must affirm that, as and before it occurs, as and before our word comes to participate in it, it obviously subsists in God Himself as the Subject and Lord who in His revelation controls His own work . . . Therefore the relationship between what He is in Himself and what He is in our work is only a relationship of similarity. Yet while this is true, it is also true that both in Himself and in our work He is not Another.[89]

The word 'analogy' is claimed by revelation itself, but like any other human word it is inappropriate in itself since it is freighted with philosophical assumptions. It is simply of no interest to Barth.

> We are not concerned with the words as such. In a sense we simply turn our back on them. We look at the true revelation of God. And by it we are pushed away from the words parity and disparity . . . And, pressed again by the true revelation of God, we are pushed on to the word 'analogy'. In itself and as such it is no better than the words parity and disparity.[90]

---

89.    Barth, *CD* 2/1, 227; cf 214, 215.
90.    *CD* 2/1, 226. GH Clark, *Karl Barth's Theological Method* (Philadelphia: The Presbyterian and Reformed Publishing Co, 1963), 142–147, misses the point of Barth's discussion as to the suitability of the word analogy. Barth's argument does not depend upon the word analogy being the 'revealed word'. The theological necessity of the word analogy resides in the distinction posited in God's self-revelation between God's being in God's self and God's being for us. If Barth's argument is to be critically examined, it is inappropriate to accuse him of a contradiction on the basis of the

The partiality of analogical predication of human words and concepts to God presupposes the distinction between God's knowing and affirming of God's self and God's knowing and affirming God's self as the creature's Lord—the Lord who determines the divine being as One who loves in freedom. This is God who determines God's self for the human creature and the human creature for God's self in the eternal Son Jesus Christ. He is the One in whom God elects God's self for humankind and humankind for God's self and in whom God is properly the Object of human thought and speech as well as the Subject. Thus, in authorising the appropriateness of human speech and language on the basis of God's self revelation, God

> takes to Himself something that already belongs originally and properly to Him . . . It is obviously His truth originally, primarily, independently and properly, because creatively. It is our truth only subsequently, secondarily, dependently and improperly, because creaturely.[91]

In his discussion of the appropriateness of analogical predication in human knowledge of God, Barth brings to expression in this area of his theological epistemology the principle that has guided his thought since his Anselm book. This is that theological thought can only move from the actuality of theological knowledge—in this case human knowledge of God in God's self-knowledge because God is the self-electing God in Jesus Christ—to the possibility of human knowledge of God. Other possible ways of thinking and speaking about the appropriateness of analogical speech about God are negated by the actuality of human knowledge of God in Jesus Christ. Since this actuality presupposes God's inconceivable act in which God posits God's self as the Lord of the human creature, the truth of human knowledge of God is

> the power of our faith . . . that God has accepted His Son in the flesh, that He has comforted this man Jesus in eternity. And in Him he has already comforted us all in advance . . . [M]oving in our *circulus veritas Dei*, we are in the sphere of Jesus Christ,

---

law of non-contradiction concerning his use of certain words: the fact that Barth speaks of a 'similarity that is not similar to ordinary similarity' (146.) In a work devoted to a study of Barth's theological method this is a conspicuous failure.

91.    Barth, *CD* 2/1, 228; cf 1/1, 39ff.

where that which in an earlier context we called the veiling and the unveiling of God, the way from one to the other, forms the household rule from which we cannot except ourselves.[92]

Thus, the actuality of creaturely knowledge of God coincides with the unity of the *Deus revelatus* and the *Deus absconditus*, that is, beyond the negative limit of human existence in that unity actualised in God's self-positing in the Holy Spirit's raising of Jesus Christ from the dead. This means, from the point of view of the human subject, that God in this self-revealed unity is the ground of the veracity of human analogical predication in speech about God.

Consequently, Barth's discussion of the doctrine of analogy, as advanced by the orthodox Lutheran theologian A Quenstedt, takes a decidedly critical turn.[93] According to Quenstedt, the question of the knowledge of God in terms of analogy arises because both univocal and equivocal predications show themselves to be inadequate explanations of the fact of creaturely knowledge of God. This is so since, on the one hand, the creature is not God and thus any quality of one cannot be predicated of the other *univoce*. God does not belong to a genus. On the other hand, Quenstedt believes that equivocal predication must be rejected too, since by itself it does no more than simply state that both sides of the analogical relation are what they are. In any case, the creature has real knowledge of God, so both of these alternatives must be rejected.[94] Quenstedt therefore rejects both *analogia inequalitatis* and *analogia proportionalitatis*. Proper analogy does not have the kind of similarity 'which exists when some determinations of two objects agree but at the same time disagree,' or that exists 'between different species of the one *genus*.'[95] Proper analogy between God and the creature must therefore be understood in terms of *analogia attributionis*. This is when 'the *analogia* is *analogans* in the first and *analogata* in the second.'[96]

What Quenstedt proposes is a relationship in which what is predicated exists first and properly in one and then, because the second is dependent on the first, in the second as well. The predication is not attributed to the secondary side of the relationship in a merely external manner but in terms of 'an *analogia*

---

92.    *Ibid*, 253, 254; see above, 53–59, and Appendix 3.
93.    *CD* 2/1, 237ff.
94.    *Ibid*, 237.
95.    *Ibid*, 237, 238.
96.    *Ibid*, 238.

*attributionis intrinsecae'.*[97] If this were not the case then one would be back in the position of equivocal predication, and creaturely knowledge of God would be impossible. So it must be the case, according to Quenstedt, that the

> analogy *proprie* belongs both to the *analogans* and the *analogatum*. It is inward both to God and to the creature, although in the last only secondarily *et per dependentiam.*[98]

Barth does not object to Quenstedt's use of analogical predication but to his reasons for its necessity.

> Although we agree with his attack on the thesis of parity and disparity between human words and divine being, in his case it has another sense than with us. With us the rejection of parity is a defence against the denial of the veiling of God in His revelation. But with him it is a defence against the denial of the distinction between absolute and relative being as such. With us the rejection of the thesis of disparity is a defence against the denial of the unveiling in God's revelation. With him it is a defence against the denial of the unity of relative and absolute being in truth.[99]

Barth sees the proper necessity for analogical predication in the nature of the self-revealed unity of God and the unity of this God and the creature—in the Father as *Deus absconditus*, the Son as *Deus revelatus* and the Holy Spirit as the inconceivable unity of both the *Deus absconditus* and the *Deus revelatus*. If Quenstedt had seen this he would not have insisted that the relationship between God and the creature is one of *analogia attributionis intrinsecae.'* For, what makes the creature into an analogue of God

> does not lie in itself and its nature, not even in the sense that God will acknowledge and accept as an analogue (in itself) something of that which lies in the nature of the creature. What converts the creature into an analogue of God lies only in the veracity of the

---

97.　*Ibid.*

98　Barth, *CD* 2/1, 238.

99.　CD 2/1, 239.

object known analogously in the knowledge of God, and therefore in the veracity of God Himself.[100]

Since Barth supports the view that creaturely knowledge of God and the creature presupposes the being of God in God's self-positing as the God of the creature on the basis of God's self-revealed unity, the only possible way in which creaturely predication can be understood as appropriately applied to God is by 'extrinsic' attribution. This is to emphasise the inconceivability of the freedom whereby God determines God's self for the creature and the creature for God. In the man Jesus Christ, the creature is analogous to the Creator '*extrinsece* in the form of *apprehensio* and not at all *intrinsece*'.[101]

It is important to realise that Barth's rejection of Quenstedt's view of analogical predication is based on his dogmatic presuppositions and not simply on the basis of an analysis of what has been traditionally understood as analogical predication in respect of speech about God. Barth grounds the reality and possibility of analogical predication in the distinction between God's being in and for God's self and God's being for and with the creature. It is the unity of this self revealing God which presupposes the reality of creaturely knowledge of God in terms of the creature's being in analogical predication.

In the doctrine of revelation, Barth understood this self-revealed unity of God in terms of a dialectic between the doctrines of *perichoresis* and *appropriation*. In the doctrine of God, the self-revelation of God presupposed God's self-election, the fact that God not only *posits* God's self in freedom but posits God's *self* as love. Subsequently, I have indicated the relationship between this aspect of the doctrine of God and Barth's analysis of the covenant as the internal basis of creation This presupposed creation as its external basis or its technical possibility. We now see that Barth's conception of the relationship between God and the creature in terms of the creature's knowledge of God and knowledge of the creature is grounded in the same revealed unity of God. The continuities and distinctions in the creature's knowledge of God and of the creature are grounded in, because they presuppose, the continuities and distinctions of the being of God the Creator and Lord.

It now remains for us to see how this conclusion explains the relationship between knowledge of God and knowledge of the creature in terms of Barth's understanding of the relationship between *analogia fidei* and *analogia relationis*.

---

100.  *Ibid*, 240.
101.  *CD* 2/1, 239.

## Knowledge of the creature in relation to knowledge of God: *analogia fidei and analogia relationis*

I have already indicated that the determination of Jesus in his cosmic or worldly relationships presupposes his being the Man for other human beings as the external expression of his being Man for God, real Man. In this determination he is identical with God's self-determination as God for the creature. Precisely because Jesus in his cosmic relationships presupposes the truth of God's own self-election, the creature which corresponds to this determination in its being for the other in the I-Thou relationship is essentially hidden from itself. In the creature's knowledge of the creature we are before the same primal mystery as that unity between *Deus absconditus* and the *Deus revelatus* beyond the negative limit of human existence, the resurrection of Jesus Christ in the Holy Spirit. In the humanity of Jesus we stand

> before the true and original correspondence . . . the fact that the man Jesus in His being for man repeats and reflects the inner being or essence of God and this confirms His being for God . . . The humanity of Jesus is not merely the repetition and reflection of His divinity, or of God's controlling will; it is the repetition and reflection of God Himself, no more and no less. It is the image of God, the *imago Dei*.[102]

To know the creature in its correspondence (as I and Thou) to the truth of Jesus Christ as the Man for others, as the One who repeats for us the being of God, God's own self-election, is to perceive that one can only know this truth in faith. Faith acknowledges that we stand before the mystery by which God distinguishes God's self from God's self and in so doing also distinguishes God's self from the creature. Barth uses the idea of *analogia relationis* to describe the content of faith's knowledge in this context.[103] *Analogia relationis* is thus primarily a christological reference. It expresses the way in which Jesus *is* the

---

102. Barth, *CD* 3/2, 219.
103. Thus Jüngel, *Gottes Sein is im Werden*, 116: 'Gott in der Offenbarung an seiner konkreten relationalen Existenz als Gott Vater, Sohn und Geist teilgibt in der Weise der Wiederholung. Die Wiederholung ist als Relation Gottes zu uns die Entsprechung zu Gottes Selbstbezogenheit: *analogia relationis*.' See also E Jüngel, 'Die Möglichkeit theologischer Anthropologie', in *Evangelische Theologie* 22 (1962), 535.

image of God, the One who presupposes the creature's existence in the unity of the Triune God. What is at stake in understanding this relationship is 'the relationship within the being of God on the one side and the being of God and that of man on the other.'[104] Christian anthropology is not derived by deducing certain truths about human beings on the basis of the humanity of Jesus, considered in the context of a general anthropological framework, but only in faith which asks after

> a basic form of humanity . . . in which there is given and revealed the fact that the man Jesus can be for them . . . How far as men they are beings which can be represented by the man Jesus in his suffering and conquering.[105]

Just as the *analogia fidei* presupposed an analogical relationship as opposed to a relationship of parity or disparity in respect of creaturely knowledge of God, so too does the *analogia relationis*. In both cases, we see that the necessity of the relationship reposes on the freedom of God to be who God is in God's self-revelation.[106]

---

104. Barth, *CD* 3/2, 220.
105. *Ibid,* 223, 224.
106. Cf Jüngel, 'Die Möglichkeit theologischer Anthropologie', 541–542. On the difference between D Bonhoeffer's use of the term *analogia relationis* and Barth's, see J Moltmann, *The Lordship of Christ in Human Society: Two Studies in the Theology of D Bonhoeffer* (New York: Scribners, 1967), 53–55. It would appear that Bonhoeffer was the first to use the term.

# Chapter Four

# The Relationship in the Dogma of the Trinity with the Doctrine of Creation
## Part Two

This chapter will critically assess the nature of the God-creature relationship delineated in Barth's theological schema in which the doctrine of the Trinity is of central significance. In our analysis we have seen how Barth's method drives inexorably towards a material unity in terms of his methodological presuppositions. These presuppositions derive from Barth's determination to understand God and the world in terms of the event of revelation. This event is such that the One who is revealed in it becomes the basis upon which Barth understands both the way in which God distinguishes God's self from God's self and distinguishes God's self from the creature. This God is the living God beyond whom or behind whom there is no transcendent depth of being, no static eternity in which this act or event takes place. This act reveals who this God is in God's self revelation; and it presupposes all the distinctions and continuities in the being of God and the creature.

Because God exists as this One who knows God's self in Jesus Christ as the Lord of the creature—of all creation and all people—the free decision in Jesus Christ to be for us humans configures the fact of our existence and knowledge of creation as coming from God.[1] The question before us is whether Barth's method of understanding God and the creature provides an adequate basis for taking account of what any Christian doctrine of creation must explicate. This is that

> created forms of rationality (are) to be distinguished from the
> eternal rationality of God. In creating and knowing them God
> remains free from any necessity in the relationship, although they
> remain grounded in the supreme truth of His being.[2]

---

1. Barth, *CD* 3/2, 41. Cf JD Bettis, 'Theology in the Public Debate: Barth's Rejection of Natural Theology and the Hermeneutical Problem', in *Scottish Journal of Theology* 22/4 (1969): 385ff.
2. TF Torrance, *Space, Time and Incarnation*, 65.

This view of the relationship between God and creation has been seen to be decisive in establishing the created integrity of the world and facilitating the development of modern natural science.[3] In giving the creation a rationality and integrity of its own on the basis of God's freely willed action, God

> endowed the universe with an immanent rationality making it determinate and knowable. Over against the creation God remains quite free in His eternal Self-existence and therefore cannot be known in the determinate way in which created things are known, but the creation also remains free in its utterly contingent character and is therefore to be known in its natural processes only out of itself.[4]

The fact that the immanent rationality of the creature cannot give a final account of itself in terms of its own inner structure can be seen as the obverse side of the truth that the connection between creaturely being and its ground in the creative will of God is 'grounded in God alone, and does not rest partly in God and partly in creation'.[5]

This view of the relationship between God and creation is one that is to be distinguished from other views concerned to express this same phenomenon. According to Foster, the Christian view that nature is created signifies 'the main difference between the methods of ancient and the methods of modern natural science'.[6] The principle practical result of this difference was that experience rather than logical axioms played the major role in understanding the world of nature.

---

3.   On this see the important articles by MB Foster, 'The Christian Doctrine of Creation and the Rise of Modern Natural Science', in *Mind* 43–45 (1934–1936): 446ff, 439ff, 1ff. See also the following: TF Torrance, *Theological Science*, 59ff and *Theology in Reconstruction*, 62ff; EL Mascall, *Christian Theology and Natural* Science, 93ff, and *Existence and Analogy*, 4ff, 10ff; G Vahanian, *The Death of God*, 172–174; A Flew and D MacKinnon, 'Creation', in *New Essays in Philosophical Theology*, 170ff, 176; C Dawson, 'The Scientific Development of Medieval Culture', in *Medieval Essays* (London: Sheed & Ward, 1953), 135ff.

4.   TF Torrance, *Theological* Science, 59.

5.   *Ibid*, 60; cf TF Torrance, *Theology in Reconstruction*, 71, 72.

6.   MB Foster, 'The Christian Doctrine of Creation and the Rise of Modern Natural Science', in *Mind* 43 (1934): 453.

Modern science describes natural substances instead of defining them, it discovers their properties by observation and experiment instead of by 'intuitive induction' and demonstration, it classifies their species instead of dividing their genera, it establishes between them the relation of cause and effect instead of the relation of ground and consequence.[7]

The Greek method involved the assumption that the form of a thing, that which makes it intelligible to reason, was the prime attribute of material things. The form makes a thing to be what it is, whereas matter does not contribute any positive element to a thing's being.

Matter is the correlative, in the object, of sense in the subject, as form is the correlative of reason; and thus the Greek assumption about science, that there can be no empirical evidence for scientific conclusions, depends upon the Greek assumption about nature which may be loosely designated the assumption of the 'unreality of matter'.[8]

The ancient Greek view entails that in relation to God neither element in nature can be seen to be dependent upon a creative power outside itself for its being what it is; neither element, matter or form, can be understood to be created. For, 'if matter were created it would possess positive being' and 'if form were created it would not be intelligible'.[9] Nature may be conceived to be dependent upon a superior power for the action whereby the two elements are brought together, but not for the being of either matter or form. Plato's demiurge functions as both informative and purposive. But it is 'confined to the information of given matter . . . and directed by the antecedent conception of an end.'[10] The same assumption, with certain qualifications, also holds for the Aristotelian view of creation.[11]

---

7.    *Ibid*, 454.

8.    *Ibid*, 455.

9.    *Ibid*, 456.

10.   *Ibid*, 459. Cf Foster, 'The Christian Doctrine of Creation', in *Mind* 44 (1935): 443ff, 454ff, for the development of Plato's cosmology. See also JH Gay, 'Four Medieval Views of Creation', in *Harvard Theological Review* 56/4 (1963): 243ff.

11.   Foster, 'The Christian Doctrine of Creation', in *Mind* 43 (1934): 460, 461; cf 44 (1935):

The distinctive characteristic of a doctrine of creation, which presupposes a Creator, rather than a manufacturer, is that instead of seeing a correlation between the divine essence and the created rationality in defining matter it will be the case that the

> *voluntary* activity of the Creator (i.e., that in his activity which exceeds determination by reason) terminates on the *contingent* being of the creature (i.e., on that element of its being which eludes determination by form, namely its matter and the characteristics it possesses *qua* material). If such voluntary activity is essential to God, it follows that the element of contingency is essential to what he creates . . . [This] element in nature which depends upon the voluntary activity of God, is incapable of becoming an object of reason, and science must therefore depend, in regard to this element, upon the *evidence* of sensation. The reliance upon the senses for evidence, not merely for illustration, is what constitutes the empirical character peculiar to modern science; and the conclusion follows that only a created nature is a proper object of an empirical science.[12]

Foster develops his thesis on the relationship between the Christian doctrine of creation and the rise of modern natural science[13] by criticising the view presented in St Augustine's work on the Trinity, in particular the relationship between the eternal Logos or Word of God and the existence of the creature, which Augustine presupposes in his thought. Augustine is seen to overcome one of the problems inherent in the Greek view of the God/creature relationship in so far as he identifies the Word of God with God's self-utterance. By linking this Word with the rationality of the creature in its broadest sense, Augustine avoids Plato's dilemma of the form and the matter of the world being co-eternal with God. God is freed from any necessary connection with the world by being the author of God's own thought. But the problem remains in Augustine of distinguishing between the Son's natural generation as the Son of God and his

---

    450ff, 460ff.

12.   *Ibid*, 464, 465.

13.   Foster, 'The Christian Doctrine of Creation', in *Mind* 45 (1936): 1ff.

incarnation in time. The world is thus presented as an inferior representation of the divine reason.[14]

Thus, a distinction is seen to be necessary which emphasises the fact that, while in creating the world God establishes a relationship with the creature, this relationship is not something which proceeds from God's nature as such. It proceeds from God's will that establishes the existence, rationality and integrity of the creature as distinct from that which is God's by nature.[15] It must be the case that the creaturely form of God's self-revelation is grounded not in the nature of God,

> but in the will of God, i.e., it is not possible to argue back from it
> to the nature of God in the sense of how God is constituted, but
> only to the nature of his will, i.e., from his will as made known in
> history to his eternal will as the will of his free love.[16]

There is thus a functional, as distinct from a structural, similarity between the being of God and that of the creature.[17] Barth is not unaware of this problem. Although it is true that his whole theological enterprise depends upon the equation that 'God's essence and His operation are not twain but one', he nevertheless maintains that 'it is necessary and important to distinguish His essence as such from His operation'.[18] The necessity for this distinction is that although the operation of God is God's essence, God's self-revealed Lordship corresponds to 'a free divine decision . . . He remains free, in operating, in giving Himself.'[19]

Foster's analysis raises the question for theology of understanding the distinction considered necessary between the rationality of God's being, which remains implacably indeterminate in God's transcendence vis-à-vis the creature, and the determinate nature of the relationship into which God enters

---

14.  Cf V Lossky, *The Mystical Theology of the Eastern Church* (London: J Clarke, 1961), 95ff, and TF Torrance, *Theology in Reconstruction*, 64–66, 78ff.

15.  See TF Torrance's analysis of Duns Scotus' solution to this problem, *ibid*, 78, 86, 273. The difficulty inherent in any distinction between God's essence and God's will is that it may open up a way to the idea that God is unknowable, inscrutable. Cf TF Torrance, *Space, Time and Incarnation*, 65.

16.  H Gollwitzer, *The Existence of God as Confessed by Faith*, 186.

17.  *Ibid*, 185.

18.  Barth, *CD* 1/1, 426.

19.  *Ibid*.

voluntarily in creation and incarnation. By emphasising either one of these aspects of the matter errors will arise.[20] Over-emphasis on the transcendence of God can make the relationship God establishes with the world accidental to God as such. We may recall in this context Barth's vigorous defence of the *filioque* in terms of his exposition of the doctrine of the Trinity. Barth's whole position in this defence was to the effect that what God is in God's self-revelation God is in God's self.[21]

> The reality of God in His revelation is not to be bracketed with an 'only', as though somewhere behind His revelation there stood another reality of God, but the reality of God which meets us in revelation is His reality in all the depths of eternity.[22]

Over-emphasising the contingent nature of created reality can tend to ignore its dependence upon the continued presence of God with and for the creature. If this happens, then the contingency of the creature's existence can be converted into a necessity that finds no room for God's participation in creaturely history. Thus, Deism asserts there is room for God only at the beginning of the created process whilst agnosticism asserts the reality of contingent necessity of nature alone. Deism or agnosticism is 'the price'[23] paid for asserting the contingent nature of created existence understood as an act of God's will which is distinguished from God's self.

In any account of the God/creature relationship, the issues raised by Foster's account of the God/creature relationship must be taken into account. This will entail ensuring in the following discussion of this issue, from the point of view of knowledge of God and knowledge of the creature, that the divine and human elements in the relationship are addressed in their distinct and related integrity.

## Catholic and Reformed understanding of the God-creature relationship

The views of EL Mascall and TF Torrance are taken to be representative of the Catholic neo-Thomist (albeit in an Anglican form) and the Reformed traditions.[24]

---

20.  TF Torrance, *Space, Time and Incarnation*, 61ff.
21.  Barth, *CD* 1/1. 548ff. See 35ff. above, 32–39.
22.  Barth, *CD* 1/1, 548.
23.  TF Torrance, *Theological Science*, 67, note 1.
24.  EL Mascall, *Christian Theology and Natural Science* (Hamden, Connecticut: Shoe

In examining their views, we will take into account the issues raised in the previous discussion related to M Foster's thesis concerning elements in the God/creature relationship which, while establishing the relationship, at the same time preserves the integrity of God's Godness and the creatureliness of the creature.

Mascall maintains that the unique Christian contribution to understanding creation in the manner outlined in Foster's thesis is best seen in the metaphysics of St Thomas Aquinas.[25] St Thomas, in contrast to Aristotle, placed emphasis on the act of existence of created things rather than their existence being defined in terms of their essence. For Aristotle essence, expressed as concepts about a thing's existence, served as the basis of major premises of syllogistic arguments and was not the object of experimentation.[26] On the other hand, when essence is understood as an act of existence its definition will receive formulation in propositions based on personal judgment that are open to experimental verification. Since St Thomas refused to hold that a thing's existence was an addition to its essence, there could be no question of the world having to conform to a predetermined scheme of universals and particulars.[27] Instead of a theory of universals and particulars, of form and matter, the relationship between the rationality of created being and its transcendent cause will be analogical. Analogical speech in this context derives its meaning from St Thomas' denial of the Aristotelian essentialist metaphysic and the substituting of his own existentialist metaphysic. This seeks to understand the creature's being in relationship to God in terms of the actual contingency of creaturely existence and does not attempt a logical correlation between the structures of reason and being.[28]

Thus, the basis upon which Mascall seeks to relate the contingent being of the creature to the Creator is by means of an analysis of creaturely existence. The distinction between God and the creature will be posited by the difference presupposed between the relationship between existence and essence in creatures and in God. The non-necessary nature of this relationship in creatures

---

String Press, 1965), and *Existence and Analogy* (London: Longmans, Green, 1949); TF Torrance, *Theological Science, Theology in Reconstruction,* and *Space, Time and Incarnation.*

25.   Mascall, *Existence and Analogy,* 4ff, 10, 44ff.

26.   *Ibid,* 19, 20.

27.   *Ibid,* 62.

28.   *Ibid,* 122–124, 126–128.

postulates their contingency in respect of the One in whom this relationship is one of necessity; this One is commonly called God.

Analogical speech about God is legitimised by the contingent relationship in which the creature stands in its relationship with God. The form of the analogical relationship will be governed by the discrepancy between the relationship between existence and essence in God and in the creature. Though existence is predicated of both God and the creature, the mode of predication differs in respect of God and creatures. Consequently, one cannot add together the relationship of existence to essence in God and the creature and make a significant statement about them. Thus, while the creature is related to God and its existence is guaranteed as a creature, there is no direct proportion between God's willing of God's self and God's willing of the creature's existence.

Mascall's analysis of the relationship between God and the creature in terms of St Thomas' existentialist metaphysic is one that entails the meaningfullness of human speech and language about God in terms of the structures of existence. God is knowable apart from any direct reference to a particular revelation.

For scientific method, this means that the definition of created reality in terms of natural laws cannot contain its description without remainder, since the creature's existence entails an act of will on the part of the Creator.[29]

Mascall holds with St Thomas that being is not a *genus;* there is nothing outside of being with which it may be differentiated.[30] From God to dust, everything is. What is true of beings in their relationship to one another is true also of the relationship between God and things. But as being is not a *genus,* the relationship between God and things is one that can only be spoken of analogically, as distinct from univocal or equivocal predication. Mascall, following St Thomas, distinguishes between two basic types of analogy, those classified as 'two to a third' and those categorised as 'one to another'. This latter type, for obvious reasons, is the only kind considered appropriate for the God / creature relationship. God could not be compared with something else in which both God and the creature participated in different ways—Barth's reason for rejecting the doctrine of *analogia entis.*[31] The analogy of 'one to another' is divided into two sub-types: analogy of 'attribution' and analogy of 'proportionality'.[32] In the analogy of attribution, the predicate belongs formally and properly to

---

29.   *Ibid,* 129–132.
30.   *Ibid,* 99ff.
31.   See above, footnote 73 and 109 footnote 82.
32.   Mascall, *Existence and Analogy,* 101–103.

one analogate, and only relatively and derivatively to the second. The analogy of proportionality rescues the analogy of attribution from being simply an assertion that if creatures are then also God is. It states

> that the analogue under discussion is found formally in each of the analogates but in a mode that is determined by the nature of the analogate itself.[33]

But if the analogy of proportionality was the only valid analogy, then it would collapse either through its univocal predication or, avoiding this, would lapse into agnosticism since there would be no way of judging what relationship the analogates stood in relationship with each other.

> Without the analogy of proportionality it is very doubtful whether the attributes we predicate of God can be ascribed to Him in more than a virtual sense; without the analogy of attribution it hardly seems possible to avoid agnosticism.[34]

The analogical relationship between God and the creature must therefore be seen to combine, 'a tightly interlocked union [of] both the analogy of attribution and the analogy of proportionality'.[35] The perfections of the creature are predicated of God eminently according to the analogy of proportionality. The issue of the theological use of analogy is that of distinguishing, on the basis of the analogy of attribution, the mode of signification of the perfection in the creature and in God.[36] The difference in the mode of signification, based on existential judgment about the created nature, grounds the theological use of analogical predication in speech about God and the creature. In this we see Mascall's attempt to explain how the transcendence as well as the immanence of God in the God/creature relationship can be held together, without compromising the integrity of either God or the creature.[37]

---

33.  *Ibid*, 104.
34.  *Ibid*, 113, 114–121. Cf B Mondin, *The Principle of Analogy in Protestant and Catholic Theology* (The Hague: J Nijhoff, 1963), 41, 42, 46, 49, 50; A Flew and DM MacKinnon, 'Creation', 182
35.  Mascall, *ibid*; cf J McIntyre, 'Analogy', in *Scottish Journal of Theology* 12/1 (1959): 13, 14, 16–17.
36.  Mondin, *The Principle of Analogy*, 50.
37.  This understanding of creaturely knowledge of God and creaturely knowledge of

Where Mascall seeks to understand the God / creature relationship in terms of an analysis of creaturely existence facilitated by Thomist metaphysics, TF Torrance seeks understanding of the same issue by means of a Reformed view of the person of Jesus Christ.[38] In considering the issues raised by Foster in respect of the structure of the Christian doctrine of creation and the rise of modern natural science, Torrance emphasises the change in the doctrine of God that took place in the Reformation of the sixteenth century. The Reformation revived Patristic insights that revolutionised the medieval worldview and were conducive to the development noted already by Foster.

According to Torrance, the Reformers destroyed the systematic connection between thought and being which had prevailed in Western theology since Augustine. This connection entailed that nature was impregnated with final causes posited by the eternal knowing and willing of the creature by God.[39] The Reformers accomplished this in two ways. Firstly, they challenged the reversibility of the relationship between God and the creature by their doctrine of election.[40] This questioned the assumption that there is an inherent relationship between the form structure of human reason and God, in this case the *logos* of God, and creaturely being. The relationship between God and the creature is freely posited by God and therefore is irreversible. The transcendence of God, signified by such a doctrine of election, is understood to safeguard the contingency of the creature in the God / creature relationship. Secondly, the contingency of created nature was affirmed as such by the nature of God's condescension to the creature in the incarnation of the eternal Son of God. Calvin, in particular, speaks of God's action in the incarnation as 'accommodating' God's self to our creaturely way of being and knowing both God and the creature.[41] This, of course, implies that human knowledge of God in relation to the creature is tied to the factuality of the event of God's self-giving, in which event God adapts creaturely knowledge of God and the creature to the divine reality of God's own being.

---

the creature according to analogical predication assumes that there is a likeness between cause and effect. On this see Mondin, 50ff and 88.

38.   TF Torrance, *Theological Science*, 59ff, and *Theology in Reconstruction*, 62ff.
39.   Cf Torrance's comment on Aquinas in this connection, *Thelogical Science*, 60.
40.   *Ibid*, 66.
41.   TF Torrance, *Theology in Reconstruction*, 70; see also *Divine and Contingent Order*, 136ff; *Space, Time and Incarnation*, 52ff; *Space, Time and Resurrection*, 159ff; *Theology in Reconciliation*, 281ff; *God and Rationality*, 31ff; *The Mediation of Christ*, 13ff.

In this schema, the actual humanity of the incarnate Son of God is critically important as the locus in which God guarantees that creaturely statements about God repose upon the reality of God's being, and that creaturely existence is confirmed in its created contingency by the free condescension of God to it in the purposive teleology of Jesus' life in history. Thus, that the Son of God is *homoousios* with the Father is foundational for the Reformers' view of the God/creature relationship as expounded by Torrance.

> Apart from the *homoousion* there is no real and objective connection between our human knowing and speaking of God, and God Himself.[42]

However, since this movement of the incarnation is from God *to* the creature, no logical correlation can be made between the structure of creaturely being and knowing and the being of God. For this reason, Torrance rejects any attempt to construct a natural knowledge of God as a prior conceptual system abstracted from the actuality of the condescension of God through which God becomes accommodated to the structures of the creature's existence—see εγενετο in St John 1:14—including the structures of the creature's being and knowing of God. Thus any natural theology for Torrance must be part of an

> integrated unity with positive theology in which it plays an indispensable part in our inquiry and understanding of God.[43]

Before passing on to consider Torrance's understanding of the part played by analogy in the creature's knowledge of God, and the relationship between God and the creature which this implies, we look at an often overlooked aspect of the Reformed approach to the question of the knowledge of God. I refer to the methodological importance of the humanity of Jesus in understanding the issue.

---

42. *Ibid*, 39.
43. Torrance, *Space, Time and Incarnation*, 70. For Torrance's discussion of Bouillard's thesis on the relationship between natural and revealed theology, see 'The Problem of Natural Theology in the Thought of Karl Barth', in *Religious Studies* 6/2 (1970): 121ff.

## The methodological importance of the humanity of Jesus in Reformed theology

To the question of how we know God, Calvin gives a clear answer. 'We must go outside ourselves and not measure God by the capacity of our minds.'[44] Faith is called knowledge in the sense that

> we intend not so much a comprehension as men commonly have of those things which fall under the notice of their senses. For it is so superior, that the human mind must exceed and rise above itself, in order to attain to it. Nor does the mind which attains it comprehend what it perceives, but being persuaded of that which it cannot comprehend, it understands more by the certainty of this persuasion, than it would any human object by the exercise of its natural capacity.[45]

The stretching of the human mind in the knowledge of faith correlates to the condescension of God in Jesus Christ to accommodate Himself to the measure of our understanding.

> As we are corporeal, always creeping upon the ground, cleaving to terrestrial and carnal objects, and incapable of understanding or conceiving of anything of a spiritual nature, our merciful Lord, in His infinite indulgence, accommodates Himself to our capacity, condescending to lead us to Himself.[46]

This stretching of the human mind in the knowledge of faith, dependent as it is upon God's act of accommodation in Christ, corresponds to the fact that it is determined by an act of divine will which relates the creature to the transcendent reality of God's eternal being. Since this act is a voluntary divine condescension, it takes place not for God's sake, as though God needs to reveal God's essence, but for the sake of restoring the relationship of the creature to the Creator. Therefore, knowledge of God is, at one and the same time, reconciliation

---

44.   J Calvin, *Commentary on the Book of Acts*, on 17:23.
45.   Calvin, *Institutes of the Christian Religion*, book 3, chapter 2, section 14; cf book 1, chapter 7, section 5, and *Commentary on Ephesians*, on 3:19.
46.   Calvin, *Institutes of the Christian Religion*, book 4, chapter 14, section 3; cf 2.6.4.

with God. In discussing Christ's humiliation, Calvin reminds his readers that it in no sense detracts from his glory.

> If it takes nothing from His glory that He was altogether 'emptied', neither does it degrade Him that He chose not only to grow in body, but to make progress in mind.[47]

> And so Christ bids him [John the Baptist] consider what was suitable to the character of a servant, which He had undertaken; for a voluntary subjection takes nothing from His glory.[48]

This paradoxical 'glory' of Christ takes place for the sake of the creature. It is a vicarious action. It is the creature's shame with which Christ clothed himself. In this 'not his but ours' lies the reason why Calvin sees a double aspect to all Christ's sufferings. He is at the same time accursed and beloved by the Father. Christ is accursed for our sake, but beloved because he is obedient to the Father's will.[49] Since God's condescension was for the sake of the creature, the glory and power of God is in no way diminished or altered by God's act of accommodation.[50]

The purpose of this examination of Calvin's thought is to link it with the emphasis we have found in TF Torrance's understanding of the God / creature relationship. Torrance is at pains to give due weight to both the transcendence of God, by use of the doctrine of election, and the intimate relationship God establishes with the creature, grounded in the voluntary condescension of the

---

47.  Calvin, *Commentary on St Luke* 2:40; cf *Commentary on Philippians* 2:6; for the incarnation as such, *Commentary on St John* 10:17; for Christ's subjection to parents, *Commentary on St Luke* 2:51; for his Baptism, *Commentary on St Matthew* 3:13; for his infirmities, *Commentary on Hebrews* 4:5; for the voluntary and vicarious nature of Christ's humiliation, *Commentary on St John* 11:53, 14:30, 18:1, 4, 8, 12, 19:12. For the question of Christ's obedience in Calvin's thought, see P van Buren, *Christ in Our Place: the Substitutionary Character of Calvin's Doctrine of Reconciliation* (Edinburgh: Oliver & Boyd, 1957), 27ff. This dissertation, prepared under Barth's supervision, shows reserve at critical points towards Calvin's emphasis on the historical humanity of Christ and the part it plays in the structure of the doctrine of God; see 11–13, 16–18, 38, 39.

48.  Calvin, *Commentary on St Matthew* 3:14.

49.  Calvin, *Commentary on St Luke* 23:28; cf *Commentary on St John* 17:24.

50.  Calvin, *Commentary on Hebrews* 5:9; *Commentary on St John* 13:32 and 17:1, *Commentary on Colossians* 2:15.

Son of God. Torrance expounds this in respect of the person of Christ by his interpretation of the doctrines of *an-* and *enhypostasis* as a commentary on the hypostatic union. This means that

> by *anhypostasia* classical Christology asserted that in the *assumptio carnis* the human nature of Christ had no independent *per se* subsistence apart from the event of the incarnation, apart from the hypostatic union. By *enhypostasia*, however, it asserted that in the *assumptio carnis* the human nature of Christ was given a real concrete subsistence within the hypostatic union—it was *enhypostatic* in the Word. *Anhypostasia* and *enhypostasia* are inseparable. In the incarnation the eternal Son assumed human nature into oneness with Himself, but in that assumption Jesus Christ is not only real man but a man.[51]

Torrance is careful to point out that these technical terms, related to the Chalcedonian decree, cannot be developed into 'a masterful idea of a system of thought', divorced from the reality to which they point: the mystery of the person of the incarnate one. He nevertheless sees their usefulness in directing us to both the 'unconditional priority of God's grace, that everything in theological knowledge derives from God's grace,' and to 'a full unimpaired place for human decision, human response, and human thinking in relation to the Truth of God's grace'.[52]

Thus, while the incarnation does not mean that God is limited by the creaturely form which is assumed into unity with God's self, the use of the terms *an-* and *enhypostasia* entail recognition of the reality of the creaturely structures of thought and being in all our relations with God. The incarnation in relation to creation establishes

> the infinite freedom and the unique kind of necessity that hold between God and the world, which not only preserve its contingence but which so ground it in the rationality of God as to provide for us in our creaturely existence an intelligible medium and objective basis for all our relations with God.[53]

---

51. Torrance, *Theology in Reconstruction*, 131, note 1; cf *Theological Science*, 217, 269.
52. Torrance, *Theological Science*, 217; cf *God and Rationality*, 137ff.
53. Torrance, *Space, Time and Incarnation*, 67, 68.

For this reason, Torrance does not see any methodological necessity to exclude the natural knowledge of created reality from playing a meaningful part in theological speech about God. In fact, he holds on the basis of the above analysis that 'it is no longer possible to operate scientifically with a separation between natural and revealed theology'.[54]

Torrance consequently has reservations about Barth's position in respect to this central issue.[55] Reminiscent of Barth's critical analysis of Quenstedt's formulation of the doctrine of analogy,[56] Torrance claims that, contrary to Barth, natural knowledge grounded in the person of Christ according to the doctrine of *an-* and *enhypostasia* must not be considered 'extrinsic but intrinsic to actual knowledge of God'.[57]

The theological relevance of Torrance's interpretation of the place of natural knowledge of God, within the context of his exposition of its Christological basis, may be seen in the way in which he relates his view of Jesus *enhypostatic* humanity to the Patristic and to Calvin's understanding of God's 'economic' condescension.

> The child Jesus 'cut his way forward' (*proekopte*) as he grew in wisdom and in favour with God and man [Luke 2:52]. In other words, Jesus' growth in wisdom was regarded as opening up a way for man to rise to true knowledge of the Father. Jesus Christ is not only the Truth who accommodated himself to us in order to reveal himself, not only the Word become flesh, but he is also Man hearing and obeying that Word, apprehending that Truth throughout his life on earth, so that he provides for us in his own obedient sonship within our human nature the Way whereby we are carried up to knowledge of God the Father.[58]

The essentially practical implication of Torrance's understanding of the God/creature relationship, in terms of knowledge of God and knowledge of the creature, is seen further in his reinterpretation of the unity of Christ's person:

---

54.   *Ibid*, 69.
55.   Torrance, *Space, Time and Incarnation*, and 'The Problem of Natural Theology in the Thought of Karl Barth'.
56.   See above, 113–116.
57.   Torrance, *Space, Time and Incarnation*, 70.
58.   Torrance, *Theology in Reconstruction*, 38; cf *Theological Science*, 218, 279.

the unity of the *an-* and *enhypostasia* in the person of the Son.[59] The unity of the person of Christ is related, in a trinitarian context, to the Eucharist and the church.[60]

However, to facilitate this practical implication it is necessary for Torrance to develop an alternative understanding of 'person' to that which has been dominant in the western theological tradition. He contends that, through St Augustine's concentration on the interior life of the believer, the idea of person became fatally twisted in an individualistic manner. It was easily identified with the logical subject of Aristotelian metaphysics. Through the influence of Boethius' definition, this became the dominant view of western theology. This is that *persona est rationalis naturae individua substantia.*[61]

Torrance seeks an alternative to this individualistic view of the person from Patristic sources, as developed by Richard of St Victor. This view is developed 'ontologically' from the doctrine of the Trinity and entails that 'person'

> is at once a relational and an ontological notion, for the relationship
> is not just a determination of our understanding but an inherent
> and ontic determination of personal existence. [So] God is personal
> in his own mode of Being involving all his existence and acts.[62]

This was the teaching taken over by John Calvin who reconstructed it in his view of the inter-relationship of the knowledge of God and ourselves that is grounded in the person of Christ. This is that knowledge of God is personal in the sense of being a

> direct dialogical encounter with God in Christ, for it is only
> through sharing in the knowledge of the Son by the Father and
> the knowledge of the Father by the Son, that we can know God as
> He has given Himself to us in Jesus Christ. Thus the organic unity
> of theology goes back in Christ to the unity of the Godhead.

---

59.   See on the following Torrance, *Theological Science*, 350ff; *Theology in Reconstruction*, 85ff, 189ff.

60.   Torrance, 'The Atonement and Oneness in the Church', in *Scottish Journal of Theology* 7/3 (1954): 249ff; cf *Theology in Reconstruction*, 131ff.

61.   Torrance, *Theological Science*, 306; cf *Theology in Reconstruction*, 85.

62.   Torrance, *Theology in Reconstruction*, 85.

Theological statements therefore 'participate sacramentally in the mystery of Christ as the Truth whom they refer to and upon which they rely for their reality'.[63]

## The doctrines of *an-* and *enhypostasis* as christological formulae

Before we assess the contributions of Mascall and Torrance to understanding the God / creature relationship in terms of knowledge of God and knowledge of the creature, we look at the criticisms that have been raised against the doctrines of *an-* and *enhypostasis*, which are central to the Reformed view as interpreted by Torrance.

According to J McIntyre,[64] the doctrine of *enhypostasia* arose out of the indecision of the Council of Chalcedon concerning the reality of the human individuality of the man Jesus within the hypostatic union. 'The vacuum which was created by the indecision of Chalcedon on the matter of an hypostasis for the human nature was one to be abhorred.'[65] This vacuum, according to McIntyre, was grounded in the Aristotelian metaphysics of those engaged in the christological controversies of the fifth and sixth centuries. The Aristotelian principle of 'no *physis anhypostatos*' is seen to be of central importance. This idea derived from Aristotle's understanding of the nature of reality as consisting of primary and secondary substance (*ousia*).[66]

The primary substance is the substance to which different predicates are referable. The actual substance is not predicable of anything; it exists in its own right. It is 'neither predicated of a subject nor exists in a subject'. Secondary substance, on the other hand, is predicated of something else and must always exist in something else.

McIntyre's thesis is that, in the christological controversies, the participants substituted this Aristotelian distinction between primary and secondary

---

63. Torrance, *Theological Science*, 138 150; cf 158, 159.

64. J McIntyre, *The Shape of Christology*, 86ff; cf A Grillmeier, 'Christ in Christian Tradition: From the Apostolic Age to Chalcedon (451)', translated by J Bowden from 'Die theologische und sprachliche Vorbereitung der christologishen Formel von Chalkedon', in *Das Konzil von Chalkedon*, edited by A Grillmeier and H Bacht, volume 1 (Würzburg: Echter Verlag, 1951; revised edition London: Mowbray, 1965), 308ff, 316–318, 336–337; GL Prestige, *God in Patristic Thought*, 271–274; AB Bruce, *The Humiliation of Christ*, 382–385; D Baillie, *God Was In Christ*, 90ff.

65. McIntyre, 88.

66. *Ibid*, 86.

substances for that between *hypostasis* and *physis*.[67] In addition, as in Aristotle, it was impossible without the primary substance for anything else to exist; in the christological context, this implies the principle of 'no *physis* without an *hypostasis*'.

In the Chalcedonian decree there could be no question of a second *hypostasis* beside that of the Word who is the subject of the incarnation. However, this seemed to mean that there could be no human *hypostasis*.[68] It is assumed in the decree that this lack does not reduce the true humanity of Christ. Leontius of Byzantium's doctrine of the enhypostatised human nature of Jesus in the *hypostasis* of the Word was meant to fill the vacuum created by the Chalcedonian view. However, McIntyre points out that if the *hypostasis* of the man Jesus were *enhypostatised* in that of the Logos, 'it would be impossible to differentiate the *man* Jesus from the man Peter or the man John unless, in some way, the human *hypostasis* was retained'. Further, 'if the *hypostasis* is an essential part of what we associate with humanity . . . then in respect of this humanity, Christ is not completely one with us.'[69] Soteriologically, this would mean that individual humans are not redeemed.

It would appear that McIntyre's strictures on the doctrine of *enhypostasis* call into question Torrance's attempt to develop the Reformed understanding of the christological basis of creaturely knowledge of God and creaturely knowledge of the creature, and thus of the understanding of the God / creature relationship it entails. For the non-particularity of the humanity of the man Jesus would mean that his knowledge of the Father would not be knowledge that could be related to our own particularity as human beings. Further, the non-particularity of the humanity of the man Jesus would compromise the priority of grace that is central to Torrance's thesis, since the act of the incarnation would not be such an act of condescension and accommodation to our creaturely status that Torrance's thesis requires.

However, there are important factors which ameliorate McIntyre's seemingly fundamental criticism of the *an-* and *enhypostatic* doctrine.

McIntyre's thesis is that the Aristotelian presuppositions of the christological debates led to the indecisiveness of the Chalcedonian settlement. It produced

---

67.   *Ibid*, 88.
68.   *Ibid*, 94.
69.   *Ibid*, 96, 97.

an 'impersonal' human nature of Jesus on the basis of the dictum derived from Aristotle, 'no physis *anhypostatos*'.[70]

It is this specifically Aristotelian view of the person which McIntyre sees as underlying the christological debate and which led to the bandaid solution of the *enhypostatic* doctrine, which Torrance rejects. He maintains it is this logical definition of 'person' that is excluded by the Christian revelation. This 'logical' definition gave rise to the Boethian definition we have already noted.[71] Against such a view of person as *naturae rationabilis individua substantia*, Torrance proposes a Victorine understanding of person which is 'relational and an ontological notion'. By this is meant that 'the divine essence and existence in the person (or persons) of God . . . is not just a determination of our understanding but an inherent and ontic determination of personal existence'.[72] God alone is

> personalising Person, and it is ultimately from His Word that all that is truly personal among us derives. We cannot understand His unique person by explaining it from our persons, but only through the fact that His person explains ours.[73]

In this essentially trinitarian understanding of person, statements about us in relation to God 'derive their basic form from the life and obedience of Jesus as the incarnate Son toward the Father in heaven'.[74] In Christ, 'there is minted out of our human life the material mode of speech and thought that is truly adapted to God'.[75]

In this, Torrance seems to be arguing for the position put forward earlier by HM Relton who, in discussing the *enhypostasis*, maintained that 'without God, human personality is incomplete, and that He alone can supply it with that which alone can help it to its full realization'.[76] Thus the humanity of Jesus, far

---

70.   *Ibid*, 94; cf 88.
71.   See above, 36–39.
72.   Torrance, *Theology in Reconstruction*, 85.
73.   Torrance, *Theological Science*, 147.
74.   *Ibid*, 160.
75.   *Ibid*, 279.
76.   HM Relton, *A Study in Christology: a Problem of the Relationship of the Two Natures of Christ* (London: SPCK, 1929), 226; cf 91ff. See also McIntyre, *The Shape of Christology*, 85: 'What we must not allow ourselves to forget is that it is the soteriological interest that is predominant in the discussion of the human nature of Christ—not the logical or even metaphysical.'

from being impersonal, is more fully personal than in any other person because of its complete union with God.

It does not seem to us to be the case that the Aristotelian logic was as all pervading in the christological debates as McIntyre claims, and that it led to the cul-de-sac of the impersonal human nature of Christ in the Chalcedonian settlement.[77] McIntyre appears to leave out of account a significant sector of the church in his view of the pre-Chalcedonian christological debates.

I refer to the way in which St Cyril of Alexandria understood the incarnation of the Logos in his confrontation with the Nestorian heresy. As distinct from the Antiochene view of *physis* as an assemblage of attributes,[78] which made it amenable to the kind of thought typified by the principle of 'no *physis anhypostatos*' which McIntyre's analysis finds so ubiquitous, St Cyril uses the word in the sense it had borne in Alexandria since the early fourth century. Its meaning was 'concrete individual, or independent existent'.[79] As such, it could be used synonymously with *hypostasis*. Consequently, when St Cyril wanted to express the unity of the incarnate one, his point of departure was always from the reality of the actual historical humanity of Christ. As a result, he spoke of the union as *kata physin* and *kata hypostasin*.[80]

We may illustrate this point by taking as an example St Cyril's defence of *Theotokos* as a title for the Virgin Mary. The term had been questioned by Nestorius who wished to use the term *Christotokos* in its place in order to indicate that Mary was not the mother of the divine but rather of the human nature of Christ.[81]

In his analysis of the christological issues in his debate with Nestorius, St Cyril uses a distinction, later taken up by Calvin, to which we have already drawn attention. This is that the actual historical particularity of the humanity of Jesus is the basis for distinguishing the voluntary activity of God in the economy of

---

77.  McIntyre, *The Shape of Christology*, 88, 89.

78.  JND Kelly, *Early Christian Doctrines*, 318.

79.  *Ibid*, 318; cf 224, and Clement of Alexandria, Mss. 1335 D in 'Early Christian Liturgies and Other Documents', in *Ante-Nicene Christian Library*, volume 24 (Edinburgh: T&T Clark, 1869), 177.

80.  *Ibid*, Cf Grillmeier, *The Council of Chalcedon*, 412.

81.  St Cyril, 'Five Tome Contradiction of the Blasphemies of Nestorius', Tome 1, 28. Quotations from St Cyril are taken from *A Library of Fathers of the the Holy Catholic Church* (Oxford: Parker & Rivingtons, 1881). It should be noted that, without exception, the translator renders *hypostasis* in St Cyril's writing as *person*. Cf JND Kelly, 320.

salvation from the nature of God's transcendent being in and for God's self. This distinction enables St Cyril, at one and the same time, to emphasise the unchangeable nature of God. The Word remains one with the Father, and yet at the same time the Word accommodates to himself the flesh of our humanity as the man Jesus. If the particularity of the man Jesus is called into question as delineating the condescension of God to the creature for its eternal salvation, then the whole process of human redemption is put in jeopardy.[82]

If this happens, as in the views espoused by Nestorius, then the humanity of Jesus can no longer be the basis for indicating the concrete actuality of God's condescension in the Word to the creature. The incarnation then simply illustrates a truth about the divine nature which may apply to all or no specific person of the Trinity. Further, if the nature of God *per se* is related to the creature in the act of incarnation then it follows, as Nestorius was always pointing out to his orthodox critics, that either the creature, in this case Mary, becomes a goddess and the deity is circumscribed by creaturely existence and thus ceases to be God, or another God comes into existence and the church is guilty of polytheism.[83]

The fundamental problem with Nestorius' position, according to St Cyril, was that he refused to understand the economy of God's movement toward the creature in terms of the particularity of the humanity of Christ as *the* incarnation, the *becoming* flesh of the Word. Instead, he chose to relate God and the creature in terms of an analysis of the relationship between the nature of God and the nature of the creature in terms of the internal being of the incarnate one.[84]

---

82. Cyril, *ibid*, 5, 6.
83. *Ibid*, 7: 'I [Nestorius] often asked them [St Cyril], do you say that Godhead has been begotten of the holy Virgin. They straightway recoil at the saying . . . then when I reply to this, What is incongruous do we say in advising to flee the word (*Theotokos*) and come to the phrase significant of the two natures . . . Either clearly acknowledge that Godhead has been born of Mary, or if you flee this expression as blasphemy, why say the same as I, dost thou feign thou sayest it not?'
84. It is no accident that the differing Latin and Greek versions of the Chalcedonian decree derive from this important distinction between Cyril and Nestorius. The unity of the person of Christ was considered as consisting 'of two natures' (εκ), according to the Cyrillian line, or 'in two natures' (εν), following the Antiochene Nestorian line. On this important question see P Schaff, *The Creeds of Christendom*, volume 2 (New York: Harper, 1919), 64, note 4; I Dorner, *History of the Development of the Doctrine of the Person of Christ*, translated by D Simon, volume 1 (Edinburgh: T&T Clark, 1861), part 2, 411; RV Sellers, *The Council of Chalcedon: a Historical and Doctrinal Survey* (London: SPCK, 1961), 217, 258; TH Bindley, *The Oecumenical*

According to St Cyril, this circumventing of the 'economy' of the incarnation in Nestorius' thought destroys both the deity of God and the creatureliness of the creature. For if the Word of God in the economy of salvation is understood simply in terms of the nature of God, it implies that Godhead is recipient of movement from place to place.

> If the Godhead be unembodied, at large and everywhere, and not in place and circumscript, how will it pass through a single body? [I]f he [Nestorius] says that the matter is true of Emmanuel singly and alone, let him teach the reason why . . . Hence not only once for all but many times over shall we find God has been made man, and not only the Word out of the Father, but I will add both the Father Himself and besides, the Holy Spirit.[85]

Not only does Nestorius' view lead to a dividing of the Godhead by assuming that in the incarnation it 'passes through' Mary, he also, despite his deepest intentions, denies the humanity of Jesus. Since Nestorius allots the human frailties of Jesus and likewise his resurrection from the dead and his exultation to his humanity, he must assume that the church's worship is directed toward a creature! The co-worshipped natures indicate that the humanity of Jesus, far from being safeguarded as humanity, is deified.

> Nestorius who feareth the charge of man worship, is caught in the act of being a man worshipper and is holden in the meshes of his own mis-counsel . . . That which is co-worshipped with another is altogether other than that which is worshipped. But *we* are accustomed to worship Emmanuel with one worship, not severing from the Word the body that was Personally [hypostatically] united to Him.[86]

---

*Documents of the Faith* (London: Methuen, 1950), 197; F Loofs, *Nestorius and His Place in the History of Christian Doctrine* (Cambridge: Cambridge University Press, 1914), 110, 111.

85.   Cyril, Tome 1, 34; cf 16, 18, 19, 35.
86.   Cyril, Tome 2, 70, 76, 77; cf 71, 72. The text is in *Cyrilli Archiepiscopi Alexandrini: Libri quinque contra Nestorium,* edited by PE Pusey  (Bruxelles: Culture et Civilisation, 1965), 122. Cf Cyril, Tome 2, 47–50.

It is therefore understandable that Dorner, on the basis of St Cyril's defence, judges that

> an unprejudiced consideration of the course which this dogma [Christology] pursued, must convince us that prior to the Council of Chalcedon, the doctrine of the duality of natures within the *unio*, was not really a doctrine of the church.[87]

From the evidence so far, it would seem that McIntyre's case for the ubiquity of the Aristotelian principle 'no *physis anhypostatos*' is not substantiated, except in so far as the Nestorian and Antiochene protagonists are concerned. It is not surprising, therefore, that both sides in the christological debate heralded Chalcedon as a triumph for Nestorianism![88]

The relevance of the above discussion on the doctrine of the *enhypostasis* of the human nature of Jesus in the Word incarnate derives from the place that TF Torrance gives to the particularity of the human nature of Jesus in his understanding of the God/creature relationship. In terms of the question of analogy, this is of decisive importance for Torrance's understanding of the God/creature relationship in terms of the question of knowledge of God and knowledge of the creature. As opposed to EL Mascall who relates the question of analogy to St Thomas Aquinas' analysis of existence in general, Torrance seeks to explicate the God/creature relationship in terms of the specific movement of God to the creature in the man Jesus Christ.[89] Thus,

---

87. I Dorner, *History of the Development of the Doctrine of the Person of Christ*, 108. The italics are in the original. Cf F Loofs, *Nestorius and his Place*, 97, 98; W Pannenberg, *Jesus: God and Man*, 287ff.

88. See A Grillmeier, 'Christ in Christian Tradition', 365, 452, 439–441; W Pannenberg, *Jesus: God and Man*, 289, 290; AB Bruce, *The Humiliation of Christ*, 49, 50; F Loofs, *Nestorius and His Place*, 90ff,190ff; JF Bethune-Baker, *Nestorius and His Teaching* (Cambridge: Cambridge University Press, 1908), 98, 99,189ff, 205, 211; D Baillie, *God Was In Christ*, 85ff, 91 note 1. For a contrary view see P Verghese, 'The Christology of the non-Chalcedonian Churches', in *Sobornost* 4/5 (1961): 255, 256; J Kamaris, 'The Problem of the Unification of the non-Chalcedonian Churches of the East with the Orthodox on the Basis of Cyril's Formula: *Mia physis tou Theou Logou sesarkomene*', in *The Greek Orthodox Theological Review* 10/2 (1964–5): 61ff.

89. Torrance, *Theology in Reconstruction*, 114.

if there is a true analogy of proportionality, as the Thomists aver, it must be grounded, not in any abstractly conceived ontological continuity between man and God, but on the *unio hypostatica* in which we have the union of God and man as God has set it forth in Christ.[90]

However, as we have seen in analysing Mascall's doctrine of analogy, the analogy of proportionality needs the analogy of attribution to save it from collapsing into univocal predication.[91] Whereas Mascall used the distinction between the mode of predication in the creature and that in God to form the basis of the analogy of attribution, Torrance seeks to use the historical particularity of the humanity of Jesus to achieve the same purpose. As opposed to the view that the *unio hypostatica* can be used to illustrate a general relationship between God and the creature, Torrance contends that the proper form of analogy should run:

> as divine and human natures are related in Christ, so in the church Christ and human nature are related . . . The analogy takes the proper form; as A is to B, so C is to D, where C is: A to B . . . . But when the false form of the analogy is drawn . . . then the human nature of Christ is omitted from it and that means that C is replaced by A in the form: as Α is to B, so A is to D. Thus this doctrine of the church turns out to be Monophysite.[92]

Thus, whilst affirming the reality and integrity of creaturely knowledge of God, Torrance is careful to relate this affirmation to the specific action of divine condescension and the accommodation of the Word of God to the conditions of creaturely existence.

> The *analogia entis* is entirely grounded upon the *analogia gratiae*, and only in an *analogia fidei* corresponding to the *analogia gratiae*

---

90.  *Ibid*; cf Torrance, *God and Rationality*, 137ff.
91.  See above, 124–129.
92.  Torrance, *Theology in Reconstruction*, 185. See also Torrance's agreement with the Catholic scholar G Söhngen who attempts to establish analogy in conformity with the movement of God to the creature, *ibid*, 116, 2; H Bouillard, *The Knowledge of God*, 123; TF Torrance, 'The Problem of Natural Theology in the Thought of Karl Barth'.

does the *analogia entis* have any truth or reality. Outside that, the truth of God is inevitably turned into a lie.[93]

Both Torrance and Mascall, in their own way, seek to understand the question of the God/creature relationship in terms of MB Foster's thesis[94] by emphasising the particularity and integrity of creaturely existence and knowledge in relationship to God the Creator. We find Torrance's presentation more convincing, not least because he is able to relate the particularity of the Christian revelation to the immanent and determinate rationality of the creature. He is able to show how, over against creation, God remains quite free in God's eternal self-existence. Yet at the same time God is free to relate to that which is not God by the ineffable voluntary condescension accomplished in the eternal Son's accommodation of himself to the way of creaturely being and knowing in order that the structures of our (fallen?) minds might be opened up to the truth of God's being and life. As a consequence of this interaction, God binds us to the created and contingent ways of knowing in all our relationships with God's self. It is on this basis that Torrance makes the statement that 'it is no longer possible to operate scientifically with a separation between natural and revealed theology'.[95] He is therefore able to give a coherent account of both

> the infinite freedom and unique kind of necessity that hold between God and the world, which not only preserve its contingence but which so ground it in the being and rationality of God as to provide us in our creaturely existence with an intelligible medium and an objective basis for all our relations with God.[96]

If we agree with the Reformed viewpoint, as interpreted by TF Torrance, concerning the part played by the natural structures of human understanding in knowing God and the world, then it follows that there are serious questions that need to be posed about Barth's method of understanding the same question. These questions will obviously relate to Barth's understanding of the Trinity as the basis of his theological epistemology and how this basis determines the answers he gives to the God/creature relationship. In terms of the question

---

93.  *Ibid,* 116; cf *Theological Science,* 273, 276, 278, 279.
94.  See above, 120–124.
95.  Torrance, *Space, Time and Incarnation,* 69.
96.  *Ibid,* 67, 68.

in relation to which we have chosen to articulate this relationship between knowledge of God and knowledge of the creature, we must raise the kind of question J McIntyre raises in his defence of Quenstedt's doctrine of analogical predication, to which Barth took such exception.[97]

McIntyre's defence of Quenstedt's analogy of intrinsic attribution affirms that 'when God creates, He creates beings whose creation constitutes their being. He [Quenstedt] is endeavouring to find out how you may speak of creatures who prior to salvation *are*, and in fact must *be* in order to be saved.'[98] We have indicated, in our appreciation of TF Torrance's presentation of the matter, that concentration of attention on the integrity of the contingent way of being and knowing of the creature does not in any way deny the transcendence and immanence of God when seen in the context of God's voluntary condescension to the creature in Christ. Here it has been seen to be true that the particularity of the humanity of Jesus expresses in itself both the freedom of God's condescension and the grounds for articulating knowledge of God and the creature in terms of the determinate way of creaturely knowing.[99]

### The viability of Barth's trinitarian method of understanding the God-creature relationship

Before we asses Barth's trinitarian method with respect to the question of the God / creature relationship in terms of knowledge of God and the creature, it will be necessary to provide the context of that assessment. This will be in terms of a review of the conclusions reached in the preceding chapters regarding Barth's methodology as it impinges upon the doctrine of creation.

The mere position of the doctrine of the Trinity in the *Church Dogmatics* is itself arresting and important in grasping its place in Barth's methodology. It appears in the context of Barth's doctrine of revelation. Barth wishes to emphasise that he is not talking about 'God' *per se*, as a theologian, but about the particular self-revealing God of the prophetic and apostolic witness in the Christian Scriptures and the church. He is writing *Church* dogmatics. The question that the actual event of revelation necessitates as elucidating its truth is one that asks after its possibility in terms of 'Who' the self-revealing God is. The freedom or

---

97.   See above, footnote 133, footnote 57.
98.   J McIntyre, 'Analogy', 17. Cf the same question, in respect of Barth's methodology, raised by H Bouillard in *The Knowledge of God*, 117
99.   Torrance, *God and Rationality,* 144ff; cf A Fairweather, *The Word as Truth,* 75ff.

Lordship, which the event of God's self-revelation presupposes, obviates any other question as to revelation's truth—a freedom of the creature for God which is not presupposed by the actuality of the event itself.

The question, then, of the nature of this self-revealing God can only follow the exposition of the doctrine of the Trinity that presupposes God's self-revelation: God's Lordship as the One who is the Revealer, the Revealed and the Revealedness in the event through which the creature is related to its Creator, Reconciler and promised Redeemer. The nature of a 'not yet trinitarian God' could only be discussed first if it is thought possible to identify God without reference to the event of revelation in which God exercises God's Lordship.[100]

The question as to the nature of the revealed God, in the doctrine of God, is expounded by Barth as an answer to the question that the revealed Lordship of God as the Triune God presupposes that God is the God who is able, who is free, to be the God of the creature. That God takes form amongst God's creatures means that God distinguishes God's self from God's self in a mode of being other than that in which God is the hidden God. The reality of Jesus Christ is the basis of this possibility in God. In being the self-revealed God, God remains who God is in and for God's self. Thus, the nature of this God must be one in which God is the God who loves in freedom. It is God's nature to be both love and freedom, but in that order. It is God's love as actualised in Jesus Christ which defines God's freedom.

The relationship between God and the creature, which emerged from Barth's exposition of the doctrines of Revelation and God, was seen to be grounded in God's self election to be the God of the creature. The eternal covenant resolved in God's being who God is as both One and Another in the unity of a Third is such that the event, in which God chooses God's self, coincides with God's resolve to be the creature's Lord in God's Son. God's self-relatedness as Father, Son and Holy Spirit is the basis of the covenant that is the both the internal ground of creation and creation is its external possibility. It is for this reason that Barth places the doctrine of election in the doctrine of God.

Thus, the distinctions and relationships in which the creature exists before and with God are characterised and known as they presuppose the reality and possibility of God's being who God is as the Creator, the creature's Lord in the event of self-revelation in Jesus Christ. That the doctrine of creation is anthropologically orientated in Barth's presentation corresponds to this fact:

---

100. See on this point K Rahner, *The Trinity*, in the important chapter 1,1–48.

that the Son of God in the inconceivable freedom in which God posits God's self as both one and another in the unity of a third, chose to be a man and not a stone or a fish. Barth's anthropology is, as the doctrine of creation as a whole, defined by God's choice to be this man Jesus. The existence of the human creature is predicated on the fact that it is the technical possibility of the realisation of the covenant that is identical with the person of Jesus Christ, as God for the human and the human for God and other human beings. As the image of God in its being both one and another, man and woman, humanity presupposes this compact and decision of God. Whether we experience our lives as such or not, this is our human reality that remains despite the onslaught of the power of evil. It remains because the one in whom humanity's being is presupposed in God remains faithful to himself. In choosing to sin, humanity chooses an ontological impossibility in view of the one who is its Lord.

This relationship between God and the creature, considered from the point of view of Barth's understanding of the basis of knowledge of the creature, the *analogia relationis*,[101] is one whose structure was determined both on the side of God and the side of the creature by the nature of the decision in which God exists as God for the creature in Jesus Christ. In our discussion of Barth's doctrine of analogy, we drew attention to the fact that his methodological exclusion of the place of creaturely knowledge of God and the creature cast doubt on the viability of his method to establish a God/creature relationship which took into account the integrity of the created structures of creaturely being and rationality.

It has been shown both from a neo-Thomist and a Reformed point of view how, in any account of the God/creature relationship, one must be able to demonstrate methodologically how God is and is not related to the contingent existence of the creature. This dialectic is unavoidable in any account of the God/ creature relationship, both in the interests of God's freedom and the created integrity of the creature's existence. Barth's method finds great difficulty in giving place to this crucial element. In considering the immanent relationship of creatures with their Creator, the continuities and distinctions of creaturely existence are postulated on the basis of God's freedom to repeat and confirm God's own self *ad extra*.[102] This has led not only critics but also Barth's friends to complain of

---

101. See above, 116–118.

102. In this context I agree with von Balthasar's comment: '*Die Gnadenordnung der Menschwerdung setz sich die Schöpfungsordnung voraus, die, von ihr verschieden, doch immer wieder zu sehr auf sie reduziert wird.*' See HU von Balthasar, *Karl Barth:*

a conceptual gap between theological dogmatics and our understanding of created existence, rational as well as physical . . . [Barth] tends to restrict the relation between them to the *event* of grace, without developing, at any rate in any adequate way, the ontology of the creaturely structures which it assumes.[103]

Thus, it would appear that Barth's development of the doctrine of the Trinity from an analysis of the event structure of God's self-revelation entails the methodological exclusion of what we have taken to be critical elements in the theological meaning of the God/creature relationship.[104]

---

*Darstellung und Deutung seiner Theologie*, 148. Cf Barth, *CD* 1/1, 426.

103. TF Torrance, 'The Problem of Natural Theology in the Thought of Karl Barth', 133, 134, and *Space, Time and Incarnation*, 65; cf Berkouwer, *The Triumph of Grace in the Theology of Karl Barth*, 56; W Kreck, '*Analogia Fidei* oder *Analogia Entis*?, in *Antwort: Kal Barth zum siebzigsten Geburtstag am 10. Mai 1956* (Zürich: Evangelischer Verlag, 1956), 273–286.

104. See G Watson, 'Karl Barth and St Anselm's Theological Programme', 31–35. Also RH Roberts, *A Theology On Its Way? Essays on Karl Barth* (Edinburgh: T&T Clark, 1991), who makes the important point, with which the general structure of my critique of Barth agrees, that Barth's reunification of the immanent and economic doctrines of the Trinity contains the potential for serious distortions. It reemphasises those characteristics of western Trinitarian thought that finally tend to deny the centrality of the Trinity in Christian doctrinal teaching. Not merely Barth's understanding of the Trinity is called into question, but the whole Western tradition. Since Augustine this has relied upon a '*filioquist*' and christologically-conditioned extrapolation of the doctrine of the Trinity expressed in both ecclesiology and spirituality which has tended towards distortion, even the disintegration of the trinitarian framework (92).

# Chapter Five

# Conclusion

The issues raised in our analysis and assessment of Barth's understanding of the God/creature relationship on the basis of his trinitarian methodology involve important questions as to the structure and meaning of dogma in the church. We have analysed Barth's presentation of the dogma of the Trinity in his doctrine of revelation as a 'critical principle' in terms of his method of achieving understanding of the event of God's self-revelation and the relationship between God and the creature.[1]

However, there is a major tradition of the church in which the dogma of the Trinity has been understood less as doctrine and more as that which expresses the life of the church lived in the Trinity as the form of the renewal of created existence. Here, the relativity of creaturely existence is taken to be part of the dogma which celebrates its ontological renewal as part of the creature's evolving relationship with its Creator and Redeemer.

## The dogma of the Trinity in the eastern and the western church

E Schlink has drawn attention to the significance of the different kinds of statements the church uses in its speech about God in a variety of settings. The contradictory but complementary statements the church makes about Jesus' historicity and his unity with the eternal God indicate that the church does not simply believe it has to do with a finite subject who can be defined in the language it uses to describe the reality to which it points. Schlink describes as 'doxological' the structure of such statements the church uses to speak about Christ's unity with the Father and his unity with human beings.[2] These are statements based on events which have been experienced as having occurred as originating from God. Since designations and relations drawn from the finite

---

1.  Barth, *Table Talk* (Edinburgh: Oliver and Boyd, 1963), 48, 49.
2.  E Schlink, *The Coming Christ and the Coming Church* (Edinburgh: Oliver & Boyd, 1967), 21, 22; Cf 16ff, 87ff; W Pannenberg, *Basic Questions in Theology*, volume 1 (London: SCM, 1970), 211ff; TF Torrance, *Theological Science*, 158–161; *God and Rationality* (Oxford: Oxford University Press, 1971), 156ff; G Ebeling, *Theology and Proclamation* (London: Collins, 1960), 82ff.

realm are transferred to the eternal God, contradictory conceptions inescapably arise. Here in the church, however, human conceptualisation sacrifices itself in the act of adoration. The nature of the reference of our words to the divine reality itself is 'withdrawn from our purview by the very act of adoration.'[3]

In using this expression 'doxological' for the reference of human language to the infinite being of God, on the basis of the experience of God's soteriological action in historical events, Schlink distinguishes it from what he calls 'kerygmatic' statements. These latter speak of earthly events that are understood to be fixed by the church's tradition. They are

> chiefly concerned with transmission of fixed pieces of church tradition. This includes the tradition of our Lord's deeds, and His passion as well as the appearance of the risen Lord.[4]

Doxological statements, on the other hand, intend to speak of God's eternal being as such. They are praise of the eternal God on the basis of God's deeds.

> Doxology is not only concerned with God's activity in history but with God Himself in His own eternal reality . . . Consequently, in the development of doxology we can observe the appearance of statements about God's existence, essence, and properties, whose purpose it is to exalt His eternal unchangeableness which comprehends all history.[5]

Doxological statements, in being offered to God in praise, are acknowledged to be 'broken open' from above in the way in which they refer to God's being. For this reason, doxological statements cannot be used as premises from which conclusions about God can be drawn without further ado. The conceptual clarity of doxological statements disappears from the horizon of the worshipper's thought. While in 'kerygmatic' statements the 'I' of the witness expressly appears and vouches for the truth that is witnessed to, in 'doxological' statements the 'I' who speaks disappears. 'The "I" is sacrificed in doxology. Thus doxology is always a sacrifice of praise.'[6]

---

3.    Pannenberg, *Basic Questions*, 219.
4.    Schlink, *The Coming Christ*, 25.
5.    *Ibid*, 21, 22.
6.    *Ibid*, 22.

If the doxological statements of the church's worship are not to be simply expressions of the subjectivity of the worshipper, it is important to realise that the liturgical structure in which doxology is celebrated is shaped by the reality it is intended to serve. In this the church is thrown back upon the strategic importance of the historical humanity of Jesus in whom God assimilates the creature's thought-forms and opens them up to the truth of God's own life. In Jesus Christ, 'we are provided with the very essence and core of man's worship of God . . . for He constitutes in His vicarious humanity the eloquent reality of our worship.'[7]

Schlink draws attention to the significant fact that the progressive deformation of the liturgical structure of the church's creedal statements took place in Western as distinct from Eastern Christianity.[8] In the West, doxological elements in the church's confession were used as major premises of arguments from which statements are deduced about the historical content of revelation. Serious logical problems arise when this happens, and these logical problems soon become theological problems.[9]

The unity and coherence of such statements, that is, the relationship between 'doxological' and 'kerygmatic' statements, is understood to be grounded in the God to whom and before whom the statements are made. There is no middle term joining the propositions as they appear. This logical discrepancy is to be emphasised since it draws attention to the peculiar status of such statements. Theological coherence can here only be expressed if the unexpressed condition of the statements is fulfilled; this is that the theologian is the recipient of the gracious encroachment of God.[10] This entails that the *Sitz im Leben* of the statements cannot be ignored when assessing their meaning. In fact, it is decisive in determining their meaning and their relationship to each other.

These considerations bear directly on the development of the church's doctrine of the Trinity and, in our view, have not been sufficiently taken into account in understanding the place and meaning of that central Christian confession. They have been shown to be of crucial importance in understanding Barth's method and, consequently, his understanding of the God/creature

---

7.    Torrance, *God and Rationality*, 157, 158. Cf *Theology in Reconstruction*, 38ff; Church of Scotland Report, *Worship in the Reformed Church*, edited by JB Torrance.
8.    Schlink, *The Coming* Christ, 42; cf 37ff, 93–95.
9.    *Ibid*, 34, 35, 66ff, 74–77.
10.   See G Watson, 'The Basis of Union Considered as a Confessional Statement', in *Colloquium* 8/2 (1976): 14ff.

relationship. Therefore, we propose to turn to the Eastern Church's view of the place of the Trinity in the life of the church to gain a perspective on its setting and meaning. We will pay particular attention to the way in which creaturely thought and experience find their place in the celebration of the God / creature relation in creation and reconciliation.

### St Basil's 'De Spiritu Sancto'

In St Basil's defence of the deity of the Spirit, we note the importance of the human experience of salvation within the liturgical structure of St Basil's argument. So it is not without significance that the dispute, which occasioned this work, broke out in relation to the celebration of the liturgy.

> When praying with the people and using the doxology to God the Father in both forms, at one time 'with the Son together *with* the Holy Ghost' and at another time 'through the Son *in* the Holy Ghost', I was attacked by some of those present on the ground that I was introducing novel and at the same time mutually contradictory terms.[11]

The deniers of the Spirit's deity maintained that, since the preposition 'in' predicated creaturely circumscription to that which is essentially uncircumscribed, then by definition the Spirit cannot be equal with the Father and the Son, which the copula 'with' implies in the doxological ascription.[12] St Basil replies that such an assertion springs from a failure to distinguish between the undivided unity of God who is the object of all doxological statements and the temporal missions of the trinitarian *hypostases*. The former, as common to all *hypostases*, cannot be thought of as divided in any sense whatsoever.[13] St Basil agrees with his opponents that if any of the divine *hypostases* are impugned, with respect to their being one with each other in the ineffable divine unity, then all are called into question.[14]

However, on that account St Basil does not deny that prepositions such as 'of', 'through' and 'in' are properly ascribed to God. The church recognises both

---

11.   Basil, 'De Spiritu Sancto', in *The Library of Nicene and Post-Nicene Fathers*, edited by Schaff & Wace, volume 8, chapter 1, section 1.3.
12.   *Ibid*, chapter 4, section 6.5.
13.   *Ibid*, chapter 5, sections 8–12; chapter 6, sections 13, 14.
14.   Basil, 'De Spiritu Sancto', chapter 6, section 15.

aspects: the ineffable undivided unity of God and the distinct *hypostases* which are associated with words which describe local movement and are taken by St Basil's opponents to divide the deity.

> I say the church recognises both uses and deprecates neither as subversive of the other. For whenever we are contemplating the majesty of the nature of the Only Begotten, and the excellence of His dignity, we bear witness that the glory is *with* the Father; while on the other hand, whenever we bethink us of His bestowal on us of good gifts, and of our access to and admission into, the household of God, we confess that this grace is effected for us *through* Him and *by* Him. It follows that the one phrase '*with whom*' is the proper one to be used in the ascription of glory, while the other, '*through whom*' is especially appropriate in giving thanks.[15]

We immediately notice that, for St Basil, the distinctions between the trinitarian *hypostases* are understood in terms of the time-conditioned elements associated with the events of the history of salvation. The unity of the *hypostases* is understood in terms of an ineffability relative to these time-conditioned elements. The unity of God is not a logical concept related to the *hypostatic* distinction, but is of a doxological nature that acknowledges the free condescension of God to the creature in creation and reconciliation and promised redemption celebrated in the liturgy. Only Arians and their like who refuse to acknowledge the liturgical basis of the church's celebration of the deity of the Spirit, 'with' and 'in' the Father and the Son, could introduce the notion of an above and a below in God, an *a priori* and an *a posteriori*.[16]

St Basil points out further[17] that the freedom of God in relation to God's action in the economy of salvation, and the voluntary nature of this action in relation to humankind, is understood in precisely the same way as the ineffable unity of God in relation to the distinctions in the economy. The economy takes place not in order that God's being may be added to but that the creature may be renewed as a creature. As the praise that is offered to God in the church's worship acknowledges God's ineffable unity to be grounded in the distinctions involved in the action of God in the economy of salvation, so too God's freedom

---

15. *Ibid*, chapter 7, section 16.
16. *Ibid*, chapter 8, section 18
17. *Ibid*.

is acknowledged as that of the creature's gracious Lord for precisely the same reason.

## The relationship between *dogma* and *kerygma* in *'De Spiritu Sancto'*

The distinction which St Basil draws between the ineffable unity of God—like the distinctions between the *hypostases* on the basis of the history of God's activity—is related to another distinction he draws: between *dogma* and *kerygma*. *Dogma* refers to God's ineffable unity and is 'observed in silence', while *kerygma* refers to the story of God's redemptive acts in history and is 'proclaimed to the world'.[18]

To prevent the kind of logical projections of which the deniers of the Spirit's deity were guilty, in which the time-conditioned predicates related to the economy of salvation were applied to the undivided unity of God, St Basil maintains that 'Dogma is made difficult to understand for the very advantage of the reader'.[19] The 'difficulty' to which St Basil refers concerns the legitimate use of both words 'with' and 'in' in the understanding of the dogma of the deity of the Spirit, in this basically liturgical structure of dogma.

The 'difficulty' refers to the suspension of logical form in the relationship between the two kinds of statements made in the celebration of the creature's renewal by God's action. This action that shapes the structure of the liturgy is the voluntary condescension of God in the economy of salvation, whereby God accommodates in the Son (since for Basil the church's teaching of *opera trinitatis ad extra sunt indivisa* is assumed) to the creaturely mode of being in relationship to God's self. By this action our creaturely being and thought are configured by God's action to the shape of God's condescension, taking into account, on the one hand, its voluntary nature and, on the other, the reality of the Son's humanity now united to his relationship to the Father and the Spirit.[20] The 'difficulty in understanding' to which St Basil refers, and which had proved a stumbling block to his opponents, is precisely the basis of the church's thanksgiving. St Basil therefore asks his opponents, 'shall this His care for us degrade to meanness our thoughts of Him?'[21]

---

18.  *Ibid.*
19.  *Ibid*, chapter 27, section 66.
20.  See the important chapter, 'The Nature of Truth', in TF Torrance, *Theological Science*, 146ff.
21.  Basil, 'De Spiritu Sancto', chapter 27, section 66.

## The deity of the Spirit

In understanding the deity of the Spirit, St Basil applies the same argument as that which he uses to defend the deity of the Son. Those predicates which the deniers of the Spirit use to degrade the Spirit as a creature—the ascription *'in'* as distinct from *'with'*—are not to be understood as though God is divided by being circumscribed by time and place. Rather, they indicate the ineffable voluntary condescension that takes place not that God's being may be added to or subtracted from, but that the creature may be renewed as a creature in relationship to God. Thus, the Spirit does not participate in the Godhead as if in need of being given anything—the Spirit is one with the Father and the Son. The Spirit is 'sent' and is 'given' not for the Spirit's sake but for our sake. The Spirit is

> impassibly divided, shared without loss of ceasing to be entire . . .
> to everyone who receives it, as though given to him alone, and yet
> it sends forth grace sufficient and full for all mankind.[22]

As with the Son so with the Spirit: to question the Spirit being *with* the Father is to divide the deity; to question the Spirit being *in* us or the church, and thus imply creaturely circumscription, is to deny the economy of salvation, God's voluntary condescension to the creature.

> For when renewing man, by breathing on the face of the disciples,
> restoring the grace, that came of the inbreathing of God, which
> man had lost, what did Jesus say? 'Receive ye the Holy Spirit.'[23]

We see in St Basil a determination to hold to the tradition of the church's liturgical celebration by explaining its words to the deniers of the Spirit's deity in such a way that the truth which it celebrates is that which configures its use. Thus, when the church considers the appropriateness or otherwise of language in relationship to God, the issue cannot be discussed apart from the context in which human beings are related to the present activity of God in the world for the purpose of their ontological renewal as human beings. This context for St Basil is the Divine Liturgy.

---

22.  *Ibid*, chapter 9, section 22; cf chapters 10–15.
23.  *Ibid*, chapter 16, section 39; cf chapter 19, section 49; 24, section 56.

## Nicaea and the unity of God

At the Council of Nicaea, Jesus Christ was declared to be *homoousios* with God the Father. The anathema of the creed against those who asserted that the Son came into existence from the non-existent, or from another *hypostasis* or *ousia* distinct from the Father, entailed that these two terms, which later became associated with the unity and the triplicity of God, 'were substantially identical.'[24]

Despite this, what Nicaea specifically excluded was what St Basil calls a unity 'as when two copper coins alike are made of the same substance, that the Father and the Son are derived from a third.'[25] A generic view of the unity of the Father and the Son is specifically excluded. Thus, the unity envisaged by the Creed was one which took as its point of departure the difference based in the economy between the appearance of God in the flesh, and on the basis of this contingent fact, God's ineffable being as the Father who sent the Son. As the particularity of the Son's revelation was the point of departure in understanding the personal divine unity in the Father, this conception of *homoousios* excluded the Sabellian error of identity of *hypostases*. A unitary object cannot be *homoousios* with itself. The use of the term *homoousios* itself implies plurality of objective *hypostases*.

I agree therefore with Prestige in his claim that,

> so far as the Council of Nicaea is concerned, the problem of the divine unity did not arise, since, the party which can later be designated Athanasian regarded the term *homoousios* as containing within itself the true and proper solution of that problem also.[26]

It is obvious that those who did not share the Athanasian approach to God's unity and diversity, on the basis of the *homoousios*, grew suspicious of the assumed identity by the Council of the terms *ousia* and *hypostasis*. At the Council of Alexandria (361)[27] under the leadership of Athanasius, it was formally agreed

---

24.   GL Prestige, *God in Patristic Thought* (London: SPCK, 1956), 168.
25.   Basil, Epistle No 52, section 1.
26.   Prestige, *God in Patristic Thought*, 213. On this important issue see St Cyril of Alexandria, 'Five Tome Contradiction', Tome 1, 28–35; Tome 2, 47–50, 53, 54, 56, 57; Tome 4, 152; Tome 5, 168–174, 177, 178, 181, and 'Scholia on the Incarnation of the Only Begotten', 186, 187, 190–192,198, 199, 202, 230, 231. See also N Nissiotis, 'The Importance of the Doctrine of the Trinity for Church Life and Theology', in *The Orthodox Ethos*, edited by AJ Philippou, volume 1, 43ff.
27.   See on the following Kelly, *Early Christian Doctrines*, 253, 254.

that the formula 'three *hypostases*', hitherto suspect by some because it sounded like three separate deities, was pronounced legitimate provided it did not carry the Arian connotation. Also the seemingly opposite 'one *hypostasis*' was equally approved provided there was no Sabellian intent.

After the work of the Cappadocian Fathers, the doctrine of the Trinity came to be formulated in the East as teaching one *ousia* and three *hypostases*. 'The unity of the *ousia*, or Godhead, follows from the unity of the divine action',[28] which we see in revelation. Gregory of Nyssa put it this way:

> If we observe a single activity of the Father, Son and Holy Spirit, in no respect different in the case of any, we are obliged to infer unity of nature from the identity of activity; for the Father, Son and Holy Spirit co-operate in sanctifying, quickening, consoling and so on.[29]

This statement of Gregory brings us back again to the central concern in the Eastern Church with the practical orientation of the church's dogma, grounded as it is in the church's liturgical celebration of the creature's renewal. It was precisely this practical concern that led to development in the East of the doctrine of the divine *energia*. This was to combat the influence of a version of western theology in which the creature's participation in the life of God through the economy of salvation, celebrated in the liturgy, was being called into question.[30] To safeguard this reality of the creature's unity with God and at the same time distinguish it from that unity achieved by God in Jesus Christ—the *hypostatic* unity—the notion of the unity according to the divine *energia* was developed. If no such distinction were developed, then the reality of God's particular unity with the creature in Christ would be called into question by being seen as an illustration of a general condition of the relationship between God and creation. Then both the Creator and the creature would be denied as a result of the creation being seen as united by nature to the Creator.[31]

---

28. *Ibid*, 266.
29. Quoted in Kelly, 266; cf Torrance, *Theology in Reconstruction*, 31–45.
30. On the following, see V Lossky, *The Mystical Theology of the Eastern Church*, 80, 81; G Florovsky, 'St Gregory Palamas and the Tradition of the Fathers', in *Sobornost* 4/4 (1961): 165ff, 175, 176.
31. Lossky, *Mystical Theology*, 73, 85, 86, 89, 93–97; RC Walls, 'St Gregory Palamas', in *Scottish Journal of Theology* 21/4 (1968): 435ff, 445, 446.

The doctrine of the union according to the *energia* designates the kind of union appropriate to creaturely existence between the Creator and the creature consequent on the activity of God in the economy of salvation. This relationship with the creature, which involves all the trinitarian *hypostases,* cannot be interiorised within the divine being as if it were a natural determination of the divine being. So, for example, the Holy Spirit cannot be reduced to being a relationship between the Father and the Son; concern for a common nature in understanding the divine unity can never pre-empt the distinctiveness of the Spirit's work in the dynamic of salvation.[32]

The conciliar decisions of the fourteenth century, subsequent to the dispute between St Gregory Palamas and the Calabrian monk Barlaam, established an

> ineffable distinction, other than that between His [God's] essence and His persons according to which He is, under different aspects, both totally inaccessible and at the same time totally accessible. This distinction is that between the essence of God , or His nature, properly so called, which is inaccessible, unknowable and incommunicable, and the energies or divine operations . . . in which He goes forth from Himself, manifests, communicates and gives Himself.[33]

Palamas' position is that the church must understand an essential union in terms of the *ousia* of God, a *hypostatic* union according to the economy of salvation and a union according to the *energia.*[34]

This development in the Eastern Church's understanding of the trinitarian dogma again emphasises the practical orientation of the dogma in the church. It

---

32.   Lossky, *Mystical Theology,* 54–57, 62, 81; W Ullmann, 'Das filioque als Problem oekumenischer Theologie', in *Kerygma und Dogma* 1 (1970): 58ff.

33.   Lossky, *Mystical Theology,* 70; cf 69ff, 76ff; J Meyendorff, *A Study of Gregory Palamas* (London: Faith Press, 1964), 191ff, 215, 216; Barth's methodological interest in the unity of the self-revealed God leads him to reject Palamas' position and take sides with Barlaam. He sees the divine *energia* as 'a half way stage of the divine, on which it becomes capable of a link with the creature and can communicate to it a higher nature'. See Barth, *CD* 2/1 332. The same sort of concern is shared by B Leeming, 'Rediscovering Eastern Christendom', in *Orthodox-Catholic Relations,* edited by AH Armstrong and EJB Fry (London: Longman, Darton and Todd, 1964), 15ff, 39, 40; but see TF Torrance, *Theology in Reconstruction,* 243.

34.   Meyendorff, *A Study of Gregory Palamas,* 183; cf 219.

is the experience of the creature's ontological renewal celebrated in the liturgy that is its locus. Schlink and Rahner also underline the point.[35] In the East, 'the Eucharistic celebration makes operative the whole economy of salvation, in which the whole Trinity is involved.'[36] This is not mere recital of words, but 'a real-ontological communication to man of the revealed reality as such.'[37]

## Tertullian and the Trinity in the West

The general phenomenon of differences between the eastern and western approaches to the trinitarian dogma has often been commented upon in theological textbooks. GLPrestige, for example, maintains that

> the groundwork of the Cappodocian Fathers' thought lay in the triplicity of equal *hypostaseis*, and the identity of the divine *ousia* came second in order of prominence to their mind.[38]

Or Karl Rahner contends that the Greeks

> considered only the (for them subsequent) problem of the unity of the three persons, whom they encountered as distinct both in their theology *and* in salvation history.[39]

In contrast with this approach for which the history of the divine economy of salvation was essential, as it provided the structure and purpose of the church's liturgical life, the western view of the trinitarian dogma 'begins with the one God, the one divine essence, and only afterwards does it see God as three

---

35. Schlink, *The Coming Christ*, 42ff; Rahner, *The Trinity*, 18ff; see also Nissiotis, 'The Importance of the Doctrine of the Trinity', 32, and N Zervov, 'The Worship of the Orthodox Church and its Message', in *The Orthodox Ethos*, volume 1 (Oxford: Holywell Press, 1964), 115ff.

36. IH Dalmais, *The Eastern Liturgies*, (London: Burns and Oates, 1960), 77.

37. Rahner, *The Trinity*, 14, note 10; A Schmemann, 'Liturgy and Theology', in *The Greek Orthodox Theological Review* 17/1 (1972): 95; TF Torrance, 'Come Creator Spirit for the Renewal of Worship and Witness', in *Theology in Reconstruction*, 240ff. See also the 'Commentary on the Divine Liturgy of Chrysostom', by Symeon of Thessalonica (d. 1429) in *The Liturgies of SS Mark, James, Clement, Chrysostom and Basil*, translated by JM Neale and RF Littledale (London: J Masters, 1865), xxiff.

38. Prestige, *God in Patristic Thought*, 242, 243.

39. Rahner, *The Trinity*, 18, note 13; the word is *italicised* in the original

persons.' Or the Latin view emphasises the fact that 'God is one Object and three Subjects (*una substantia, tres personae*).[40]

Consequently, as Rahner emphasises, the western dogmatics were characterised by a separation between God's threefoldedness and God's unity, the latter taking precedent over the former. The result is that the doctrine of God 'becomes quite philosophical and refers hardly at all to salvation history.'[41]

Thus, when we look at the way Tertullian understands the threefoldedness of God in his treatise *Ad Praxean*, what strikes us is that the term 'economy' is used to explain the eternal intra-divine relationships on the principle that division of authority does not entail division of nature.[42] Attention here is focused away from the history of salvation to the question of how threefoldedness and unity can be *understood* as real yet not self-contradictory. Thus, Tertullian sees the unity of God as

> single individual rule, which does not, because it is government of one, preclude him whose government it is, either from having a son, or from having made himself actually a son to himself, or from ministering his own monarchy by whatever agents he will.[43]

Tertullian then goes on to refer to the comparison of this reality to the relationship in one person between thought and consciousness. This would assume particular importance in St Augustine's later formulation of the trinitarian doctrine for the Western Church. This comparison governs Tertullian's notion of the distinction between the persons rather than the distinctions being related to the history of salvation.[44] The consubstantiality of the Son is understood in terms of his being the Reason or Wisdom of God; and that which is the Reason or Wisdom of all created rationality cannot itself be without substance.

---

40.  Rahner, *ibid*, 17 and Prestige, *God in Patristic Thought*, 235; cf Kelly, *Early Christian Doctrines*, 272ff.

41.  Rahner, *ibid*, 18.

42.  On the following see the translation of Tertullian, *Ad Praxean* in *Ante-Nicene Christian Library*, volume 15, number 11; cf also Prestige, 97ff; A von Harnack, *History of Dogma*, volume 2, 257ff.

43.  Tertullian, *ibid*, chapter 3, 338.

44.  See above, 102ff.

Whatever, therefore, was the substance of the Word that I designate a Person, I claim for it the name Son, and while I recognise the Son, I assert his distinction as second to the Father.[45]

Harnack maintains that a distinction drawn on this basis is nothing but a 'juristic distinction' and a 'legal fiction'.[46] It must be admitted that Tertullian's approach to the divine economy is one in which

the conception of function is becoming very prominent . . . The economy of which Tertullian is speaking is not that of the Son, whether in redemption or any other connection. It is expressly 'his economy', that is the economy of the being of God . . . [I]t is not an economy of redemption nor an economy of revelation, but an economy of divine being.[47]

The Holy Spirit is seen in terms of the economy of the divine being as a relationship between the Father and the Son. 'Just as the fruit of the tree is a third from the root, or as the stream out of the river is third from the fountain, or as the apex of the ray is third from the sun.'[48]

This idea of unity has been aptly described as 'organic', in that it is established by a unifying and organising source that administers its authority in a threefold manner.[49]

Since the content of the history of salvation is not the basis upon which the unity of God is confessed, the relationship between God and the creature, which this conception entails, will be quite different to that encountered in the Eastern Church's conception. Instead of allowing the particularity of the history concerned to enter into the meaning of the freedom and transcendence of God who condescends to the creature, the intra-mundane relationships will tend to become a reflection of the internal life of deity itself. It is not surprising then,

---

45.  Tertullian, *ibid*, chapter 7, 345, 346.
46.  Harnack, *ibid*, 282, 283.
47.  Prestige, *ibid*, 105, 106.
48.  Tertullian, chapter 8, 348.
49.  Prestige, 97. Cf 101, 102; JHS Burleigh, 'The Doctrine of the Holy Spirit in the Latin Fathers', in *Scottish Journal of Theology* 7/2 (1954): 113ff, 123–125; J Meyendorff, *The Orthodox Church: its Past and its Role in the World Today* (Crestwood NY: St Vladimir's Seminary Press, 1996), 196, 197.

as Harnack has noted,[50] that there is a direct link between Tertullian's turn to Montanism and his view of how God and the creature are related in the economy of salvation. Tertullian sees a structural relationship between the dispensations of the Father and the Son in the history of the world that is passed and now a dispensation of the Spirit and the history that is to come. World history is thus structured according to the economy of the divine being. It becomes a pale reflection of eternity in a manner that would be anathema to the Greeks and the eastern tradition. As Grillmeier sees it,

> creation and history threaten to become factors in the inner processions of God. The neat distinctions between the *processiones* and the *missiones* outside Him [God] must be developed in a careful process without the two being separated. Only in this way can the danger of pantheism, and also of subordinationism, be avoided. The tremendous attempt to make the doctrine of the Trinity and the Incarnation into a *Weltanschauung* had come to grief on this idea of *oikonomia*.[51]

## Tertullian and St Irenaeus on the economy

It will illustrate the point we are seeking to emphasise—the differences between the east and the west with respect to the trinitarian dogma—if a comparison is drawn between Tertullian and St Irenaeus and their approach to the meaning and place of the 'economy' in their respective theological systems.

Harnack draws attention to an important aspect of this matter (even though he in no sense can be regarded as sympathetic to what he understands to be the 'physical' view of salvation common in the Eastern Church), that

> whereas Tertullian developed the Logos doctrine without reference to the historical Jesus, the truth rather being that he simply added the incarnation to the already existing theory of the subject, there is no doubt that Irenaeus, as a rule, made Jesus Christ, whom he knew as God and man, the starting point of his speculations.[52]

---

50. Harnack, *ibid*, 311.
51. Grillmeier, 'Christ in Christian Traddition', 133; cf 142, 143.
52. Harnack, *History of Dogma,* volume 2, 262. Cf on the same issue the significant differences found in the church confessions found in the writings of Irenaeus and Tertullian in Schaff, *The Creeds of Christendom,* volume 2, 13ff.

The central importance of the historical humanity of the incarnate Son for St Irenaeus' view of the economy may be gathered from his key concept of 'recapitulation'[53] that he uses to expound the work of Christ. The foundation of this idea is that, in the humanity of the Son of God, the Son in the reverse direction traverses the pathway of fallen humanity in Adam so that he becomes a new Adam and the author of a new humanity.

> He therefore, in His work of recapitulation, summed up all things, both waging war against our enemy, and crushing him who at the beginning had led us away captive in Adam . . . in order that, as our species went down to death through vanquished man, so may we ascend to life again through a victorious one.[54]

In fulfilling his work of recapitulation, the strategic importance of Jesus' humanity is evident in that at every point he placed himself in the same circumstances as Adam and was confronted with the same choices. Thus was wrought in the human and creaturely sphere the decisive victory, the benefits of which can pass to all human kind because Christ acted as their representative champion.[55] Under these conditions Christ kept the commandments of the law, in spite of the temptations of the Devil. 'As a consequence, there was done away that infringement of God's commandment which had occurred in Adam.'[56] St Irenaeus emphasises that this was a grim struggle in which the Son of God was engaged for his fellow human beings against all that negates their humanity in relationship to God and each other.[57] The importance of this human struggle of the Son of God is the foundation for St Irenaeus' view of the relationship established by the risen Christ with humanity in the church. The dominating

---

53. The translation of Irenaeus, *Adversus Haereses* (2 volumes) is that found in the *Ante-Nicene Christian Library*. On 'recapitulation' see book 1, chapter 10, par 1; book 3, chapter 16, par 6; see also G Aulen, *Christus Victor* (London: SPCK, 1953), 32ff; W Pannenberg, *Jesus: God and Man* (Philadelphia: Westminster, 1968), 381; TF Torrance, *Conflict and Agreement in the Church*, volume 1, 258ff; A Nygren, *Agape and Eros*, 400ff.

54. Irenaeus, *Adversus Haereses*, volume 2, book 5, chapter 21, par 1.

55. Volume 1, book 3, chapter 19, par 3; volume 2, book 5, chapter 21, par 2. For the parallel thought in St Anselm's soteriology see above, 25–29.

56. Volume 2, book 5, chapter 21, par 2.

57. Volume 2, book 5, chapter 23, par 2; volume 1, book 3, chapter 18, par 6; volume 1, book 2, chapter 20, par 3.

conception is that humans participate in the human relationship which the incarnate one established for them with the Father. This may be described as a *theosis*.[58] 'Man is rendered spiritual and perfect because of the outpouring of the Spirit.'[59]

In this account of St Irenaeus' view of the soteriological effect of the incarnation, we also see the basis for St Irenaeus' view of the relationship between God and creation. God relates to creation by means of God's 'two hands'. In opposing the Gnostic separation of Spirit and flesh, God is understood to be immediately present and active in creation in God's Word and God's Spirit.

> It was not angels, therefore, who made us and formed us . . . For God did not stand in need of these, as if He did not possess His own hands. For with Him were always present the Word and Wisdom, the Son and the Spirit, by whom, freely and spontaneously, He made all things.[60]

As the 'hands' of God express the immediacy of God's presence, the unity of the Son and the Spirit is implied.

> The Father planning everything well and giving His commands, the Son carrying these into execution and performing the work of creating, and the Spirit nourishing and increasing . . . this is He who is the only true God.[61]

We bring our discussion of the differing views of the economy of salvation in apterthe Eastern and Western Churches to a conclusion by indicating the significance of these differences. As we have seen, they principally relate to the part played by the historical humanity and human experience of the incarnate one in understanding the dogma of the Trinity, its setting in the church's celebration of human redemption, and the relationship between God and the creature that

---

58.  See TF, Torrance, *Theology in Reconstruction*, 243.
59.  Irenaeus, volume 1, book 5, chapter 6, par 1. Cf volume 1, book 3, chapter 19, par 1; book 3, chapter 10, par 2; book 4, ch 20, par 4; volume 2, book 5, chapter 27, par 2; volume 2, book 5, chapter 17, par 1.
60.  Volume 1, book 4, chapter 20, par 1; cf book 2, chapter 2, par 4; book 4, chapter 19, par 1.
61.  Volume 2, book 4, chapter 38, par 3; cf volume 1, book 3, chapter 24, par 2.

it presupposes. The differences come together in St Augustine whose view of the trinitarian dogma has had such a decisive influence in western Christianity. He takes up and develops ideas found in Tertullian's view of the Trinity in which, as I have noted, the idea of unity rather than the distinctiveness of the *hypostases* is predominant. The idea of divine unity is associated with the idea that 'in the mind itself, even before it is a partaker of God, His image is found', so that 'there is set forth an inherent kinship between the divine and human being or a pre-established harmony between ultimate truth and human truth'.[62] As a result, the significance of the particularity of the human life of Jesus, the Son of God, will be less than a view which sees this particularity and the way he went as indicating the basic structure of the God/creature relationship. For such a view

> fails to wrestle seriously with the basic fact upon which the Christian gospel rests and with which it stands or falls, the condescension of God to enter our lowly and creaturely existence in Jesus Christ, to break through the discrepancy between us and God . . . and restore man to union with God.[63]

It is therefore not surprising that the conception of the nature of the distinctions in the Godhead, in relation to the issue of unity, posed somewhat of a problem for St Augustine's trinitarian theology. These distinctions, which for the east were concerned to express the reality of God's condescension and God's self-communication to the creature in creation and reconciliation, are primarily understood by St Augustine from the point of view of intra-trinitarian relationships. As the Father and the Son are Begetter and Begotten, the Spirit is the relationship of mutual love of the Father and the Son.[64]

K Rahner has indicated the methodological difficulties in attempting to understand the dogma of the Trinity on this basis. Not only does it produce

> the impression that it can only make formal statements about the three divine persons, with the help of concepts about the two

---

62.    TF Torrance, *Theological Science*, 189; cf JND Kelly, *Early Christian* Doctrines, 272.

63.    *Ibid*, 190.

64.    Augustine, 'On the Trinity', in *The Works of St Augustine*, volume 8 (Edinburgh: T&T Clark, 1873), book 1, chapter 7; cf book 9, chapter 17; book 15, chapter 45. See also Lossky, *The Mystical Theology of the Eastern Church*, 33, 45, 56, 57, 158, 169.

processions and about the relations. [But] even these statements, however, refer only to a Trinity which is absolutely locked within itself—one, which is not, in its reality, open to anything distinct from it.[65]

The problem, as Rahner sees it, can only begin to be addressed in the West if, in understanding the relationship between God and the creature, it is recognised that

we know about the Trinity because the Father's Word has entered history and given us his Spirit . . . [T]his starting point should not only be tacitly presupposed; the treatise [on the Trinity] should really start by positing it as such.

As a western theologian[66] Barth shared the particular dogmatic tradition of the Reformed church. It is certainly not a limitation that a particular theologian belongs to this or that tradition of the Christian church. However, in appreciating the breadth and depth of the church's tradition it is important to realise the problems attendant upon the focus of a particular strand of that tradition, structured as it is by historically divisive issues.

It is our view that Barth's comprehensive dogmatic labours[67] have been impaired in their reception by his failure to give an adequate account of the relationship between God and the creature. This is so precisely because he has not taken into account the place the liturgy had and has in the structure and meaning of the central Christian confession of the Trinity, celebrating as it does the ontological renewal of the creature in history. The polemical atmosphere in which Barth formulated his renewed *Dogmatik* precluded him from appreciating this vital point.

It is for this reason, as we have noted in our exposition of Barth's theology, that at each significant point the question of the God/creature relationship has been called into question by the inability of Barth's method to take account of a creaturely freedom that does not at the same time impugn the freedom of God. But the creature was created to participate in the fullness of the divine life—this is its vocation. It is called to make this union a reality in free harmony of the

---

65.    K Rahner, *The Trinity*, 18. Cf R Prenter, *Creation and Redemption*, 37ff, 50, note 8.
66.    Barth, *Table Talk*, 48.
67.    See TF Torrance, 'Karl Barth', in *Scottish Journal of Theology* 22/1 (1969): 1ff.

created will with the divine will. The soteriological purpose of the economy of salvation, celebrated in the liturgy, establishes the grounds for this reality for sinful creatures. This is the mystery of the church inherent in creation.[68]

The inadequate dogmatic basis of Barth's presentation of the dogma of the Trinity obviates positive appreciation of the God / creature relationship as a vital part of that dogma. For this reason, Barth's dogmatic method requires critical reappraisal in a genuinely ecumenical spirit and context. We have attempted to indicate some of the basic questions this appraisal must address if the dogma of the Trinity is to play its central role in western Christian thought.

---

68.   V Lossky, *The Mystical Theology of the Eastern Church*, 112ff. Cf RH Roberts, *A Theology On Its Way?* 93; BL Hebblethwaite, 'The appeal to Experience in Christology', in *Christ, Faith and History: Cambridge Studies in Christology*, edited by S Sykes and J Clapton (Cambridge: Cambridge University Press, 1972), 263ff; J Moltmann, *The Trinity and the Kingdom of God* (London: SCM, 1981), 5, 63, 64.

# Appendix 1

The problem with Schleiermacher's theology, as Barth saw, it may be illustrated from Schleiermacher's philosophical writings.

In his *Dialektik*,[1] Schleiermacher gives the following exposition of the relationship between God and the world. The idea of the world is expressed as *'die Grenze unseres Denkens'*. Since the transcendental ground of thought lies outside thought itself, the expression of the concept of the world as a finite limit gives only *'den Weg zum tranzendenten Grunde.'*[2]

In this relationship between the incompleteness of finite thought and the transcendental ground of its possibility as a limiting concept, we have the complement to Schleiermacher's idea, which plays a significant role in his theology, that of the unmediated self-consciousness.

However, while the idea of the world and God are correlated they can never coincide. The reason is that

> im Gedenken ist die Gottheit immer als Einheit gesetzt ohne
> Vielheit, die Welt aber als Vielheit ohne Einheit: die Welt ist Raum
> und Zeit erfüllend, die Gottheit raum und zeitlos; die Welt ist die
> Totalität der Gegensätze, die Gottheit die reale Negation aller
> Gegensätze. Zu denken ist aber eins nicht ohne das andere.[3]

Here the relationship is dialectically balanced on the basis of the given plurality and antitheses of temporal knowing and being and their negation in the divine transcendent ground of being. But the correlation is positively grounded in the fact that *,wir nur von dem durch die Welt in uns Hervorgebrachten auf Gott kommen.'*[4]

Schleiermacher finds support for his position in the fact that it is seen to overcome the problems involved in the old difficulty of conceiving God as existing either 'outside' or 'inside' the world. On the one hand, to think of God outside the world means that one *'setzt einen Gegensatz, der notwendig rückwirkend*

---

1. F Schleiermacher, *Dialektik,* edited by I Halpern (Berlin: Meyer und Müller, 1903).
2. *Ibid,* 224.
3. *Ibid,* 227.
4. *Ibid.*

*in Gott einen Gegensatz zwischen Selbstätigkeit and Empfänglichkeit hervorbringt, wie davon die natürlichen Theologien, welche auf der Schöpfungstheorie ruhen, voll sind.'* [5] On the other hand the problem is, *'das innerhalb geht wesentlich züruck darauf, Gott zu natura naturans und Weltordnung zu machen.'* [6]

Despite Schleiermacher's insistence on the integrity of the dialectic, the question arises that if the conception of God is meaningful, as the dialectic presupposes, then such meaning that it has can only be derived from the kind of relationship that is specifically excluded by Schleiermacher, namely, causal dependence. This relationship is excluded on the basis of excluding from the concept of God *'einen Gegensatz zwischen Selbstätigkeit und Empfänglichkeit.'* [7] The validity of Schleiermacher's enterprise depends upon the possibility of comparing absolute and relative in an absolute but non-conceptual manner. [8] As the hermeneutical basis for Christian dogma, it entails that dogma can only be understood as descriptions of the determinations of human self-consciousness in its relation to the comprehensive feeling of absolute dependence.

This feeling of absolute dependence, in which the relationship between God and the world is established, can only be known in the time-conditioned descriptions of these various states. Thus, it can be known only indirectly. [9]

---

5.     *Ibid*, 228.

6.     *Ibid*.

7.     *Ibid*.

8.     This appears to have been overlooked by H Richard Niebuhr, *Schleiermacher on Christ and Religion* (London: SCM, 19164), 184, 185. Here he simply states that 'Schleiermacher does not permit any cognitive dissolution of the finite-infinite distinction, for it is the relation and not the identity of terms that he stresses in his description and analysis.'
To justify this statement in terms of the phenomenological givenness of existence only begs the question why this dissolution is not possible. There would need to be introduced extra logical factors, necessitated by, say, the historical relationship between the incarnation of the Word and human kind to establish Schleiermacher's argument. But it is just this relationship which Schleiermacher excludes in the interests of what Barth terms the higher concept of human nature.

9.     F Schleiermacher, *The Christian Faith*, Sec 30, 125ff. On this question see Schleiermacher, 'On the Discrepancy Between the Sabellian and Athanasian Method of Representing the Doctrine of the Trinity', in *The Biblical Expositor's Quarterly Observer* 6/9 (1835): 1ff. Of course, on the basis of his understanding of Christian dogma Schleiermacher supports Sabellius' view of the Trinity precisely because Sabellius rejects the view that the historical differences and relationships presupposed by the history of the economy of salvation do not as such enter into

Schleiermacher posits a direct non-cognitive relation between God and the world which is found as given but not known in the feeling of absolute dependence, just as the actuality of knowledge amidst change is given in the non-deducible basis of the *Dialektik.*[10]

---

the definition of the *hypostatic* distinctions and God's unity. Since the doctrine of the Trinity assumes distinctions in the divine being, it can never be an immediate utterance of Christian self-consciousness but only a combination of several such utterances. (Section 170, 738ff)

10.    Schleiermacher, *Dialektik*, 143; cf 136.

# Appendix 2

We find it difficult to understand why E Brunner should suggest that, in Barth's development of his doctrine of the creature in *Church Dogmatics* Volume 3/2,

> Barth himself will surely not contest the fact that what stands in this sixth volume is in contradiction to much that was said in earlier volumes.[11]

There are two main points that give rise to Brunner's confusion concerning Barth's presentation. Firstly, he appears to understand by 'Real Man', in Barth's terminology, the one who in Barth's view exists for God, as 'man as he actually exists'.[12] Therefore, Brunner cannot see why Barth should criticise his view of man as presented in his anthropology as a 'mere potentiality', for he has taken as his point of departure existing man.

Such a complete misunderstanding of Barth is hard to imagine. It is therefore no wonder that Brunner, having assumed that Barth means by 'Real Man', empirical man and man as he actually exists, views the way in which Barth develops his views as 'irreconcilable with the Christian doctrine of sin'.[13] By this he means Barth's 'Real Man' is ontologically immune to sin.[14]

If Brunner had understood that Barth's 'Real Man' presupposes the inconceivable freedom and love in which God posits God's self as God for man and man for God in Jesus Christ, then he would have realised that the ontological immunity of 'Real Man' to sin corresponds to the self-determination of God which is identical with who God is. For Brunner, consequently, 'real man' is to be understood as man as he actually is in contradiction to God; Jesus Christ is True Man who contradicts this man of sin, that is, 'real man'. If Brunner had not seemed so concerned to find in Barth a confirmation of his own teaching[15] and attended to what Barth had actually written, he would not have been at all sanguine about a possible rapprochement with Barth in the area of anthropology.

---

1.  E Brunner, 'The New Barth', in *Scottish Journal of Theology* 4 (1951): 123, 124.
2.  *Ibid*, 125. Cf Barth, *CD* 3/2, 132ff.
3.  *Ibid*, 126.
4.  *Ibid*, 129.
5.  *Ibid*, 125: 'the main point common to us both'!

Secondly, Brunner fails to understand the meaning of Barth's view of the *analogia relationis*. Brunner maintains Barth teaches that

> the I-Thou relationship between God and man and between man and man are related to one another . . . Between these I-Thou relationships there exists, says Barth, an analogy, that is an *analogia relationis*.[16]

But Brunner finds difficulty in accepting that this relationship is a determination of man's being, 'that it is an ontological determination'.[17] Brunner believes, with R Prenter, that this means that the *analogia relationis* becomes an *analogia entis*.[18] What Brunner fails to notice is that he has not stated Barth's definition of the *analogia relationis* at all. Just as he failed to appreciate the basis of Barth's exposition of his anthropology in terms of the 'Real Man', Jesus Christ, who is identical with the act of God's self-positing, here too the *analogia relationis* is Jesus Christ as man for God and man for other men in precisely the same way. This *analogia relationis* excludes an *analogia entis* precisely because it posits a relationship whose distinctions and continuities presuppose God's own self-positing and are as inconceivable in terms of who the creature is as is this act of God. The comparison involved in the *analogia relationis* is not a comparison between the being of God on the one hand and the being of the creature as such on the other. As I have indicated and as Barth himself indicates, on the page reference given by Brunner (!), it is a matter 'of the relationship within the being of God on the one side, and the being of God and that of man on the other', that is in Jesus Christ.[19]

6.    *Ibid*, 127.
7.    *Ibid*, 127.
8.    *Ibid*.
9.    Barth, *CD* 3/2, 220; cf 262.

# Appendix 3

McIntyre seeks to explain[20] Barth's rejection of Quenstedt's improper presentation of the doctrine of analogy by a misunderstanding of the question of analogy Quenstedt seeks to address.

> Quenstedt discerns the inadequacy of the analogy of attribution in respect of extrinsic denomination, namely, that this analogy does not affirm anything of the internal nature of the secondary analogates; and further, that he wishes to emphasise that when God creates, He creates beings whose creation constitutes their being. He is endeavouring to find out how you may speak of creatures who prior to salvation *are*, and in fact must *be* in order to be saved.[21]

However, it would appear that McIntyre overlooks the fact that, according to the presuppositions of Barth's dogmatic method, it is not possible to consider the existence of the creature prior to the event of God's self-revelation. The existence of the creature and the creature's knowledge of God and other creatures presupposes the unity of God's being who God is in the event of God's self-revelation. To consider the existence of the creature apart from this event in which God is the God of the creature is to presuppose a freedom of the creature for God that is not presupposed by the freedom of God for the creature. This would result, in Barth's terms, either in the creature being deified or God being divided.

The same sort of question is addressed to Barth by H Bouillard.[22] He asserts that, according to Barth,

> the truth which our words have in God does not become truth for us except when the grace of revelation lends them analogy with God . . . This gift can never be transformed by us into a given. What comes to us through revelation is not something we would know outside of it . . . It is a work of grace, a mode of divine revelation.

---

10. J McIntyre, 'Analogy', in *Scottish Journal of Theology* 12 (1959): 1ff.
11. *Ibid*, 17.
12. H Bouillard, *The Knowledge of God*, 97ff.

Thus the partial correspondence implied by analogical predication means

> that even within revelation God remains hidden . . . we are sent
> back to the reciprocal immanence of veiling and unveiling . . .
> When we speak of partial correspondence between our words
> and the being of God, the word 'partial' recalls God is hidden
> and thus designates the limit of our knowledge; but the link to
> revelation which the word correspondence evokes is also the
> promise which accompanies our enterprise of knowing God if it
> is undertaken in obedience.[23]

Bouillard, in contrast to McIntyre, has seen the connection between Barth's doctrine of analogy and his doctrine of revelation, in which God is at one and the same time hidden and revealed; as the the *Deus absconditus* and the *Deus revelatus* beyond the negative limit of human existence in death through the resurrection of Jesus Christ. This unity between the knowledge of God and the creature expresses the truth of the being of the creature as presupposing the event of revelation that is configured by the relationship between the Father, Son and Holy Spirit. But has Bouillard seen this link correctly? We think not.

Bouillard notes that, for Barth, 'partial' in analogical predication is posited by the relationship God establishes between God's self and the creature in the event of revelation. However, this limit does not consist in one considered as a limit to creaturely knowledge. The partiality of which Barth speaks corresponds to the way in which God, in positing God's self for man in Jesus Christ, repeats in him *ad extra* what God is in God's being for God's self. The *self*-revelation of God presupposes this self-election of God in the inconceivable freedom and love in which God exists. The word 'partial', therefore, does not refer to a limit of creaturely knowledge of God, but to the fact that the reality of creaturely knowledge of God presupposes this freedom of God to be for us what God is for God's self. It is this mystery to which Barth draws attention in his insistence on *extrinsic* as opposed to *intrinsic* analogical predication. Thus, when our human language truly speaks of God,

---

13.    *Ibid*, 100, 101.

God establishes the one truth, His own as the truth of our views, concepts and words ... When He claims them, He does not confirm Himself but us. But in them He does in fact confirm Himself.[24]

It really appears as if Bouillard wishes Barth to abandon the context of his dogmatic method in which he defines his understanding of analogical predication, of partiality, in favour of the Thomist method of 'negation of the mode of predication'.[25] However, as in the case of McIntyre, there can be for Barth no neutral sphere of creaturely existence in which words and concepts may be judged more or less appropriate to God. All words and concepts, in and of themselves are inappropriate, but all can be appropriate depending on the decision and action of God in being who God is in and for God's self, for us.[26]

14.  Barth, *CD* 2/1, 229.
15.  H Bouillard, *The Knowledge of* God, 115.
16.  For more on this question see the following: TF Torrance, *Theology in Reconstruction*, 116; B Mondin, *The Principle of Analogy in Protestant and Catholic* Thought, 164ff; C O'Grady, *The Church in the Theology of Karl* Barth, volume 1, 95ff; W Pannenberg, 'Zur Bedeutung des Analogiegedankens bei Karl Barth', in *Theologische Literaturzeitung* 1 (1953): 17ff; W Pannenberg, 'Analogy and Doxology', in *Basic Questions in Theology*, volume 1, 211ff, 214 note 3; J Hamer, *Karl Barth*, 39–52, 66, 67, 69ff; HU von Balthasar, *Karl Barth: Darstellung und Deutung*, 120ff; E Jüngel, 'Die Möglichkeit theologischer Anthropologie', 536, 543ff; W Kreck, '*Analogia Fidei* oder *Analogia Entis*', 272ff.

# Bibliography

Anselm, St, *Concerning the Truth*, translated by J Hopkins and Richardson (New York: Harper, 1967).

-------*Dialogus de Veritate*, Migne PL Tomus 58.

-------*Monologion: Proslogion: Cur Deus Homo and Apologetic on Behalf of the Fool*, translated by S Dean (La Salle, Illinois: Open Court, 1962).

Anstey, CRP, 'St Anselm Demythologised', in *Theology* 64 (1961): 17–23.

Athanasius, St, *Letters Concerning the Holy Spirit*, translated by CRB Shapland (London: Epworth, 1951).

-------*The Incarnation of the Word* (London: Mowbray, 1953).

-------'Four Discourses Against the Arians', in *Select Library of Nicene and Post-Nicene Fathers*, volume 4, edited by P Schaff and H Wace (Grand Rapids: Eerdmans, 1957).

Augustine, St, 'On the Trinity', translated by AW Hadden, in *The Works of St Augustine*, volume 8, edited by M Dods (Edinburgh: T&T Clark, 1873).

Aulen, Gustav, *Christus Victor*, translated by G Hebert (London: SPCK, 1953).

Baillie, Donald, *God was in Christ* (London: Faber, 1961).

Baillie, J, *Our Knowledge of God* (London: Oxford University Press, 1949).

Balthasar, Hans Urs von, *Karl Barth: Darstellung und Deutung seiner Theologie* (Köln: J Hegner, 1951).

Barth, Karl, 'A Theological Dialogue', in *Theology Today* 19/2 (1962/1963): 171–177.

-------*Anselm: Fides Quaerens Intellectum: Anselm's Proof of the Existence of God in the Context of his Theological Scheme*, translated by I Robertson (London: SCM, 1960). German original *Fides Quaerens Intellectum: Anselms Beweis der Existenz*

*Gottes im Zusammenhang seines theologischen Programs* (Zürich: Evangelischer Verlag, 1958).

-------*Die Christliche Dogmatik im Entwurf* (München: Kaiser, 1927).

-------*Church Dogmatics*, volumes 1–4; authorised English translation of *Die Kirchliche Dogmatik,*

1932ff, edited by TF Torrance and G Bromiley, 1936ff. This translation, abbreviated as *CD*, is followed unless otherwise indicated.

-------*Fragments Grave and Gay*, translated by E Mosbacher (London: Collins, 1971).

-------*From Rousseau to Ritschl*, translated by B Cozens (London: SCM, 1959).

-------*How My Mind Has Changed*, edited by J Godsey (Virginia: John Knox, 1966).

-------'Liberal Theology: Some Alternatives', in *Hibbert Journal* 59 (1960/1961): 213–219.

-------*The Epistle to the Romans*, translated by E Hoskyns from the 6 edition of *Der Römerbrief*, 1928 (Oxford University Press, 1933; second edition 1950).

------- 'Parergon', in *Evangelische Theologie* 8 (1948): 268–282.

-------*Schicksal und Idee in der Theologie*, Gesammelte Vorträge, Band 3 (Zürich: Evangelischer Verlag, 1957).

-------*Table Talk*, edited by J Godsey (Edinburgh: Oliver & Boyd, 1963).

-------*The Göttingen Dogmatics*, 2 volumes, edited by H Reiffen, translated by G Bromiley (Grand Rapids: Eerdmans, 1990).

-------*The Resurrection from the Dead* (London: Hodder & Stoughton, 1933).

-------*The Word of God and the Word of Man* (London: Hodder & Stoughton, 1928).

-------*Theology and Church*, translated by L Smith (London: SCM, 1962).

Barth, Karl and Eduard Thurneysen, *Revolutionary Theology in the Making:*

*Correspondence 1914–1925*, translated by JD Smart (London: Epworth, 1964).

Barth, Karl and Emil Brunner, *Natural Theology: Comprising 'Nature and Grace' by Professor Dr Emil Brunner and the Reply 'No!' by Dr Karl Barth* (London: G Bless, 1946).

Basil, St, 'De Spiritu Sancto', in *The Library of Nicene and Post-Nicene Fathers*, edited by P Schaff and H Wace, volume 8 (Grand Rapids: Eerdmans, 1894).

Bennett, JC, 'Comment on "Letter to American Christians" by Karl Barth', in *Christendom* 8 (1943).

Berkouwer, GC, *Man: the Image of God*, translated by D Jellma (Grand Rapids: Eerdmans, 1954).

-------*The Triumph of Grace in the Theology of Karl Barth*, translated by H Boer (London: Paternoster, 1956).

Bethune-Baker, JF, *Nestorius and his Teaching* (Cambridge: Cambridge University Press, 1908).

Bettis, JD, 'Theology in the Public Debate: Barth's Rejection of Natural Theology and the Hermeneutical Problem', in *Scottish Journal of Theology* 22/4 (1969): 385ff.

Bindley, TH, *The Oecumenical Documents of the Faith* (London: Methuen, 1950).

Bonhoeffer, D, *Act and Being*, translated by B Noble (London: Collins, 1962).

Bouillard, H, *The Knowledge of God*, translated by S Femiano (London: Burns & Oates, 1969).

-------*Karl Barth: Genese et Evolution de la Theologie Dialectique, Part 2. Parole de Dieu et Existence Humaine* (Paris: F Aubier, 1957).

Bruce, AB, *The Humiliation of Christ* (Edinburgh: T&T Clark, 1881).

Brunner, E, 'The New Barth', in *Scottish Journal of Theology* 4/2 (1951): 123ff.

Bultmann, R, *Essays: Philosophical and Theological*, translated by GC Greig (London: SCM, 1955).

-------*Existence and Faith: Shorter Writings of Rudolf Bultmann* (London: Collins, 1964).

-------*Theology of the New Testament*, 2 volumes (London: SCM, 1952-1955).

Burleigh, JHS, 'The Doctrine of the Holy Spirit in the Latin Fathers', in *Scottish Journal of Theology* 7/2 (1954): 113–132.

Calvin, J, Commentaries on *St Luke; Philippians; St John; St Luke; St Matthew; Hebrews; St John; The Book of Acts; Colossians*, translated by THL Parker, edited by TF Torrance & DW Torrance (Edinburgh: Oliver & Boyd, 1963ff).

-------*Institutes of the Christian Religion*, 2 volumes, translated by H Beveridge (Edinburgh: T&T Clark, 1863).

Camfield, FW editor, *Reformation Old and New: A Tribute to Karl Barth* (London: Lutterworth, 1947).

Clark, GH, *Karl Barth's Theological Method* (Philadelphia: The Presbyterian and Reformed Publishing Co, 1963).

Clement of Alexandria, MS 1335 D in 'Early Christian Liturgies and Other Documents', in *Ante-Nicene Christian Library*, volume 24 (Edinburgh: T&T Clark, 1869), 177.

Come, A, *An Introduction to Barth's Dogmatics for Preachers* (London: SCM, 1963).

Cyril, St, *Cyrilli Archiepiscopi Alexandrini: Libri Quinque Contra Nestorium*, edited by PE Pusey (Bruxelles: Culture et Civilisation, 1965).

-------'Five Tome Contradiction of the Blasphemies of Nestorius' and 'Scholia on the Incarnation of the Only Begotten', in *A Library of the Fathers of the Holy Catholic Church* (Oxford: Parker & Rivington, 1881).

Dalmais, IH, *The Eastern Liturgies* (London: Burns and Oates, 1960).

Dawson, C, 'The Scientific Development of Medieval Culture', in *Medieval Essays* (London: Sheed & Ward, 1953).

Diem, H, *Kirkegaard's Dialectic of Existence* (Edinburgh: Oliver and Boyd, 1959).

Dorner, IA, *History of the Development of the Doctrine of the Person of Christ*, 2 volumes, translated by D Simon (Edinburgh: T&T Clark, 1861).

Downing, FG, *Has Christianity a Revelation?* (London: SCM, 1964).

Ebeling, G, *Theology and Proclamation*, translated by J Riches (London: Collins, 1966).

Flew, A and A McIntyre, editors, *New Essays in Philosophical Theology* (London: SCM, 1955).

Florovsky, G, 'St Gregory Palamas and the Tradition of the Fathers', in *Sobornost* 4/4 (1961).

Foster, MB, 'The Christian Doctrine of Creation and the Rise of Modern Natural Science', in *Mind*, 43/45 (1934/1936).

Gay, JH, 'Four Medieval Views of Creation', in *Harvard Theological Review* 56/4 (1963): 243–273.

Gilson, E, 'Sens et Nature de l'Argument de Saint Anselms', in *Archives d'Historie Doctrinale et Litteraire du Moyen Age* 9 (1934): 5–51.

Godet, F, *Commentary on the Gospel of St John*, translated by F Crombie and M Cusin (Edinburgh: T&T Clark, 1876).

Gollwitzer, H, *The Existence of God as Confessed by Faith*, translated by J Leitch (London: SCM, 1965).

Grillmeier, A, 'Christ in Christian Tradition: From the Apostolic Age to Chalcedon (451)', translated by J Bowden from 'Die theologische und sprachliche Vorbereitung der christologishen Formel von Chalkedon', in A Grillmeier and H Bacht eds, *Das Konzil von Chalkedon*, volume 1 (Würzburg: Echter Verlag, 1951; revised edition London: Mowbray, 1965).

Harnack, A von, *History of Dogma*, 2 volumes, translated by N Buchanan (London: Williams & Norgate, 1897).

Hartwell, H, *The Theology of Karl Barth: An Introduction* (London: Duckworth. 1964).

Hebblethwaite, BL, 'The Appeal to Experience in Christology', in *Christ, Faith and History: Cambridge Studies in Christology*, edited S Sykes and J Clapton (Cambridge: Cambridge University Press, 1972).

Hector, KW, 'God's Triunity and Self-Determination: a Conversation with Karl Barth, Bruce McCormack and Paul Molnar', in *International Journal of Systematic Theology* 7/3 (2005): 246ff.

Hendry, GS, 'From the Father and the Son: the *Filioque* After Nine Hundred Years', in *Theology Today* 11/4 (1954/1955): 449–459.

-------'The Dogmatic Form of Barth's Theology', in *Theology Today* 13/3 (1956/1957): 300–314.

-------*The Holy Spirit and Christian Theology*, revised edition (London: SCM, 1965).

Herberg, W, *The Social Philosophy of Karl Barth* (New York: Anchor Books, 1960).

Hodgson, L, *The Doctrine of the Trinity* (London: Nisbet, 1943).

Hoogland, M, *Calvin's Perspective on the Exaltation of Christ* (Kampen: J Kok, 1966).

Irenaeus, St, *Adversus Haereses*, 2 volumes, in *The Ante-Nicene Christian Library* (Edinburgh: T&T Clark, 1868).

Jenson, R, *Alpha and Omega: A Study in the Theology of Karl Barth* (Edinburgh: Nelson, 1963).

Jüngel, E, 'Die Möglichkeit theologischer Anthropologie auf dem Grunde der Analogie: eine Untersuchung zum Analogieverständnis Karl Barths', in *Evangelische Theologie* 22 (1962): 535–557.

-------*Gottes Sein Ist Im Werden* (Tübingen: JCB Mohr, 1965); ET, *God's Being Is In Becoming* (Edinburgh: T&T Clark, 2001).

Kamaris, J, 'The Problem of the Unification of the non-Chalcedonian Churches of the East with the Orthodox on the Basis of Cyril's Formula: *Mia Physis tou Theou Logou Sesarkomene*', in *The Greek Orthodox Theological Review* 10/2 (1964/1965).

Kelly, JND, *Early Christian Doctrines* (London: Black, 1958).

Kierkegaard, S, *Philosophical Fragments*, translated by H and E Hong (Princeton University Press, 1985).

Kreck, W, '*Analogia Fidei* oder *Analogia Entis?*' in *Antwort: Karl Barth zum siebzigsten Geburtstag* (Zürich: Evangelischer Verlag, 1956).

Kuitert, HM, *Gott in Menschengestalt: eine dogmatisch-hermeneutische Studie über die Anthropomorphismen der Bibel* (München: Kaiser, 1967).

Leeming, B, 'Rediscovering Eastern Christendom', in *Orthodox-Catholic Relations*, edited by AH Armstrong and EJB Fry (London: Longman, Darton and Todd, 1964).

Lehmann, P, 'Barth and Brunner: The Dilemma of the Protestant Mind', in *Journal of Religion* 20 (1940): 124ff.

Loofs, F, *Nestorius and His Place in the History of Christian Doctrine* (Cambridge: Cambridge University Press, 1914).

Lossky, V, *The Mystical Theology of the Eastern Church* (London: J Clarke, 1961).

Mascall, EL, *Existence and Analogy* (London: Longmans, Green, 1949).

-------*Christian Theology and Natural Science* (Hamden, Connecticut: Shoe String Press, 1965).

McIntyre, J, 'Analogy', in *Scottish Journal of Theology* 12/1 (1959): 1–20.

-------'The Holy Spirit in Greek Patristic Thought', in *Scottish Journal of Theology* 7/4 (1954): 353–375.

-------*The Shape of Christology* (London: SCM, 1966).

Meyendorff, J, *A Study of Gregory Palamas* (London: Faith Press, 1964).

-------*The Orthodox Church: its Past and its Role in the World Today* (Crestwood NY: St Vladimir's Seminary Press, 1996).

Molnar, Paul D, *Divine Freedom and the Doctrine of the Immanent Trinity: in Dialogue with Karl Barth and Contemporary Theology* (Edinburgh: T&T Clark, 2002).

Moltmann, J, *The Lordship of Christ in Human Society: Two Studies in the Theology of Bonhoeffer* (New York: Scribners, 1967).

-------*The Trinity and the Kingdom of God* (London: SCM, 1981).

Mondin, B, *The Principle of Analogy in Protestant and Catholic Thought* (The Hague: J Nijhoff, 1963).

Niebuhr, H Richard, *Resurrection and Historical Reason* (New York: Scribners, 1957)

-------*Schleiermacher on Christ and Religion* (London: SCM, 1964).

Niesel, W, *The Theology of Calvin*, translated by H Knight (Philadelphia: Westminster, 1956).

Nissiotis, N, 'The Importance of the Doctrine of the Trinity for Church Life and Theology', in *The Orthodox Ethos*, edited by A Philippou, volume 1 (Oxford: Holywell Press, 1964).

Nygren, A, *Agape and Eros*, translated by P Watson (London: SPCK, 1957).

O'Grady, C, *The Church in the Theology of Karl Barth*, 2 volumes (London: G Chapman, 1968).

Ogden, SM, *Christ Without Myth* (London: Collins, 1962).

H Ott, 'Der Gedanke der Souveranität Gottes in der Theologie Karl Barths', in *Theologische Zeitschrift* 12 (1956): 409ff.

-------'Objectification and Existentialism', in *Kerygma and Myth*, edited by HW Bartsch, volume 2 (London: SPCK, 1962).

Paliard, J, 'Priere et Dialectique: Meditation sur le Proslogion de Saint Anselme', in *Dieu Vivant* 6 (1946).

Pannenberg, W, *Basic Questions in Theology*, volume 1, translated by GH Kehm (London: SCM, 1970).

-------*Jesus: God and Man* (Philadelphia: Westminster, 1968); translated by L Williams and D Priebe from *Grundzüge der Christologie* (Gütersloh: Gerd Mohn, 1964).

-------'Redemptive Event and History', in *Essays on Old Testament Interpretation*, edited by C Westermann (London: SCM, 1963), 314ff.

Prenter, R, *Creation and Redemption*, translated by TI Jensen (Philadelphia: Fortress Press, 1967).

-------'Die Einheit von Schöpfung und Erlösung', in *Theologische Zeitschrift* 2 (1946): 161ff.

-------'Dietrich Bonhoeffer and Karl Barth's Positivism of Revelation', in *World Come of Age: a Symposium on Dietrich Bonhoeffer*, edited by RG Smith (London: Collins, 1967), 93ff.

-------'Glauben und Erkennen bei Karl Barth', in *Kerygma und Dogma* 2 (1956): 176–192.

Prestige, GL, *God in Patristic Thought* (London: SPCK, 1956).

Rahner, K, *The Trinity*, translated by J Doncell (London: Burns & Oates, 1970).

Relton, HM, *A Study in Christology: The Problem of the Relationship of the Two Natures of Christ* (London: SPCK, 1929).

Roberts, RH, *A Theology on its Way? Essays on Karl Barth* (Edinburgh: T&T Clark, 1991).

Rödding, G, Das Seinsproblem in der Schöpfungslehre Karl Barths', in *Kerygma und Dogma* 10 (1964): 1–47.

Schaff, P, *The Creeds of Christendom*, 3 volumes (New York: Harper, 1919).

Schilder, K, *Zur Begriffsgeschichte des 'Paradoxon' mit besonderer Berücksichtigung Calvins und des nach-Kierkegaardschen,Paradoxon'* (Kampen: B J Kok, 1933).

Schleiermacher, F, *Dialektik*, edited by I Halpern (Berlin: Meyer & Müller, 1903).

-------'On the Discrepancy between the Sabellian and Athanasian Method of Representing the Doctrine of the Trinity', in *The Biblical Repository and Quarterly Review* 5 (1835): 265–9353, and 6 (1835): 1–116.

-------*The Christian Faith*, translated by D Baillie *et al* (Edinburgh: T&T Clark, 1928).

Schlink, E, *The Coming Christ and the Coming Church* (Edinburgh: Oliver & Boyd, 1967).

Schmemann, A, 'Liturgy and Theology', in *The Greek Orthodox Theological Review* 17/1 (1972): 86–100.

Schrey, HH, H Walz, and WA Whitehouse, *The Biblical Doctrine of Justice and Law*, Ecumenical Biblical Studies 3 (London: SCM, 1955).

Sellers, RV, *The Council of Chalcedon: A Historical and Doctrinal Survey* (London: SPCK, 1961).

Sykes, SW editor, *Karl Barth: Studies in His Theological Method* (Oxford: Clarendon, 1979).

Symeon of Thessalonica, 'Commentary on the Divine Liturgy of Chrysostom', in *The Liturgies of SS Mark, James, Clement, Chrysostom and Basil*, translated by JM Neale and RF Littledale (London: J Masters, 1865).

Smart, JD, *The Divided Mind of Modern Theology* (Philadelphia: Westminster, 1967).

Tertullian, 'Ad Praxean', in *Ante-Nicene Christian Library*, volume 15 (Edinburgh: T&T Clark, 1870).

Torrance, JB, 'Interpretation and Understanding in Schleiermacher's Theology: Some Critical

-------Questions', in *Scottish Journal of Theology* 21/3 (1968): 268–282.

Torrance, TF, *Conflict and Agreement in the Church*, volume 1 (London: Lutterworth, 1959).

-------*Divine and Contingent Order* (Oxford University Press, 1981).

-------*God and Rationality* (Oxford University Press, 1971).

-------'Hermeneutics According to FDE Schleiermacher', in *Scottish Journal of Theology* 21/3 (1968): 257–267.

-------'Karl Barth', in *Scottish Journal of Theology* 22/1 (1969): 1–9.

-------*Karl Barth: An Introduction to His Early Theology 1910–1931* (London: SCM, 1962).

-------*Space Time and Incarnation* (Oxford University Press, 1969).

-------*Space, Time and Resurrection* (Edinburgh: The Handsel Press, 1976).

-------'The Atonement and the Oneness of the Church', in *Scottish Journal of Theology* 7/3 (1954): 245–269.

-------'The Ethical Implications of St Anselm's *De Veritate*', in *Theologische Zeitschrift* 24 (1968): 307–319.

-------*The Mediation of Christ* (Exeter: Paternoster, 1983).

-------'The Problem of Natural Theology in the Thought of Karl Barth', in *Religious Studies* 6/2 (1970): 121–135.

-------*Theological Science* (Oxford University Press, 1969).

-------*Theology in Reconstruction* (London: SCM, 1965).

Ullmann, W, 'Das *filioque* als Problem oekumenischer Theologie', in *Kerygma und Dogma* 1 (1970): 58ff.

Vahanian, G, *The Death of God* (New York: Braziller, 1961).

van Buren, P, *Christ in Our Place: The Substitutionary Character of Calvin's Doctrine of Reconciliation* (Edinburgh: Oliver & Boyd, 1957).

Verghese, P, 'The Christology of the non-Chalcedonian Churches', in *Sobornost* Series 4/5 (1961).

Walls, RC, 'St Gregory Palamas', in *Scottish Journal of Theology* 21/4 (1968): 435–448.

Watson, G, 'A Study in St.Anselm's Soteriology and Karl Barth's Theological Method', in *Scottish Journal of Theology* 42/4 (1989): 493–512.

-------'The Basis of Union Considered as a Confessional Statement', in *Colloquium* 8/2 (1976): 14ff.

-------'The *Filioque:* Opportunity for debate?', in *Scottish Journal of Theology* 41 / 3 (1988): 313–330.

-------'Karl Barth and St Anselm's Theological Programme', in *Scottish Journal of Theology* 30 / 1 (1977): 31–46.

Welch, C, *The Trinity in Contemporary Theology* (London: SCM, 1953).

West, C, *Communism and the Theologians: Study of an Encounter* (London: SCM, 1958).

Whale, JS, *Christian Doctrine* (Cambridge University Press, 1941).

Williams, RD, 'Barth on the Triune God', in *Karl Barth: Studies of his Theological Method,* edited by SW Sykes (Oxford: Clarendon, 1979), 170ff.

Willis, ED, *Calvin's Catholic Christology: The Role of the So-Called 'extra Calvinisticum' in Calvin's Theology* (Leiden: EJ Brill, 1966).

*Worship in the Reformed Church,* Church of Scotland Report, edited by JB Torrance.

Zervov, N, 'The Worship of the Orthodox Church and its Message', in *The Orthodox Ethos,* volume 1 (Oxford: Holywell Press, 1964).

# Index